W9-DBU-496

The COOL GENT

THE NINE LIVES OF RADIO LEGEND
Herb Kent

HERB KENT AND
DAVID SMALLWOOD
Foreword by Mayor Richard M. Daley

Lawrence Hill Books

Library of Congress Cataloging-in-Publication Data

Kent, Herb.
The cool gent : the nine lives of radio legend Herb Kent / Herb Kent and David
Smallwood ; foreword by Mayor Richard M. Daley.
  p. cm.
Includes index.
ISBN 978-1-55652-774-6 (hardcover)
  1. Kent, Herb.   2. African-American disc jockeys—Biography.   I. Smallwood,
David.   II. Title.
ML429.K47A3 2009
791.44'3—dc22
   [B]   2008022412

Cover design: Scott Rattray
Cover photographs: microphone: iStock.com; photos courtesy of Herb Kent
Interior design: Pamela Juárez

Published by Lawrence Hill Books
An imprint of Chicago Review Press, Incorporated
814 North Franklin Street
Chicago, Illinois 60610
ISBN: 978-1-55652-774-6
Printed in the United States of America
5 4 3 2 1

To my mother, Katherine Kent.
God bless you, mom.

—Herb

CONTENTS

Foreword   ix

Acknowledgments   xi

Preface: Please Allow Me to Introduce Myself   xiii

1   1928 _____ **1**

My Peeps   2

Falling in Love with Radio as a Kid   11

From Dreams of Monsters to Radio Dreams   17

Wars: What Are They Good For?   24

You Want Me to Do What?:
    My First Encounters with Racism   30

2   DEVELOPING AN ON-AIR STYLE _____ **41**

Yes, Sir, or Yowsuh?: Early Black Radio
    and the Commercials of Yesteryear   42

Getting My Act Together in the 1950s   51

When Doo-Wop Was King   58

How I Jack Them Jams Like a Big Dog   62

Shock Jocks, Freedom of Speech, and the N-Word   69

3 THE BLACK GIANT ———————————————— **79**

WVON: The World's Greatest Radio Station   80

Thank Goodness for Pig Ears   89

All About the Promotions   93

Meeting the Jacksons at the Airport   98

Partying at the Time Square   101

Kickin' It at the Kappa Karnival   106

The Big Bike Rides   111

Staying Awake for Black Power   114

4 THEATER OF THE MIND ON RADIO ———————— **119**

Ivy Leaguers Versus Those Evil Gousters   120

Grunchions, the Gym Shoe Creeper,
   and a New Teenage Language   124

The Wahoo Man   127

The Electric Craaazzzy People!   133

5 TALES FROM THE COOL SCHOOL ———————— **137**

Jeez, the Experiences a Deejay Can Have   138

Grand Ballrooms and a Whodunit   149

My Friend, Smokey Robinson   155

Visiting "the Godfather" James Brown in Jail   162

Swimming with Mean Sharks:
   The Business Side of the Music Game   170

6 ABOUT FAME AND CELEBRITY ———————— **183**

The Price of Fame   184

Gangsters, Molls, and Friends   191

Sex: What's Love Got to Do with It? And, Well, *Love*   198

7   HITTING ROCK BOTTOM _____ 207

Jailhouse Rock   208
The Two Dead Girls   211
Drinking and Drugging, Big-Time   214
My Sixth Life   223
The Great Deejay Massacre at WVON   227
One Lonely Night   231

8   REDEMPTION _____ 237

Burning a Car, Saving a Life   238
Climbing Back and Punking Out   242
The Intervention: Damn, They Caught Me!   245
My Private Dance with the Big C   251

9   BACK TO THE FUTURE _____ 259

Twenty Years with My V103 Radio Home   260
Star of TV and Movies   264
From the Hall of Fame to the Mayor of Bronzeville   270

10   LOOKING BACK ON A LONG ROAD _____ 277

Sweet Soul Music You Must Have on a Desert Island   278
Joy Inside My Tears: Appreciations and Regrets   284

Index   289

Foreword

RICHARD M. DALEY, MAYOR, CITY OF CHICAGO

Certain elements contribute to the pulse of a city, and in Chicago there is much we can point to—from the beautiful lakefront to the historic elevated-train system to the innovative architecture. The core elements for Chicago, its heart and its soul, are the people and the neighborhoods where they live and enjoy their cultures and traditions.

No one knows this better than Herb Kent, because he is one of those people. While growing up in the Ida B. Wells housing community on Chicago's South Side, Herb began his career in radio as the teenage host of a music program for WBEZ. In the late 1940s he began playing records for other radio stations, sharing with legions of listeners his love for music. As Herb came of age, so did black music and black radio stations, and each played a significant role in the social change that was occurring during the 1950s, 1960s, and 1970s.

Today, Herb Kent is truly a legendary radio personality. His iconic status was acknowledged by his industry colleagues in 1995 when Herb became the first African American disc jockey to be inducted into the Radio Hall of Fame. One year later, residents in the community where Herb was raised demonstrated the depth of their admiration for a favorite son when they named him the honorary "Mayor of Bronzeville." Another example of the public's affection for Herb is the honorary Herb Kent "the Kool

Gent" Drive, which runs from the 6000 to 6700 block of Stony Island Avenue, one of the longest stretches of honorary street in Chicago.

Simply put, I am a huge Herb Kent fan, and I enjoy hearing him play my favorite dusty records like no one else can! Like all of his adoring fans, I applaud Herb for his sixty-five years of contributions to Chicago's radio airwaves and for furthering his inspirational reach through this book.

Acknowledgments

My most profound appreciation to my daughter Robin and radio executive Marv Dyson—without their efforts during a crucial period of my life, I probably wouldn't even be here to write a book.

Thanks to Chicago Review Press and Susan Betz for thinking that my life has been interesting enough to write about.

To Earl Jones, president and market manger of Clear Channel Radio Chicago, it's been a joy working with you.

And finally, I'd like to acknowledge all my fellow deejays and announcers who have struggled and worked so hard to reach the top through trials and tribulations. Some reached it, some didn't, but God bless them all.

—Herb Kent

This goes out to family—Louise, Danielle, Emerin, Clarissa, Chris, Damon, Mom, Jerry, Lettie, Ed, Darnell, Curt, Lois, Rose, Jeff; special friends—Ngina, Jennifer, Zondra, Farrah, Sonya Shesmiles, Marcia, Sharon the Pocketbook Lady, Michelle B. (wherever you are); the boys—Ted, Sir Sim, Andre, Kev, Mr. Zeke, Steven M.; to the illustrious contractor Paul King, an early believer; N'DIGO publisher Hermene Hartman; *Real Times*

Media CEO Hiram Jackson; Dr. Terry Mason; WVON's Melody Spann-Cooper; Mayor Richard Daley; Gov. Rod Blagojevich; and literary agent Manie Baron.

To the many people through the years who kept saying, "Y'all ain't finished with that book yet?!"—well, now we are. Thanks, everybody, for your sacrifice, input, and/or inspiration.

—*David Smallwood*

PREFACE

Hi, I'm Herb Kent.

If you're reading this book, chances are you know who I am. And if you're reading this book, I hope you bought and paid for it and didn't use the five-finger discount on your way out the store.

If you don't know me, I'm a deejay based at radio station WVAZ (V103) in Chicago, and by all accounts I've been playing music on the air continuously longer than anyone else in the history of radio—for sixty-five straight years. During the process, I managed to become the top deejay at the most powerful black station in the country—WVON during the 1960s and 1970s—and I was proudly and humbly inducted as the first black deejay to enter the Radio Hall of Fame in 1995.

I'm known as the Cool Gent; the King of the Dusties (I invented the term "dusty records"); the Mayor of Bronzeville in Chicago; the Pied Piper of Teens; and the Black Dick Clark. But you can call me just plain ol' Herbie, Baby.

I started on the air in 1944, when I was sixteen. The real Dick Clark is a year younger than me and started in radio a year later as a weatherman and news announcer. He didn't start playing music until 1952. Casey Kasem, Dick Biondi, and Pervis Spann, nationally known disc jockeys all, started in radio in the 1950s as well.

The legendary announcer Hal Jackson might have a challenge to my longevity but not my continuity. Hal began broadcasting in 1939 and is still on the air today doing the Sunday Classics show on WBLS in New York. Hal is in his early nineties now and entered the Radio Hall of Fame in the same class as me, bless his heart. But he left the air to go into radio management for many years.

Canadian folk singer Oscar Brand has hosted a weekly folk music show on WYNC in New York since 1945, so he's my first runner-up. And the only person who's been on radio longer than me, period, is Paul Harvey, who started in 1933. But he's a newscaster and commentator, of course, not a music man.

I've been on the air long enough to entertain moms and dads, then entertain their kids, and now I'm entertaining *their* kids. And what I'm proudest of is that through all my years in radio, I have just dominated the ratings. As I've gotten older, I've been referred to as a "beloved icon," but let me tell you, brother, these radio stations won't keep you on the air if you aren't pulling in the numbers, no matter how cuddly or well-known you might be.

My ratings started to explode in the 1950s, and ever since I've been number one or two in my time slots wherever I've been, and I've deejayed for eleven different stations.

I think my success has had much to do with the way I appeal to my listeners as well as how I tap into the vein of what I call Cool School music. It doesn't matter if it's old school or new school— there's a certain quality to some music that just makes it good, makes it timeless, makes it... *Cool School.*

And I have a natural God-given ability to know how to deliver this kind of music to my listeners—whether over the radio or in the clubs or at the sets—and that's what has kept me contemporary through all these years. Motown, R & B, soul, doo-wop, funk, black punk—I've been at the forefront of all those trends, and my radio shows have delivered the edgiest music of those different styles to my listeners. That's my Pied Piper appeal, and at every radio station I've worked at, I have been greeted with the same unbridled enthusiasm from the listeners.

It has really been really great. But by no means has it been easy. You don't get to the top and stay at the top just by wishing it. I'm only eight years younger than the advent of modern radio as we know it, and although I wanted to be in radio since I was five years old, that just wasn't happening for black people back in the early days of the medium.

In fact, my college broadcasting professor at a prestigious university told me, as he was giving me my final grade (which was an A), "You have the best voice in the class, Mr. Kent, but you'll never make it in radio because you're a Negro."

In a nice piece of irony for my college professor, not only did I make it in radio, I'm now a college radio instructor myself, and I treat my students with a little bit more benevolence and encouragement than he did me.

Being one of the first black deejays, I had to summon the drive to overcome the kind of crap my professor laid on me, as well as other tremendous obstacles and adversity throughout my career. I did it not only to achieve personal success but also to blaze trails for other African Americans. I was the first and/or only black disc jockey at many of the stations that employed me, and I was an equal-opportunity ratings butt-kicker at every one of them.

But I've also had to overcome personal demons that threatened to destroy me, derail me, certainly, as much or more than any outside influences like racism.

As an impoverished kid from the projects, I always wanted to be in the industry, and I did make it to the top of the radio game. But I lost it and fell all the way to the bottom. But then, with perseverance and plain stubbornness, I climbed my way back to the top again, older and wiser.

That is what this book you're holding is about—the story of a little guy who wanted to be on the radio since he was a whippersnapper, finally gets in, succeeds greatly, crashes, recovers, and rises to the top of radio again. You want it, you get it, you lose it, you get it back.

It's a tell-all of my life and career with stories I've never told before. Not just your typical "Woe is me; I'm a po' black man just trying to beat the odds, massa!" stories, but also strange and amusing anecdotes about my seven decades in the music and radio industries and the colorful characters who inhabit those worlds.

Do you know that I shadowboxed with Muhammad Ali? Played hoops against the Harlem Globetrotters? Visited James Brown in prison down south? Conducted a séance with the O'Jays? Held high school record hops featuring Aretha, Smokey, and the Jackson 5?

For the past twenty years, people I met in passing said, "Man, you oughta write a book!" Maybe they want to read it to relive the memorable times they had listening to me through the years as much as for anything deep that I might have to say. Time passes so fast. I'm eighty now, been on the air for sixty-five years, been at V103 for twenty years. Everything's symmetrical, nice round numbers coinciding; the stars are in alignment. I guess it's time to tell my story.

So come along and experience some of the wild and colorful adventures of my life and career in the pages of this book. There's weepy dramatic narrative. Tall tales. Celebrity gossip and namedropping. Fashion. History. Racism. Outlandish promotions. Shady commercials. Murder. Interracial romance. Charlie Chan. Best-of-the-best music lists. Insightful observations on the music and radio industries. Philosophy. *Amos 'n' Andy*. Gangsters, crooked cops, and groupies. Sin and redemption. All wrapped up in a feel-good happy ending.

We'll even throw in some trivia questions at the beginning and end of each chapter to test your musical IQ.

You'll laugh. You'll cry. You'll disagree. You'll think, *Oh wow*. And your butt cheeks will go to sleep from sitting in one place reading for such long periods of time.

Be warned, though, in all seriousness. This book contains adult situations, graphic language, sexual content, and strong drug and alcohol references. That is what happens in an adult life, and I'm not trying to sugarcoat it here. I'm trying to be sincere on these pages and give a real depiction of events as I came to experience them.

Oh, by the way, maybe you're wondering about the book's subtitle, *The Nine Lives of Radio Legend Herb Kent*. Well, a radio legend I suppose I am. And you don't live for more than eighty years without almost getting close to meeting your Maker at least a few times, I think. Some of my nine lives have been rather funny, some mystical, some dark and anguished. And the fact is, by all accounts, I could just as easily be dead right now as sitting in a radio booth still broadcasting or writing a book.

If you listen to some of the things that I tell you in these stories, you'll know that God has really been on my side and that I'm a survivor.

But hey, let's start at the beginning, somewhere around the time I got run over by a car as a small child, then popped right up, ran upstairs to tell, and got a whupping because they thought I was lying.

See ya at the end of the book. Sit back and enjoy!

1
◆◆◆

1928

My Peeps

Amos 'n' Andy debuted on radio in 1928, but those were not the characters' original names. What were Amos and Andy first called?

(ANSWER ON PAGE 10)

Ahhh, 1928. It was a very good year.

The United States was in the midst of Prohibition, but the good times of the '20s were still roarin'! Calvin Coolidge, who uttered the famous line "The business of America is business," was the lame duck president about to be succeeded by Herbert Hoover, and Al Capone was somewhere planning the St. Valentine's Day Massacre that would take place the following February.

Wings, released in March, would win the first Academy Award for Outstanding Picture the next year; there was no such animal as television; and the music charts were topped by Duke Ellington's "Diga Diga Doo," Louis Armstrong's "West End Blues," and "It's Tight Like That," by Tampa Red and Georgia Tom Dorsey.

Mickey Mouse, Rice Krispies, Louisiana Hot Sauce, and penicillin all made their debuts, and a first-class stamp was two cents.

Let's take a look at some of the notable African Americans who slid down the baby chute in 1928: Fats Domino, February 26; Drew Bundini Brown (Muhammad Ali's trainer), March 21; writer Maya Angelou, April 4; musicians Maynard Ferguson, May

4, Horace Silver, September 2, and Julian "Cannonball" Adderley, September 15; civil rights organizer James Forman, October 4; noted historian, author, and *Ebony* magazine editor Lerone Bennett Jr., October 17; and badass bluesman Bo Diddley, December 30.

Shout-outs also to 1928 babies: Adam "Batman" West, composer Burt Bacharach, *The Exorcist* author William Peter Blatty, Shirley Temple, hairdresser Vidal Sassoon, singer-sausage man Jimmy Dean, and two of my favorite actors, James Garner and James "Our Man Flint" Coburn. James Brown is listed in some sources as being born in 1928 in Pulaski, Tennessee; other sources claim he came along on May 3, 1933, in Barnwell, South Carolina. Only the Godfather of Soul could pull off the feat of being born twice, in two different locations at two different times.

Future career broadcaster Herbert Rogers Kent, yours truly, joined this illustrious group on October 5, 1928, born in Cook County Hospital, in Ward 52. Some people joke that "in the beginning, God created Herb Kent," but hey, I'm not that old.

My father was a pharmacist named Herbert Williams; my mother's name was Katherine Kent. They were not married, and I didn't know my father. I guess he was obviously some type of boyfriend to my mother, but I guess she may not have liked him much because he never came around. I don't know where he is—or was, I'm sure he's dead by now—or what kind of support he provided us.

I had grandparents on my mother's side who lived in Harper's Ferry, West Virginia, but I never saw them either. There's a lot of history in my family. A lot of my family members were mostly Native Americans with a little black.

My mother was part that and part black; she was fair. She was from Virginia and went to Storer College in West Virginia. After working as a schoolteacher there she came to Chicago to seek her fortune, as many people from the South did during those years as part of the Great Migration of southern blacks to Chicago.

In Chicago my mother found a job as a domestic, and she was a very hard worker. She worked for the same white woman for years. We were living at Fifty-Eighth and Prairie on the South Side, not far from where bluesman Willie Dixon ultimately lived, but not at that time.

I was an only child being raised by my mother, and I do remember that she had to go to work many times and leave me all alone. I was four or five. She would put me in the bed in some kind of way where I couldn't roll off, and I'd have to stay there alone. I would be very frightened because I was by myself, and I cried all the time, every time it happened. That's one of my first memories. But she had to work, and sometimes there was no one to look after me.

How about this for another early memory? Mom often left me with a woman called Aunt Mary, and she just thought Aunt Mary was the most wonderful person in the world. So one night I'm there with Aunt Mary, and I'm about five years old. She takes a bath and says, "Come in here." I went into the bathroom and she said, "Get in the tub with me." I'm a little kid and I got in, and she made me suck her titties, which was a pretty disgusting thing to do to a kid.

I hated titties for a long time after that. I still have this feeling about super-big titties that I could get smothered, and it came from that experience. But I didn't tell my mother. I was afraid to.

When I was six, we moved into a boardinghouse at Thirty-Seventh and Giles. My mother only made ten dollars a week as a domestic, and the lady who owned the house would charge us five dollars a week to stay there. So my mother only had another five bucks to ride the streetcar, which was about seven cents, and to buy us the barest necessities at secondhand shops.

The woman who owned the boardinghouse was very mean, very cruel, and used to beat me for doing small stuff. She took it upon herself to do that. I stole a quarter one time, and she beat the shit out of me. The only good thing I can say about that was I've never stolen anything since that time.

Except bread. Living in the boardinghouse, I never got enough to eat. I was very thin, so at night I would go downstairs and steal bread. I was hungry. All the biggest portions of the food would go to the boardinghouse owner, and she would send me to school with brain sandwiches. I complained to my mother once, and the lady got pissed off. Man, a piece of bread with some brains on it—pig brains—I couldn't eat that mess.

One day while we were living at the boardinghouse—and this is a true story, and also the first of my nine lives used up—a car ran over me. I swear. I was six years old, playing in the alley, and this guy had bad brakes, I guess. He bumped me and couldn't stop the car in time. It knocked me over, and the car ran over my midsection, just like that. The guy got out and felt me for injuries, and I remember a girl who was standing there just fainted dead away because it looked so horrible.

But it didn't hurt, didn't break any bones, didn't even break any skin, so I jumped up, ran upstairs, and told the boardinghouse lady.

"I just got run over by a car," I said.

And she gave me a whupping because she said I was telling a lie.

Was it an angel lifting the car off me? I dunno. You hear stories like that—and that God takes care of fools and babies.

◆◆◆

America at the time was in the midst of the Great Depression. Everybody in the neighborhood was poor, and a lot of them were poorer than me. Some thought I had money, that's how poor those kids were.

You'd go in their houses, and you would smell Fly Dead, which was an insecticide. It was everywhere killing them damn roaches, and you could smell it. You could smell that and pee. Little kids would have peed in a pile of clothes or something like that. But I was quite used to it, absolutely quite used to it.

How poor was I, and did I know it? I knew that I didn't have as much to eat as many of the other kids. I especially knew it at Christmastime. Some of the kids I knew had wonderful Christmases with cap pistols, bow-and-arrow sets, bikes, and all kinds of stuff. I would have a stocking with maybe an apple, a pecan nut, a peppermint candy stick, maybe some gloves and a scarf. But I was happy to get it.

My mother and I had to live in the same room at this boardinghouse. One year shortly before Christmas—I guess I was about nine—I kept hearing this sound, every night, the same sound, a rattling, paper-shuffling kind of sound, and I couldn't figure out what it was.

I finally found out on Christmas Day. My mother opened the closet door to surprise me with this big, thick, long peppermint stick she had bought me and hidden there—but it was destroyed, eaten away! I just started crying because I knew that sound I kept hearing was the damn mice, night after night, eating up my peppermint stick. Damn Christmas mice.

To make up for that terrible experience the next year, when I was ten, my mother gave me a radio, which I think was the best gift I ever got. It cost eight dollars brand-new. That was almost her entire week's salary.

◆◆◆

During my years from ages four to ten, I would sum things up by saying I was an only child, very skinny, and a scaredy kid. I got beat a lot and was hungry a lot. Made me scaredy—I was like a tiny Don Knotts, scared of my own shadow.

I was very protected—a momma's boy—and shunned everything. Maturity came to me slowly, gradually changing me from a momma's boy into a man. I haven't the slightest idea why; who knows? I sometimes think I'm still not as mature as I should be.

I also don't know why my mother never had any more kids. We never talked about it. I always wanted a sister, somebody that I could be close to, but other than that, I wasn't lonely.

That seems like a quirky thing. I was a loner, but I wasn't lonely. I played with the girl down the street, then I met my three buddies—Charles, Lawrence, and Herman—at the tail end of grammar school, when we were ten, eleven, or twelve, and we became inseparable. When they weren't around for whatever reason, I had little toy soldiers that I played with. I listened to the radio. I was never a lonely kid and always found something to do.

◆ ◆ ◆

And in fact, even though I was a scaredy kid, I was pretty independent. My mother would take me to church—she loved that church—until I was old enough, like six or seven, to ride the streetcar. Then I'd just get on the streetcar and go to church by myself. I also would walk to school by myself at an early age.

Kids did that kind of thing back then. You didn't have the predators that you have now. Or maybe they were there, but people just didn't know about them, because it was nothing to be seven years old and walk to school or get on the streetcar.

Your mother would say, "Get on the streetcar and tell the man where you want to get off." So you'd get on the streetcar and tell the man, "I want to get off at Forty-Fourth Street," and he would set you up.

Times have really changed. My mother and I also used to sleep in the park, especially in Washington Park, around the time of the annual Bud Billiken Parade. You could just sleep out, camp out, and no one would bother you. It was a more innocent time, and of course you cannot do that type of thing today without ending up as a crime statistic or in jail because sleeping in the park is no longer legal.

◆ ◆ ◆

I was a smart kid—a very smart kid—which is one reason my mother trusted me to go to church and walk to school by myself. Never really been dumb. Always got good grades, though I got better grades in college than high school.

I played around in high school. I had a great memory, and the teachers were always pissed at me because I wouldn't do homework. I didn't have to; I was very smart, remembered stuff, passed tests. All except math—I wasn't very good at that. Everything else, no problem. In grammar school, in fifth grade, I was smarter than anybody. I was just a genius. I always could read very well.

I attended three grammar schools—Carter, Raymond, and Sexton, where I graduated. My mother kept moving me from school to school, always searching for the school that would be the best for me. One thing I just loved her for is that she had this thing about education, and she felt I had to be in the best school possible.

She was very strict with me—a lot of stuff other kids were allowed to do, I was not—but she was a good mother and instilled in me the idea to be a notch above everybody in whatever I did and to succeed in life. She taught me that, and taught me that, and taught me that. I guess I get my drive from her; she wanted me to be somebody.

So when I graduated from Sexton, which was a predominantly white school at Sixtieth and Cottage, I wanted to go to Wendell Phillips High School, but she said no, you're going to Hyde Park High School, a public school located near the University of Chicago, now called Hyde Park Career Academy. She thought that Phillips didn't match up to Hyde Park academically.

But I didn't want to go to Hyde Park, which was also nearly all white, and I cried like a baby. I didn't have anything against white schools per se; I just wanted to go where my friends went, and that was to the neighborhood schools, which were generally all black. She enrolled me there anyway, and the first day I went to Hyde Park, the first thing I saw was this shapely blonde standing in front of me waiting to go in. My tears vanished.

I'm glad I went and graduated from there, though, and not just for the girls. A lot of good people came out of Hyde Park High School—Steve Allen, Mel Torme, Herbie Hancock, and Minnie Riperton come immediately to mind; I'm sure there are a lot more distinguished Hyde Park alums.

At the time, everything on the other side of Drexel Avenue on the South Side of Chicago was white, all of it. Blacks lived on Federal Street over by the railroad tracks and along South Parkway (now King Drive) up to Sixty-Third Street, and after that, it was mostly all white.

You'd think it would have been difficult to get into Sexton and then Hyde Park, but all we did was give them phony addresses about where we lived, and they never questioned it.

♦♦♦

OK, so this is where my "killer cousins" come in. I did have extended family. I had five girl cousins who were really like sisters to me, and every Sunday my mother would take me to visit her sister, Aunt Dora, who was the girls' mother, and we would have Sunday dinner.

All those girls are dead now, every last one of them. I guess I've just about outlived everybody I know, and actually, that's a little scary. But I feel pretty good healthwise, and maybe I'll still be telling these same stories to people fifty years from now.

One of the girls was younger than me, one was my age, and three were slightly older than me. They went to Sexton, too—it was Aunt Dora's address that I used to get in there and Hyde Park—so in addition to seeing my cousins on Sundays, I'd stop by during the week after school.

Some of those girls hated me, brother, because not only was I a momma's boy, I was also a snitch. I told Aunt Dora and my mother if I saw them kissing boys or smoking cigarettes. To get even with me, what they did was play this game called Be Brave.

In a house near where they lived there was a really mean dog. One time, they told me, "Go in there and pet that dog."

I was real little at the time, but I said, "I'm not crazy, that dog is mean."

They shouted, "BE BRAVE!"

So I said OK, jumped in there, and that dog bit the shit out of me.

Another Be Brave moment I never will forget happened when they were living in a third-floor walkup apartment on St. Lawrence Avenue. The girls put me in this green buggy and said, "Are you going to BE BRAVE?" I said, "Uh-huh," and they pushed that buggy down the whole three flights of steps!

Oh man, they hated my guts. I could have been mauled to death by the dog or broken my neck careening down those stairs in the buggy, so there's two and three out of my nine lives that I used up with my cousins, I guess.

◆◆◆

My cousins called me a nerd because I told on them all the time, but I wasn't a nerd. I was just a smart little kid who liked to draw. I thought I could draw, and maybe I could some. Not very well, but good enough to get a little scholarship to the Art Institute after high school. That wasn't really my calling, however. The radio thing was what I wanted . . . and ultimately what I got.

(ANSWER TO QUESTION ON PAGE 2)

Amos 'n' Andy originally debuted in 1926 on WGN radio in Chicago as *Sam 'n' Henry*, a drama about two black men from Alabama who came to Chicago to start the Fresh Air Taxicab Company. After a falling-out with WGN, the two white creators of the show, Freeman Gosden and Charles Correll, moved over to WMAQ in 1928, but they were legally barred from using the title *Sam 'n' Henry*. So they changed the characters' names to Amos and Andy. Sponsors forced the show to be located in Harlem instead of Chicago and turned it into slapstick comedy instead of drama.

Falling in Love
with Radio as a Kid

> What artist has had the most number one R & B hits?
>
> *(ANSWER ON PAGE 16)*

One of the reasons I wasn't lonely as a child was that I could listen to the radio. That was my first love, man, I loved radio—loved it, loved it, loved it. I guess I was just kind of born into radio; it's my thing, it's always been part of my life.

I was barely tall enough to turn the radio on—I had to stand on tippytoes to reach the knobs—but turn it on I would, and constantly. It was just the most amazing thing to me. I was fascinated by it.

I used to listen to Jack L. Cooper, Chicago's first black deejay. He had a program called *Red Hot & Lowdown*, where they played all this music, and I was just jamming. And later, as I was growing up and the technology developed, I'd be under the covers with a portable radio. Man, at night, listening to a turned-down radio was just . . . . oh, wow!

When I got into high school, I started making radios—actually making them, soldering and all—because I loved the way they smelled, the way they sounded. You have to realize that this was a tremendously new phenomenon. Radio as we know it has only been around since the early 1920s, so it is only eight years or so older than me. It was technologically as explosive in its time as the Internet is today. Let me give you a brief, informal history on how this amazing new method of communications evolved in its early stages.

Somewhere around the 1880s, people started to notice that when you send a heavy current of electricity through a large coil wire and make it spark, a similar spark appears in a coil of wire miles away. So they made this real long wooden rod to activate these sparks, which you could form into dots and dashes, and these spark messages could be received miles away.

Ocean liners were among the first to use these wireless telegraph, or radio, transmissions. They kept perfecting these techniques until ships could stay in touch with their home base anywhere around the world. Some of the most important work in developing the technology was done in the 1890s by Nikola Tesla and Jagdish Chandra Bose—yeah, the guy the speakers are named after.

In 1909, an electronics instructor in San Jose, California, named Charles Herrold constructed the first broadcasting station, which he named San Jose Calling. There were no call letters at the time, obviously, since there were no other stations. I think San Jose Calling eventually turned into KCBS, which still broadcasts from San Francisco today.

Charles Herrold, by the way, coined the term "broadcasting" to define transmissions intended for a general audience, as opposed to those destined for a specific ship at sea, which he called "narrowcasting." To help spread his radio signals in all directions, so that he could broadcast, Herrold designed omni-directional antennas that he put on the rooftops of various buildings in San Jose.

So radio, as we know it, became a practical, usable technology. After Herrold's first station, a number of people and entities created amateur stations before the first publicly licensed commercial broadcasting station, KDKA in Pittsburgh, received that designation in 1920.

A University of Wisconsin station in Madison began broadcasting speeches in 1919 and is still on the air today as WHA, and a Detroit station, now known as WWJ, began airing a regular schedule of programming two months before KDKA became the first publicly licensed station. Ironically, even KDKA's engineer, Frank Conrad, had been broadcasting from his own amateur station since 1916. Between 1920 and 1923, certainly by 1925, every state in America, and most countries throughout the world, had publicly broadcast radio stations.

Here's something for you trivia buffs: the first radio news program was broadcast on August 31, 1920, on station 8MK in Detroit, and the first Rose Bowl was broadcast January 1, 1923, on the Los Angeles station KHJ. And, wouldn't you know it, in 1922 WEAF in Camden, South Carolina, had the dubious honor of being the first station to accept paid advertising in the history of radio. Actually, Charles Herrold was the pioneer of that, too, because in the early 1910s he gave a local record store free publicity in exchange for records they gave him to play on the radio—and that game hasn't stopped since.

This was the broadcast side, mind you, and you can browse the Web to find out about this stuff in detail. But now, let me tell you about the receiver side.

The most common early receiver of these broadcast signals—an actual radio—was a crystal set, and boy, did I make many of those. Very simple operation. Crystal radios don't need batteries; you just hook them to the bedspring, put earphones on, and you can listen to programs all night long. To make a crystal radio, I'd take a little crystal, fool's gold—what they call iron pyrite, it's some kind of sulfide—and that's all sitting in a cup. I'd put in a little wire and move it around until I got my music live and clear. I'd leave it there—not touch it—and usually about five or six stations came in at the same time. I'd devise some little ingenious wave trap to tune it. A wave trap is a tuning device made out of a bunch of wires wrapped around a toilet paper tube that you put into the circuitry. Then I'd put one wire to the radiator for a ground and another to my bedspring. And that was it—crystal radio! And the earphones back in the day were supersensitive. They'd pick up the slightest sound, not like the utilitarian earphones of today. Those back then picked up the faintest sound and turned it into something you could hear, just the faintest little piece of electricity.

Pretty deep, huh? No, actually, pretty simple. I guess you might ask how I knew to do this at such an early age. In high school, I got these plans from the old magazine *Popular Mechanics* and went down to the Allied Radio shop—which was a forerunner of today's Radio Shack—for supplies and just put the thing together. And it worked.

I don't know if they still do it, but for years the Boy Scouts of America had their boys make crystal radio sets as crafts projects to introduce them to the world of electronics. They were so simple to make that the Boy Scouts used to call them "the radio that runs on nothing, forever."

After crystal radio sets, what really made broadcast radio available to almost every home was the advent of the vacuum tube, which simplified creating, switching, and amplifying electronic signals. The vacuum tubes benefited transmitters and receivers and led to widespread growth and commercialization of radio broadcasting as a household medium.

The problem with vacuum tubes was that they were big and cumbersome. The more vacuum tubes in a radio, the heavier that sucker was. Maybe you've seen pictures or heard stories from your parents or grandparents, or even are old enough to have owned one yourself, God bless ya, but some of those huge old floor radios had forty or fifty tubes. After dinner, the entire family would gather around these heavy monsters and listen to stories and dramas. Of course at this time, there was no such thing as TV.

In high school, as a sophomore, I graduated from crystal sets. I went back to Allied Radio, bought a tube, and made my first one-tube radio, and I started making more. I was so good at it that I even made my own microphones. I'd take a small loudspeaker, reverse the wires, hook them in a radio's input tubes, and the speaker would change into a microphone. I'm telling you, I've lived and breathed radio my entire life, and I've got quite the collection of antique radios to show for it.

But more than just building radios, I wanted to be *on* the radio. I remember one of my early influences was a guy named Martin Block, who was the first radio announcer to achieve stardom. Matter of fact, the term "disc jockey" was created by the legendary journalist Walter Winchell to describe Martin Block.

Martin's claim to fame came in 1935 at New York's WNEW station when Charles Lindbergh's baby was kidnapped. That was such a big deal, you wouldn't believe. As listeners sat glued to their radios waiting for the latest breaking news, Martin Block built his audience by playing music between the Lindbergh baby news bulletins.

He was so successful at it that he got a show called *Make Believe Ballroom* in 1935, where he created the illusion that he was broadcasting from a ballroom with the top bands in the country performing live. I think Martin hosted that show for more than twenty years, and I really dug it. I wanted to do that.

My oldest living friend is a guy named William Harvey; he was there with me at the beginning and can vouch for my intentions. I met Bill in the Christian Science Church at Forty-Fourth and Michigan Avenue that my mother and I attended, well, religiously. We met in Sunday school in a club called Youth Forum.

Bill and I were both about three at the time, and we shared a lot together growing up. He lived up on Wells or Orleans, one of the last areas of the Chicago to be completely electrified—we're talking in the 1930s, really. I used to go to his house often while we were in grammar school, and his family had kerosene lamps and wood stoves.

Bill was the first person who told me he knew I was going to have a career in radio. We weren't yet twelve years old, but he knew. I'd even try to do radio stuff in church, pretending to broadcast the Sunday school services, and Bill noticed I always tried to talk like a radio announcer.

When I went off to high school, Bill's pronouncement began to take root.

(ANSWER TO QUESTION ON PAGE 11)

Aretha Franklin has twenty-one number one R & B hits.

From Dreams of Monsters
to Radio Dreams

What R & B artist has had the most crossover hits in
music history?

(ANSWER ON PAGE 23)

M y dreams started when I was left alone in my bed at night
beginning at the age of four because my mother had to go
to work.

One night I was lying in the middle of the bed, alone as usual,
when I suddenly heard a frightening noise: something or someone
was running down the hall toward my room. A big hairy beast
burst in, jumped up on my bed, and breathed its hot breath in my
face. Its eyes burned red like hot coals. It was so real to me! I don't
know if it was my imagination or just a nightmare. Whatever, I
was scaaaared!

A few years later my mom gave me a paper circus, where all the
animals and sideshows could be punched out with little tabs on
them so that they could stand up. There were hundreds of pieces
to it, lions and tigers and clowns with bright colors. I spent hours
on the floor moving things around. It was incredible how it just
became everything to me, my favorite toy to play with. That little
circus was just colored cardboard, but it developed my imagina-

tion in ways that I have used throughout my entire life and career, to the great enjoyment of my listeners, I might add.

As I grew older and my imagination expanded, I would imagine being watched by hundreds of people as I knelt on one knee, slowly drew back my bow, set my sights on an object three miles away, and let my arrow go. And true to its mark, it sliced a human hair in two.

I had many variations of this one. Sometimes I was a captain in the army. I would be an expert rifleman, a crack shot. I never shot at people, only apples and golf balls and things like that. I would always shoot objects that were quite a distance away, and I would never miss. Subconsciously, was I perhaps thinking that a radio career for a young black boy was such a very long way away but that I would still be able to achieve it?

I remember directly fantasizing about being on the radio at about age five, and it was always in the back of my mind. As I grew older, I guess I dreamed about more mature things, but no matter what it was, I wanted to be the best at it, brilliant at it.

◆◆◆

Life took a good turn for me when my mother and I moved from the boardinghouse shortly after I reached double digits in years. We moved into the Ida B. Wells public housing development, or projects, as such housing has commonly become known.

Despite the stigma attached to projects—and the people living in them—over the past three or four decades, they were a godsend for many people when they were first constructed. They were what they were supposed to be: protected havens where single parents could raise their children or low-income families could live and try to thrive.

In the early 1940s, my mother and I moved into the two-story Ida B. Wells developments, and people were really screened before they were allowed to move in. I think my block may have had six or seven buildings, maybe twenty families, and I know that just my block alone produced a doctor, a jazz musician, and me, a radio deejay. I'm sure that success was replicated on almost every block when the projects originally were developed.

Why they went into such utter decline through the years is not for me to speculate. Some say that the tall projects, like the infamous Robert Taylor Homes, were just concrete warehouses that incarcerated their residents more than housed them, but the low-rise projects suffered their share of grief and misery, too.

We stayed in the Ida B. Wells projects until I was nineteen. If between the ages of four and ten I was a scaredy kid, during the Ida B. Wells years I was a dreamer, pretty damned innocent, and I discovered that I had a creative bent and a vivid imagination. I'm talking about real dreams, not wide-awake fantasy wishing, though I had my share of that, too.

At fifteen, I was a frail kid: six feet, a hundred and forty pounds. I was so thin my nickname was "Lanky Lou." When they asked all the other boys in gym class at Hyde Park High School to try out for the football team, they wouldn't even talk to me. They just left me in the gym all by myself, dejected.

I compensated for that by joining the ROTC, and I got to be a captain. But at night I would dream about being a football player. I loved those uniforms, and I would imagine putting on those heavy pads, grabbing my jersey with my number on it, and strapping on that glorious helmet. I'd fantasize that I was on the football field and our team was losing, then the quarterback would throw the ball to me. Leaping high into the air, I'd catch the ball, and all the great-looking girls in the bleachers would shout, "Go, Herbie, go!" Then I would zig and zag with my arm outstretched, weaving through the tacklers who would miss me. On and on I'd run, amid cheers from the stands.

Suddenly, three big players converged on me—none of whom was under three hundred pounds—and I bowled them over like tenpins. The goal posts were in sight, the cleats in my shoes were pulling up huge patches of grass, one more tackler missed me, and it was TOUCHDOWN!

I had that fantasy for years until I played in a real football game, an ROTC game in which the noncommissioned guys played the officers. Being a frail person, I was picked on. The other players kept running that ball toward me, and I got knocked out twice. That was real! Somewhere during that game, I dropped my football fantasy and began to think more seriously about radio.

I had lots of fantasies and dreams. I had a dream that I would get this gorgeous girl and we would walk hand in hand into the woods. And we would keep walking until we were covered with this bright light, which meant that we would be in love forever. I never really thought about sex, I just wanted the love to be beautiful.

I was kind of sheltered, and it took a while to learn what life was really about. I lived in a dream world a lot; in fact, I absolutely almost believed in Santa Claus until I was fourteen. In my own little world, I loved the *Nutcracker Suite*. I knew classical music and loved to listen to it. Fortunately, it was a very creative world, which ultimately turned to my advantage when I got into radio because I was able to create all kinds of different things and I became a different type of person than most other announcers.

More than anything, I dreamed of being in radio, and of all my dreams I thought it would be the hardest to attain. But it came true . . . and I still dream.

◆◆◆

There were two distinct incidents in high school that put my feet on the actual path toward a radio career. The first was a field trip.

You know, field trips are very good for students because a kid can discover a lot of stuff on a field trip, even if it's only to the zoo, a candy factory, a downtown office, or a courtroom for civics classes.

In the ROTC we took a field trip to WGN radio. They had a broadcast every Saturday called *Something of the Air,* and the top floor of WGN back then was a theater. This Saturday broadcast featured a lady named Marian Clair, who was a soprano, and they did operettas. I love classical music, and we went up there to watch this operetta.

While we were waiting for them to get started on the radio, this white guy came out with a big shock of white hair. He stood in front of the microphone and started talking, and I just couldn't believe that a human being had a voice like that. It was just—Holy Moses! I was mesmerized. I was absolutely mesmerized and I said, "That's what I want to do." I know I was fourteen at the time, but I knew that's absolutely what I wanted to do.

So I joined the radio club at Hyde Park. But that was caused by the second incident—and don't you know that a woman would be involved? Isn't that always the way in life? Always a woman involved.

Well, this wasn't a woman, she was a teenage girl, my girlfriend at the time. I was with her all the time, and man, was she fine! But to me it was just sweet and innocent. We kissed and stuff, but we never went all the way, because I was pretty square. I didn't think it was right, even though some young boys twelve years old or so can be getting it on.

One day I was sitting in my window at home and she walked by with her stomach really distended, and it slapped me upside the head that she was pregnant, very pregnant. I liked her, but I wasn't fast enough to have sex with her, and this older guy at the Melody Milk store pumped her up. He wasn't wasting any time on sweet nothings!

Here I was at fourteen, and all I could say was, "Oh, gee!" But that really hurt, so I had to find something to do. I broke up with her—didn't have much of a choice really.

Berry Gordy, of Motown Records fame, used to say, "Bad things work into good things for you." And that's what really brought it to a head; I had to do something. I was just going to go nuts, so I joined the radio club to take my mind off the situation. That hastened my decision for sure.

This event happened shortly before the ROTC field trip, so maybe that's why I liked hearing that guy's voice and maybe that's what drove me to join this radio club.

Hyde Park High School wasn't very black at that time, I say jokingly. In reality, there may have been only six or seven black students out of the entire student body, certainly not more than ten. I was the only black student in the radio club.

But the white teacher was prejudiced—when I got in it, she dropped out. Sometimes I wonder why she left instead of just stopping me from getting in in the first place, but maybe that was an impossibility at that time. Maybe she just threw her hands up and wanted nothing to do with it.

The club was made up mostly of girls. There were about twenty of us, and we said to hell with the teacher and just went and had a great old time. There was a Jewish guy in the club and they made him president, but the girls didn't like him so they kicked him out and installed me. I ran it pretty well.

We went around to different organizations, churches, stuff like that; we'd get invitations to perform. We'd get behind a curtain and we had an amplifier, speakers, microphones, and a little console. We wrote the scripts and did radio shows. Afterward, the curtain opened up and we'd be there to take a bow.

I was always afraid of what was going to happen when they saw a Negro up there. But nothing ever happened. They just gave us some nice applause, we picked up our stuff, went back to school, and put it back where it belonged. All white people weren't like that one teacher, even back then.

But starting just a couple years later, I was to run into more than my share of racism. I'll tell you about that in a little while.

From that experience of being in the radio club as a freshman in high school, I was consumed with the desire to be on radio for real. While all my friends were out doing normal teenage things, I was at home studying to become an announcer. I used *Reader's Digest* to improve my reading skills.

While my friends might have been in their bathrooms secretly reading something pretty scandalous, I spent my time in the bathroom reading announcing books, trying to make my voice deeper.

I'd shut the door and talk into the corner to develop a resonance in my voice. The bathroom was ideal because it was like a tiny enclosed studio and I could hear my voice bouncing off the walls, which allowed me to study it and experiment with it.

All my work paid off in 1944, my sophomore year, when I was selected to be in the highly prestigious, highly renowned WBEZ Radio Workshops series and got to talk on the air for the first time on a real radio station. I was sixteen at the time, and I've been on the air ever since.

(ANSWER TO QUESTION ON PAGE 17)

James Brown had an unbelievable eighty-nine crossover hits in his career!

Wars: What Are They Good For?

In the 1950s, when your radio broke, why would you just go to Walgreens instead of calling the radio repairman?

(ANSWER ON PAGE 29)

Another notable thing happened to me when I was sixteen, other than being on real radio for the first time. In 1944 World War II was raging, and a white buddy of mine and I tried to enlist in the Merchant Marines. But they wouldn't let us in; we were too young.

I missed World War I in 1918, which was ten years before I was born. I think I was twelve or thirteen, in grammar school, when things started happening with World War II and Pearl Harbor, and the war continued through my high school years.

What I remember most about that period is that everybody thought Hitler was just all fucked up. Everybody hated him. Black people, too. We drew pictures of him in school like he was the devil.

We all followed the war from the very beginning. Hitler started his mess in 1939, and we knew what was going on because we had newsreels and received radio updates from President Franklin D. Roosevelt.

24

I was walking down the street from Aunt Dora's house one day when the word came: *"Japanese Sneak Attack on Pearl Harbor!"* The newsreels showed ships on fire. News arrived almost immediately that the United States had declared war on Japan. A couple days later, we declared war on Germany.

The government began preparing the public, telling us what we had to go through. We started to ration gas, and ladies didn't have any nylon stockings—they had to paint stockings on, and that was something to behold. And that's when I remember people first started making a dollar an hour at the defense factories—if you had a job making a dollar an hour, man, you were the top dog in the neighborhood. Umh, huh!

Then there were the blackouts. The American public practiced blackouts just in case we had air raids. This was some serious stuff because these were serious times. During a blackout, you had to cover your window and all lights *must* be out so the area you were in would be completely and totally dark. That was because if the enemy planes came over and any single light was on, they'd be able to see where to bomb. The planes then didn't have very good radar, or any radar, so they couldn't see where to drop their loads.

We were all convinced that we could be attacked right here in America, on our own domestic land, right in our homes. After Pearl Harbor, when we were attacked on our soil, we didn't think it farfetched at all that those planes could come over the oceans again and bomb the shit out of us, especially the cities on both coasts.

I remember we had a blackout one night where they turned all the lights out. They had these air-raid wardens who wore big white hats—and during the height of this particular blackout with everything off, somebody turned a light *on*. I remember hearing this air-raid warden shout at the top of his lungs, "HEY, TURN THAT MOTHERFUCKING LIGHT OUT, MOTHERFUCKER!"

I'm telling you, this was some serious stuff—you could go to jail or someone might kill you for turning on a light during a blackout. We didn't have them as frequently as they did in Europe, where they did get the hell bombed out of them, like in London. But it was not a good time. We were even told to get gas masks and helmets, just in case.

I was a kid, but it wasn't scary. I wanted to go to war. All us young boys were fascinated by the war planes—we knew the names of all the different models: Messerschmitts, Hurricanes, Spitfires, Thunderbolts, Mustangs. We knew all that stuff. I loved those airplanes.

So my friend and I tried to join the Merchant Marines, where you'd work on cargo ships, like oilers and tankers or something like that. In truth, we didn't really know what the Merchant Marines did or were; we just wanted to join and be part of the war effort. Out of patriotism.

There was a helluva lot of patriotism all over the country back then, among all races—something just didn't feel right about somebody coming on your turf stealing on you, trying to kick your ass. Black or white, what the Japanese did to us at Pearl Harbor made us all Americans first. I'm fortunate to have lived so long, but unfortunate in that I had to witness both Pearl Harbor and 9/11. Pearl Harbor felt like 9/11.

We relied a lot on the newsreels, so you'd go to the movies every week, where they showed the newsreels that would tell you what was going on with the war. Then you had the foreign correspondents on the radio like Carlton Bourne and Edward R. Murrow, and they'd come on and give you their synopsis of the news. How many people got killed that day. They told us about Dunkirk, D-Day, the various theatrical operations.

Hollywood eventually made a movie about D-Day called *The Longest Day*, and blacks boycotted that movie because there were so few black faces in it. Shit, there were all kinds of black people going over to the war and dying! They put us on the front lines, man. Oh, yeah. They've always done black soldiers like that.

And the military was segregated. You were either in a white unit or a black unit. If you were in the navy and black, you were a mess boy. You were a sailor, but you weren't a regular sailor; it was a service kind of position. But boot camp taught them how to handle weapons and stuff like that, so a lot of guys were doing the machine-gun thing. The black war hero, Dorie Miller, was over there and did his thing.

I don't recall in *Saving Private Ryan* that they had any black people with Tom Hanks up there at the front, either, but in reality you better believe black people were there, up there at the front, getting killed first, in World War II. Black soldiers fought and died, and went to prison camps, too. You had the Tuskegee Airmen, who fought well, and some of them got shot down and imprisoned.

But the sad part about the blacks in the military during World War II is that they returned to a country with the kind of racist environment that produced the Emmett Till murder in the mid-1950s. It was horrible situation. The black soldiers had to fight and risk their lives away from home, then come back to the nation they defended where they were prohibited from eating in the same restaurant with white people.

But at the time I wanted to join, that was far from my mind. In fact, my friend and I were sad that we didn't get picked for the Merchant Marines. In this book we're talking about my nine lives, but funny, in this case, it never crossed my mind that I might get killed if I had joined up and fought in this war. Kids don't think about stuff like that in general, and specifically, they glorified this war. They made it out to be that Americans were heroes, and the newsreels didn't show the reality of the blood and guts.

So all the guys all over America were bragging, Yeah, I'll go over there and I'll die, but you never thought that your brains might be splattered out or that you'd be blown up in the air like a rag doll while you were in the middle of a sentence. It wasn't portrayed realistically like it is today, where you can actually see how devastating combat is.

I graduated in 1947 when World War II was just over, and I was actually drafted for the Korean War because I was old enough then. But this war was a different ballgame. I went down for my physical, filled out the questionnaire, and answered all the questions—everybody else was pretending they couldn't read and shit like that.

The examiner told me, "This is interesting—you're the first guy in a long time that's scored ninety-eight points!" out of the one hundred possible on the test, and the test wasn't hard at all.

Nobody wanted to go. But the draft guys made them. They said, "Y'all gotta go, no matter what your score, so come back here tomorrow morning with a toothbrush, toothpaste, and a little overnight bag."

Truthfully, I had injured my knee in high school, and I asked them to x-ray it. They thought I was throwing them the bull and didn't want to go, but I said please do it. They did and found cartilage deposits, so they had to reject me even though I scored so high on the test.

That was fortunate, because I didn't want to go to Korea. The difference between wanting to fight in World War II and not wanting to fight in Korea was that I wasn't a kid anymore and knew what it was all about. Hell, nobody wanted to get shot and killed.

And this one in Korea wasn't a clear-cut deal like World War II, where everybody hated Hitler and wanted to go kill him. In Korea it just seemed like it was all about fighting on these hills. Hill 702, Hill 703, take them hills—that's about what it amounted to, and I don't think we won that one, or at least not decisively.

Besides, at this point, in 1950, I had gotten my first paying radio gig and had definitely decided that radio was going to be my future. Going into the army would not help that future at all.

During the Vietnam War in the 1960s I was at the height of my popularity, and we sent tons of my WVON tapes to Vietnam because the soldiers wanted to hear the music of the day from back home. They wrote asking particularly for my tapes because I had the hottest show, but eventually all the jocks at WVON, and probably other stations across the country, started sending tapes as well. I talked to some of the soldiers when they came home—either on leave, discharged, or because of injuries—and they said they'd be listening while they were fighting. I don't know how they did it, but somehow they had some kind of tape player and earphone plugged up, and they'd take that hookup and just go off shooting.

One guy told me that when he was patrolling, he played a tape I made with the song "I Only Have Eyes for You" on it. He said it calmed him down. The tapes really sustained them, they all said. Just the thought of home—you're a long way from home and just to hear that music was something, I guess.

I didn't understand Vietnam any more than I did Korea, but I didn't have any particular antiwar feelings about Vietnam, which was common during the 1960s. My thoughts were just to help lift the morale of the guys who were fighting and dying over there.

(ANSWER TO QUESTION ON PAGE 24)

When your radio was broken back in the day, you would take all the tubes out and take them to Walgreens to check them on the tube tester. It would say good or bad, and depending on your result you may just have had to buy some new tubes to be back in business.

You Want Me to Do What?

My First Encounters with Racism

> What Chicago South Side nightclub did Elvis Presley frequent as he began his rise to stardom?
>
> *(ANSWER ON PAGE 39)*

Since Hyde Park was such an overwhelmingly white high school, it was actually almost a protected environment for the ten or so black students there. We were absorbed into everything and basically moved right along with the rest of the kids. In that way we were kind of sheltered from racism.

Even though we were in the middle of a sea of whites, we were like a drop of spit in the ocean to them—there wasn't any need for them to be racist to us in general. The only time you have racial problems, the way I see it, is when you have fifty-fifty on each side. Then there's a power struggle. Or even an eighty-twenty white-to-black ratio—whenever blacks start to move in with some

YOU WANT ME TO DO WHAT?   31

number, there are going to be problems. That's when the pushing and shoving begins.

To illustrate this point, a few years ago I went to a motorcycle rally with my friend and fellow Chicago deejay Kevin Matthews. I'm a Kev-head, as his fans are called, and I've always enjoyed listening to him. Kevin is white, and he took me to South Dakota for this annual bike rally they have, and this thing is just humongous.

The rally draws about 450,000 motorcycles, and out of this huge crowd of hundreds and hundreds of thousands, there had to be maybe—maybe—one hundred black people. After a while, the white crowd didn't pay any attention to me, man. They'd slap me on the back, shake my hand—"Say, buddy, howya doin'? How are ya? Sit down and talk."

They had clubs with these little freaky waitresses, scantily clothed, who'd rub their breasts up against you if you gave them a dollar. White guy said to me, "Hey guy, did you like that? Give her another buck!" No racial incidents at all.

So despite the unfortunate experience with the teacher in the radio club, I was OK in high school. But I was in for a rude awakening after I graduated. The white teachers couldn't prepare me for racism. Being black, I had to go out there and find out that in the public's eye I truly was not equal to these white people and the kids that I had graduated with.

◆◆◆

While I did radio in high school with WBEZ and did some other radio things after I graduated from Hyde Park, they were on a nonpaying basis, and I still had to eat. So after graduation I took a job at a huge insurance company, as did a lot of my fellow graduates. I had been a good student, but unfortunately I was not prepared for the real world, I guess, because when I joined this company, right away I was hit with my first taste of racism. I had experienced maybe some minor racial incidents at Hyde Park but nothing like what I was about to experience on that job.

First of all, my white high school friends who were also working at this insurance company sat at desks up in the front of the office while I was sent to the back to sweep the floors.

My "office" was a little coatroom, and they told me I had to wear a white jacket and some kind of cap with a bill on it, kind of like a Pullman Porter hat. Only the few blacks who worked at the company had to wear this getup. I think there were three or four of us.

I had to carry heavy packages all over downtown Chicago. They bonded me and sent me to the bank with large sums of money, but basically I was a gofer. I worked the mimeograph and photostat machines and shaved wax cylinders for Dictaphone machines. I did a lot of trivial things, and for all of this I got paid $135 a month, about 30 bucks a week after taxes.

At one point, the insurance company hired a guy from Germany who was my age. This had to be around 1947 or 1948, and World War II was over by then. But this guy had been part of the Hitler Youth, the militant group of young people Hitler wanted to propagate what he called the master race. Well, this German guy and I worked together when he first got there, but he didn't have to carry packages or do any gofer-type work. Matter of fact, he was highly favored and rose very quickly through the ranks of the company. The German dude, he was a fairly decent guy to be honest about it, and we became friends, despite the Hitler stuff and his ascendancy through the insurance company.

I still had the desire to be in radio full-time, but in the meantime I was being racially abused and becoming very stressed out about it. The three or four of us black folks who worked there were housed in the back, wearing these porters' outfits, putting clean towels in the bathrooms for the other employees, and doing that kind of thing.

Very quickly I began to hate the situation, hate being a second-class citizen. I remember once I was sitting at work with a copy of *Popular Mechanics*, and a white employee asked me why I was reading it. He told me I would never get to the point where I would be able to use that kind of knowledge. Of course, he didn't know I had been using *Popular Mechanics* and *Popular Science* magazines to build radios as far back as my early teens. But it was just all that sort of garbage, constantly, just blatant racism.

After a while, I stopped wearing the little hat and porter's outfit. We had this older black guy there named Joe who told me, "You better put those clothes back on!" Old Joe would buck and dance and sing for those white folks. But I wasn't that kind of guy. I was eighteen, very ambitious, and not only could I not take all the racism, I didn't take it very humbly, either. I wouldn't shuffle, I wouldn't go along to get along, and, eventually, before my first year was even over, they called me in and fired me. It was just what I needed. They did me a favor.

◆ ◆ ◆

Once I got fired, I did some true self-inspection and realized that if I was serious about being in radio I had to go for it. So I forced myself to pick up the phone and call NBC in Chicago. What was this, 1948, I think?

Amazingly, I was able to get through to the head of personnel, a Mr. Glen Uhles, and he thought I was so personable and had such a nice speaking voice that he hired me on the spot, over the phone, and told me to come to work the next day.

When I showed up at NBC in the Merchandise Mart in downtown Chicago and met the man who had hired me, Glen took one look and said, "I didn't know you're a Negro! But I like you anyway. You still got the job." And thus I became the first black hired at NBC in Chicago. That's a piece of history I made that I'm real proud of, and Glen and I stayed friends for many years after that. He was a dear, sweet man, and I've thought about him often and appreciated and missed him much since he's passed on.

At NBC I worked in the mailroom with a bunch of very hip white dudes, and we all became very close. It was a totally different ballgame than the insurance company had been—I didn't experience any racism, and I didn't feel any. Not to be naïve—I suppose there was some there because the world is not perfect, certainly wasn't at that time anyway, as I was finding out—but by and large I was accepted as a fellow worker.

And I was where I needed to be to advance my broadcasting career, at a big radio and TV station operation. I met Kukla, Fran, and Ollie, and their creator, Burr Tillstrom. I also met Dave Garroway, the guy I used to listen to under the covers, who was a big-time deejay and the first host of the *Today Show*. And I met one of my most important mentors, veteran news broadcaster Hugh Downs, who later coanchored the popular *20/20* TV newsmagazine show for so long. Hugh really reached out to me and encouraged me to become a deejay, and oh man, how much I wanted to become a staff announcer.

While I was working for NBC they paid for me to take some college courses. They were hooked up with Northwestern University, and many of the university's courses involved NBC's broadcast studios. My training was thorough, and I got all As.

But that's where my radio professor told me, "Mr. Kent, you have the best voice in the class. It's too bad you'll never get anywhere in radio because you're a Negro." Maybe my college professor was really trying, in his way, to help me when he said that. Maybe he didn't want me to hold on to false expectations. Even though I had such a nice voice, it truly was difficult for blacks to get anywhere in radio at the time. So what he said may not have seemed derogatory to him at all, nor ill-intended. But that possibility didn't stop me from getting pissed off. I said something to him like, "You just give me my grade—my A—and let me worry about the rest!"

If anything, he could have said something like, "Hey, Herb, just keep trying and maybe one day you'll be able to break that color line!" Instead, it seemed more like, "Hey, you got a nice voice, nigger, now why don't you go work in the meat-packing place."

By that time I had been taught by many professionals, both at WBEZ and at Northwestern. And NBC occasionally held workshops for the teens and young adults they employed where we'd go out to dinner at the end of the workday, then come back to the studio and do radio drama. They would even let us use their ace sound-effects guy, Kurt Mueller.

I was thrilled when NBC gave me an announcer's audition when I was nineteen. But, man, that audition was harder than times during the Depression. I mean, it was *hard!* I was asked to say stuff like, "An egregious and lugubrious envoy greeted me as I entered the room." I messed it all up, but they gave me the script to keep, and I practiced it on my own. I memorized those lines and can still say them today off the top of my head.

◆◆◆

When I think of NBC and my experiences there, I think of the spirit and camaraderie. But there was one incident I remember that really shook me up.

Every year NBC had a big golf outing, and this particular year the event was held at a huge country club. So I was out on the course with my mailroom buddies, learning how to play golf, when a man came up and told me I had to leave. The look in his eyes told me they had absolutely no use for any blacks at this exclusive club.

When word of this encounter reached our general manager, Jules Herbuveaux, who was just a tremendous guy, he got furious. Jules said, "If you make Herb leave, we all leave—and don't forget, we are NBC!" The country club guy backed down, and I stayed and we partied, but inside I felt really awful. After that incident I actually wanted to leave, to go someplace to lie down and cry. But I stayed and tried my best to enjoy myself.

It's a memory I'll never forget, and I will always be grateful to NBC for taking that stand. Shortly afterward, one of the station's announcers pointed me to a real, paying radio job in Gary, Indiana. So I resigned from NBC and headed out to start my professional broadcasting career.

◆◆◆

Television was just starting to hit, and it's interesting to me that, although I wanted to be a broadcaster and all, when TV came along I never even thought about going that way. Black people at that time just didn't think about being on TV, not unless you were going to be Mantan Moreland, who acted in the old Charlie Chan movies.

Talking about racism, that reminds me of an episode of Charlie Chan—and this doesn't have anything to do with my life story, but it was so funny: These bad guys were waiting outside for Charlie Chan, his number-one son, and the chauffeur, who had his hat on (I guess it was actor Willie Best at this time).

The three of them ran downstairs right into the bad guys, and Willie Best said, "Don't worry about nothin'!"

And Charlie said, "Why?"

Willie Best said, "I can fix it."

Charlie asked, "How's that?"

Willie Best said, "I got a gun."

And everybody scattered. Bad guys and all.

It was so obviously racist, man, the implications—all Negroes carry guns!

◆◆◆

I had a couple other experiences in my radio career that smelled of racism to me. I'm not sure, though. I'll tell them to you, and you toss them around in your mind. These incidents concern trying to get hired for the thing you know you do best, and I know many of you can relate to how hard it is to try to get ahead only to be rejected.

The first incident occurred right before I took the job with the insurance company. At the age of seventeen, before going to NBC, I tried to get my first paying job in radio; until then, I had worked for free. I bought a little ad in a magazine called *Broadcasting*, stating that I was a Negro, young, had ability, and would love to work at a radio station. (How about that word *Negro*? Ha, ha!)

Very shortly after, I got a response from a radio station in Williamson, West Virginia, a small station, buried in the mountains, with a broadcast radius of about ten or fifteen miles. The station needed a deejay and asked me to audition. I'll never forget: I was living in the Ida B. Wells projects on the black South Side of Chicago, and I was headed to white mountain country, of all places. But I packed my bags and kissed my mother good-bye.

I got in my car, a Pontiac Silver Streak, got my road maps together, and took off. I took a lot of bags because I figured that I wouldn't be back in Chicago for a long time; I knew I was going to get hired. This was going to be it, after working for free and practicing in the bathroom on Saturday nights when I should have been out at a party. All of this was finally going to come to fruition. I drove on and on and on, my heart bursting with pride that I was finally going to be a paid professional radio announcer.

Incidentally, have you ever traveled a long distance on just two-lane highways with no toll roads or superhighways? It was a trip. I went through so many small towns that I can still see them in my mind's eye. Finally, after about a day and a half, I arrived.

Down around that part of the world there are a lot of mountains, and this station was in a valley. The mountains restricted the broadcast range. I entered the station and was greeted by the white lady who ran it. I figured it probably was a family station that needed a black deejay to add a little spice to it in the evenings, as many white stations did back in the day.

The lady took me in for my audition, and I was totally ready. I really cannot remember what I read, but I know I gave it my best shot. On these deals, what you generally do is sit in one room while those auditioning you sit in another room behind a glass partition and listen.

I tried to read the faces of the people I was auditioning for: sometimes they were frowning, sometimes looking passive, and sometimes smiling. Anyway, the lady came in once I had finished, and guess what she told me? You won't believe this, but she told me that she didn't like it. She did not like my audition! I asked why, and you know what she said? "You sounded like you were singing."

Well, that was my first experience with the other side of radio—the not-so-nice, heartbreaking side of radio. I was so disappointed that I didn't sleep much that night, and I headed out early the next morning to go home.

About an hour out of Williamson, it happened. I had no experience driving through mountains, and I was going too fast when a sharp curve loomed ahead. I slammed on the brakes.

My car swerved, and I could see that I was approaching a huge cliff. The car spun in a big circle, and I screamed, "Oh, sweet Jesus, please help me, please help me! I don't want to die!"

Miraculously, that car stopped right at the edge of the cliff. I will never forget that for as long as I live. A crowd of about twenty people gathered around to see what had happened, and at the edge of this small town, I forgot all about not getting that job—in addition to using up the fourth of my nine lives.

I'm not sure about racism in the West Virginia audition because they knew I was black, and why have me drive all the way out there just to not hire me because of my skin color?

But let me tell you about another failed audition. Sometime later, after I had some years of experience, I heard that WIND in Chicago was looking for an announcer. I figured I could do this one. WIND was a big station, and I knew that it would pay big money. Gosh, how I wanted this job, but there were about twenty of us after that one position. We began to read for the spot, and it was a process of elimination. 'Round and 'round we went until there were ten of us. They kept calling me back, so I knew I had a chance.

Then there were five, and finally there were two, me and some other guy. Both of us waited in the studio for the decision. The gentleman giving the audition told me, "Herb Kent, you almost won, but I'm afraid you lost just by a hair." And I asked, "Just how close is close?" He said that on one word I had a downward inflection instead of an upward inflection.

I later became friends with that man, but had I gotten hired, I would have been the first black full-time announcer that WIND had. I often wonder if the guy was afraid to be the first to install a black on the staff. Or did his bosses persuade him not to hire a black because the station wasn't ready? Or if I had gone up instead of down on that inflection, would I have gotten that job?

One thing for certain is this: when these disappointments threaten to make your world collapse, you just have to try again, and try harder. At no time should you not pursue the things you want—just keep at it.

(ANSWER TO QUESTION ON PAGE 30)

Elvis loved the Club De'Lisa at Fifty-Fifth and State Street in Chicago. It's rumored that he got his slick gyrations from watching the chorus girls there wiggle about.

2

◆◆◆

DEVELOPING AN
ON-AIR STYLE

Yes, Sir, or Yowsuh?

*Early Black Radio and
the Commercials of Yesteryear*

What popular Grammy-winning crooner was once
managed by the late Sam Cooke and created the
telethon for the United Negro College Fund?

(ANSWER ON PAGE 50)

After I failed my audition in West Virginia, I returned to Chicago to take that wretched job at the insurance company, where they wanted me to play Stepin' Fetchit. When I had moved on to NBC, one of the staff announcers gave me the heads up about the opening at WGRY, the station in Gary.

I got the job, my first paid professional radio announcing gig, at thirty-five dollars a week. It was 1949, and I was about to become perhaps the first contemporary black announcer who crossed all lines.

To explain fully what I mean, I need to give you a brief rundown on black radio of yesterday, when soul brother deejays took their own records to the radio station and played what they wanted to play. I had had the good fortune to listen to radio's first black disc jockey, Jack L. Cooper, who began playing records on WSBC in Chicago in 1929, when I was a kid. Jack was an urbane dude who sounded like he was white. The other blacks following him in Chicago were Al Benson, Sid McCoy, and Daddy-O Daylie.

In 1947 there were only sixteen black deejays in the entire nation. They were a colorful lot, and all had colorful nicknames and taglines, such as Al Benson, the Old Swingmaster; Rock with Rick; Your Boy Sid McCoy; the Geeter with the Heater. Down south, there were black jocks with monikers like Oke Doke and Honey Boy. It was a male-dominated field, and women were a rarity, but there were a few—Your Musical Hostess That Loves You the Mostess, Boss Lady, the Queen Bee Merri Dee, and a few others.

Everybody had a theme song, and when you heard it kick in you knew that your favorite deejay was coming on the air. Some deejays clapped their hands, snapped their fingers, and talked through the whole record. Some gave big public dances and blues shows. All in all, they did quite well.

Many of the jocks were family men and very decent individuals. The black jocks in Chicago helped initiate a lot of record deals between artists and record companies, since the deejays could play whatever they liked and could talk about the records as much as they wanted to increase record sales.

I have to admit that, back in the day, some radio stations would hire black guys to be on the air who had no formal training. But when they got into that studio, they developed a style and could really jam. Al Benson, for instance. He was a southern preacher and vaudevillian who came to Chicago, got a show on WGES in 1945, and became just the biggest thing in Chicago radio. He appealed strongly to the newly arrived southern migrants, who identified with him because of his thick Mississippi Delta accent and because he played the down-home gutbucket blues they were familiar with.

So his speech wasn't polished; in fact, some of Al's fans called him "Old Mushmouth." But he knew *how* to talk to folks, and when you tuned him in, you'd get his familiar, soothing sound. He far surpassed Jack Cooper in popularity because while Jack was a little more dignified than Benson, he couldn't hit the nerve in communicating with the audience like the Old Swingmaster could.

Some of the black deejays could scream, some guys could moan, and it was all good—they could chop the language up, play those blues or whatever, and they had a big following. I would give anything to go back to them days and turn the radio on and listen to those guys; that would be great.

And they sounded blacker than I ever could. I was envious because their sound was so awesome. I didn't have a black accent when I first started out in radio, but I developed one as I grew, and that was deliberately done.

I was gifted with a great, beautiful voice, and as a young adolescent I went from soprano to baritone in one week. My voice just abruptly broke one Sunday morning while I was singing in church when I was twelve. One minute I was squeaking and the next I was Barry White.

But even though I had a God-given gift of a good voice, I worked on it all the time. Remember, I practiced for years sitting on the toilet speaking into the corner of the bathroom to let the echo help me learn how to get resonance in my voice, while my teenage friends were out dating and being hormonal.

In addition, when I first went on the air in 1944 with WBEZ, it was the Chicago Board of Education's radio station, so it was particularly strict about using language. The WBEZ workshops showed me how to bite off my words, how to articulate, and how to breathe diaphragmatically. The WBEZ people told us that the idea was to be unidentifiable on the air, so through training I developed a radio speaking style that I used to call "my academy voice."

You couldn't tell what race I was. I was unidentifiable on the air, and just as easily sounded as white as I did black, which is what

I meant at the beginning of this chapter when I alluded to being the first contemporary black announcer to cross all lines.

For instance, at my first job at WGRY, I played all kinds of music. They gave me a "race show"—they called the all-Negro show the race show—but also in my itinerary I had a Polish polka show and a country music show. I did it all. You couldn't tell what I was on the radio, so management took advantage of that, which worked out well for them considering that the station only had two disc jockeys.

See, I learned radio old-school style, pronouncing words correctly and stuff like that. I came up in an era where a black person would try to get a radio job and people would say, "We can't use you because you sound too black. Pronounce your words." I think it was a device used to keep African Americans out of radio.

Today I still have mixed emotions when I hear black announcers mispronounce words. There's a guy who always says "Sat-a-day," and it's like fingernails on a chalkboard to me: "It's happening Sat-a-day!" "Come on out this Sat-a-day!" He won't pronounce the r, and it just pisses me off.

You have people like Steve Harvey, who mangles the language on his syndicated show, but he's a comedian and I give comedians a break. But I think a person who's going to be an announcer by profession should pronounce everything correctly, I really do.

I have no problem with people sounding black, but you can be black and correct with your English. Some people are just lazy and they're not going to learn those words; they don't care and they just spit them out. I think that's bad for a lot of people listening, because if you say "axed" on the radio instead of "asked," people listening will also say "axed."

◆ ◆ ◆

As I worked at a string of radio stations throughout the 1950s, playing R & B music, people took bets as to whether I was black or white. I started including the slang terms that went along with what I was doing because I really tried to develop a black sound.

But because of my professional training, I came off as a white man trying to sound black.

But you know what? Some black people could instantly tell that I am black. When I was working at WGRY, a large dancing school chose me to voice-over their commercials after they heard me on the air and liked my voice. They didn't know what race I was; they had only heard my voice. But then this school got mad and canceled when they found out I was black. It seems as though a number of black people started showing up for their dance lessons after hearing my commercials. The school wasn't sure why, but that was unacceptable to them so they came to the station to inquire. After they saw that I was black, it was adios to me doing that account.

That was funny, though—all those black folk headed out to the dancing school at my suggestion and I was getting paid to promote it. So in fact the spot was a success. But I'm still not sure how they could tell that it was a brother voicing those spots.

That same thing repeated itself at WGRY. Since I was doing the race, Polish, and country-western shows, I could play any kind of music, all kinds of music. I thought I was really playing some nice music when I first started, but again some black people could tell I was black from the git-go. This black dude called up one day and said, "Man, when you gonna play some blues? Play some blues, goddamn it!"

So I started playing some blues tunes and found out that I liked the music, and I've been playing mostly black music ever since. And as the years have passed and I have mellowed, I just about have my soul sound where I want it. But after all these years, I'm still working on it.

◆◆◆

Slowly, things have changed in radio. Great voices are always in demand, but today the emphasis is on communication. If you are a good communicator, you do not need a great voice. In fact, you can have a high-pitched voice, or even an everyday-sounding voice, and get over.

However, I think the announcers with voices of character that stand out are still more successful today. A few years ago I was in a nightclub when this lady who was feeling really good came up to me and said, "Oh, hey, Herb Kent. I knew it was you because I *saw* your voice." I've had people recognize me by my voice alone everywhere from barbecue joints to gas stations to candy stores.

That voice recognition's got an awkward side to it, though. Once I took this girl to a hotel and suddenly there was all this scuffling outside the door. I heard a chambermaid say, "It's Herb Kent! He in there, yeah he is!" And then all this running around as people came to the door!

But today, it's New Jack Radio. Nobody wants to spend time training their voices anymore; they just want to get on the radio and go, and that's possible now. Some folks come right out of radio school and go big time. It used to be that a radio station wanted you to have four to five years of experience in the smaller markets before they let you on the air in a big city like Chicago or New York. But in radio, it's always a new day. No one really cares if you have perfect pronunciation or articulation; people still love you. In fact, unless you're doing talk radio, the music stations would prefer that you talk less—if you have to say anything at all other than their call letters.

Some radio stations now are even using celebrities—comedians, musicians, and singers—as their announcers. Deep down inside, I'm not sure I like it—Hey, Kenny G., I don't go around trying to play the kazoo like you, so why are you on the air taking a job away from a legitimate deejay who spent time getting trained? Some of them are pretty good and entertaining enough—Steve Harvey, Whoopi, Ramsey Lewis.

Comedians, rappers, and a lot of talk shows now heavily influence radio, and I love it because it relates to our lifestyle and our growth. In fact, I imagine that if I was nineteen again, I'd be trying to slide in on one of these rap stations; in fact I know I would, since that's a good way to get over these days.

With regard to how people sound, I'd like to do a certain gimmick on my show. On one set of lines, I would like to have people of various ethnic persuasions call in and speak, and on the other, have people call in and guess the ethnic persuasion of the people on the first line. Is caller A white or black, is caller B Chinese, and then we'd give T-shirts to those who guessed correctly. Of course, I could never really do that because a lot of people would be offended. To be perfectly honest, nowadays it really does not make a difference if you say, "Yes, sir," or "Yowsuh!"

◆◆◆

Commercials were one of the most important parts of early black radio. A lot of these jocks sold their own radio time, got their own sponsors, and wrote their own spots. They knocked down a 30 percent commission doing this, which was a nice little take. That's how a lot of these guys even got on the air, by brokering time.

While driving my new red Williams Cadillac on a warm, beautiful day, my mind began to ponder the backbone of radio—the commercials . . .

The aforementioned Cadillac dealer, Williams, is a black-owned, very posh, plush dealership in Tinley Park, a southern suburb of Chicago, and by mentioning that I drive this beautiful new red car, I just did a commercial for Williams Cadillac in print, which gives me the opportunity to keep driving it for free, since that's part of my deal for being their spokesman. I am also a spokesperson for some other very reputable folks. My other clients include Alcala's Western Wear, Gillette, Island Furs, Seaway Furniture, State Farm, Miller, Budweiser, Heileman's Old Style, and several other on-the-up businesses.

By comparison, you were not sure what you were getting in terms of "reputable" in the commercials of yesteryear, which were sold by deejays just walking up and down the street trying to find clients. And the commercials themselves on black radio are much different now than those in the 1940s, '50s, and '60s. Back then, there were a lot of commercials for hair preparations, such as Dixie Peach and Royal Crown hair dressing. We advertised skin bleaching products and many medicinal bromides, such as Black Draught, which was a laxative, and Three 6's for colds. We advertised local mom-and-pop restaurants, mom-and-pop grocery stores, mom-and-pop filling stations, and mom-and-pop record stores. We had a lot more local business then than we do today. There was Chicken-in-a-Box, Chicken-in-a-Basket, shrimp houses, and dozens of barbecue joints.

Those were all pretty cool, but then we also had some questionable sponsors, like this furniture company that advertised three rooms of furniture for $159 with no money down, complete with pictures for the walls. But the trick was that when you went to buy it, all the $159 stuff was nailed down and glued to the floor. They made excuses as to why they couldn't sell it to you and would lead you to higher priced furniture, which still ended up being cheap furniture.

Another example: Once I was at a girlfriend's house sitting on the couch getting some smooches in when there came a sharp knock on the door. A loud voice said, "We came for your TV set because you didn't make your payments!" The lady said, "Please go away, I'll pay you next week," whereupon the door crashed open, two thugs walked in, took the TV set, and left. Unfortunately, this came from one of the clients that I had advertised on the air, and I felt really bad about it.

There was also a chain of stores that bought bruised, beat-up chickens, soaked them in bleach for a couple of days until they looked fresh again, rinsed them off, and sold them. And a preacher who came to town once a month or so and would buy an hour on Saturday nights to pitch some "blessed" crosses that were supposed to cure cancer, mental illness, and everything in between. They were even supposed to bring your loved one back if he or she had strayed. Mind you now, these were little ten-cent crosses that he sold for thirty-five dollars apiece. This guy had a silver tongue, and he jammed those phone lines, not only on Saturday nights but for several days after.

What else? I also had some pretty shady insurance companies as clients. This one guy had his Corvette stolen and the insurance company jacked him around; they wouldn't replace it. So he came to the radio station because his belief in me had led him to buy the policy in the first place and he was mad at me.

Another time, when I had a beautiful '57 T-Bird with vinyl seats, an outfit came along with this new vinyl paint that could change the color of the seats or put designs on them—you know, tougher, stronger, lasts longer. Since I let them be on my show, they agreed to paint mine for free, so I gave them my car.

They brought it back a couple of days later, seats repainted with some funny design. I can still smell the paint—it had a peculiar odor. Just two weeks later, my seats fell apart. The paint had flat out just ate them damn seats up.

These things truly happened back in the day, but people and radio stations are more enlightened now. As deejays back in the 1950s and '60s, we had no idea that we were endorsing products that were unethical; even for those that we placed on the air ourselves, we had no idea that we were being used.

I don't want to give the impression that old time radio had nothing but a bunch of crooked commercials; we of course had some very fine clients. But, thank God, I'm glad those thirty-five-dollar crosses and bleached chickens are a thing of the past.

You can read more about the history of black deejays and early black radio in another book that I highly recommend, *Chicago Soul* by Robert Pruter.

(ANSWER TO QUESTION ON PAGE 42)

Lou Rawls was once managed by Sam Cooke.

Getting My Act Together in the 1950s

> What was Chuck Berry's profession before he made it big?
>
> *(ANSWER ON PAGE 57)*

As a disc jockey, if you work very hard and are lucky enough to land a job in radio period, then your real job has just begun. Next you need to make a name for yourself, and you've got to get good ratings.

That was the mission when I got my first paid radio job at WGRY in Gary, Indiana, in 1949 at the age of twenty. I kissed my mother good-bye again, like I had done when I went on the audition in West Virginia when I was seventeen. But this time it wasn't an audition; it was a real job, and I figured to be in Gary for some time. With her only son having left the nest, my mom moved to New York City to be closer to some of her other family members. I lived in Gary with a family we knew. They were a traditional lot and told me to stay off the streets, don't go out, etc., and I tried to do that. I was still really shy.

Before I left Chicago I was a member of the Skyloft Players. It's what we used to call "little theater," for budding actors and actresses. There were a few such groups in Chicago, and ours was all black; there were maybe thirty of us. We had a theater in the

51

top of the Community Service Building, a very cozy thing that might have held about eighty people, if that many. We did plays like *Streetcar Named Desire*—not one-act plays, but plays that needed no changes in scenery. We did build scenery, however. We learned how to do everything: apply makeup, deliver lines, how to block.

It was very good, very intense training that benefited me for a long time. It was a perfect testing ground for developing the improvisational skills required to host a radio program, and I excelled there. Being in the Skyloft Players helped me develop a concept I call "theater of the mind on radio," which I'll talk about in later chapters.

One of my closest friends in the Skyloft ensemble was Lynn Hamilton, who was from Chicago Heights. She and some of the other members left the group and went to New York to seek their fame and fortune. Lynn ended up playing Redd Foxx's girlfriend on his show *Sanford and Son*. She also had a nice role on *The Waltons* for a while and was in several movies.

I left the group to seek fame and fortune as a radio deejay at WGRY, and I was *hot* from the minute I hit the air! I discovered I truly had a talent for radio and began to get large audiences immediately. I would get over sixty cards and letters a day, people loved my show that much—and it was a small radio station. The boss thought that I was writing them myself. He thought I went home every day and wrote sixty letters with different handwriting. He just couldn't believe it.

Working at WGRY was a great learning experience about the rudiments of radio. There were only two deejays, and we worked twelve-hour shifts seven days a week. So in addition to polishing my on-air presence with my race, polka, and country-western shows, I also produced, wrote, interviewed personalities, typed my own log, and did my first remote on-location broadcast.

It was the shows that were making me a name, however, and we were on a roll with that until the station hired a lady deejay named Vivian Carter. She came in with sponsors and brought a lot of money to the station. Vivian just flat out didn't like me. I guess I was very good at what I was doing and maybe she thought I was standing in her way. She wanted to take my time slot on that radio and do what she had to do. So she came in and convinced the boss that she needed my time to make the station more money. He bowed to her wishes and fired me.

Vivian left him about a year later to form Vee-Jay Records—that was one ambitious old broad!—and the boss called and said he really regretted letting me go and asked me to come back. But it was too late; I had moved on and already found another radio job.

That was the first time I was fired. But it's no sin to be fired at a radio station, believe me, because it's not the most secure job in the world. I guess I've been fired five or six times by different stations, but I've also been rehired by those same stations. Working in radio is a trip!

◆◆◆

I left WGRY in 1950, the start of a new decade and a new start for me. I went back to my old job in the NBC mailroom, but Sam Evans, a jock from WGES, quickly came to get me.

There were no all-black stations in Chicago at the time and black people listened mostly to WHFC, WOPA, and WGES. These stations put their black deejays and black music in the mix with all their other ethnic programming—German, Greek, Italian, whatever.

But WGES had more black programming than the other stations and a Big Three disc jockey lineup of the Old Swingmaster Al Benson, Richard Stamz, who did a lot of black comedy stuff along with his music—his show was called *Open the Door, Richard!*—and Sam Evans.

Sam was a big enough force that he promoted concerts in the area, and he brought in some good money to WGES. All these guys worked on the brokered system: you buy your time from the station and then go out and sell advertising to recoup that money and make some for yourself. The more money you brought in, the more hours the stations would let you buy.

I had managed quite a little reputation for myself very early at WGRY, so Sam wanted me to work for him to attract listeners. He had four hours a night and he gave me one of his hours, and he was going to sell it. I turned him down at first, but he talked me into it. You know the old adage: If you ever want to get anywhere you have to leave where you are and put both your feet in it. So I left NBC again and went to WGES. I did very well, actually. I gave Sam a lot of good ideas, and I also learned how to sell time. I got ahold of some sponsors from a shrimp house who saw this as an opportunity, so they bought up all the time from me instead of Sam. Sam fired me.

But Al Benson picked me up under the same kind of deal and let me do fifteen or twenty minutes a night with him. Then he must have gotten pissed off at me for some reason, and he fired me, too. But Al and I became good friends in the long run, and he taught me so much.

After Benson let me go, station management at WGES figured that I must have been doing something right, so they gave me my own time, and I was independent of everybody. But in order to take the hours they gave you, you had to get out in the streets and sell radio spots. And that I did. Eventually, an announcing job opened up at a new station in Harvey, Illinois, called WBEE. It looked like a better opportunity because WBEE was committed to doing all-black programming, so I quit WGES and went there.

I guess I was with WGES from maybe 1952 until 1955, when WBEE came on the air, but I'll never forget that one of my high-lights at WGES was working with Mahalia Jackson, the gospel legend. I used to be Mahalia's announcer for her time slot on WGES, and I would broadcast from her house on the South Side of Chicago. I don't know how long we did this, but I would bring the remote amplifier out to her beautiful home. We would set up in her kitchen and she would talk and we'd play records and she would cook breakfast for us.

I'll certainly never forget having breakfast with Mahalia Jackson. What a wonderful woman she was. And man, could she cook! This was the first time I was ever that close to a famous celebrity—the first of many, many times.

I went over to WBEE and my career really took off. Just, zoom! It just catapulted. I started to get real hot and really realized that I had a big following and that I was a big talent. I did the afternoon show, anywhere from two to five, or two to eight or nine, because it was a sunup to sundown station. In the summer we stayed on longer and in winter I was only on for a couple of hours. I had an interesting work day. Played a lot of doo-wop records. Did some record hops and promoted some shows. I had Howling Wolf once.

I got an unbelievable load of cards and letters and visitors to the studio. And a group of my ardent listeners developed a fan club around me and gave me the title of Herb Kent, the Cool Gent! It seems to have stuck. That nickname had everything to do with my personal style and the image I projected. I was tall, handsome, debonair, very stylish and fashionable, ultra-cool, and classy. I had what someone once called a "cognac smooth" voice that I used conversationally on the air. I was articulate, a smooth talker, and I didn't holler and scream. I was just strikingly different from the typical black radio announcer of the day—I was the brash, flashy Cassius Clay to their mumbling Sonny Liston, I guess. And you know what? I just loved being cool. Still do.

Something else that's stuck with me throughout my career is "dusty records." I'm also known as Herb Kent, King of the Dusties. I created the term while I was at WBEE, but I got the thought from the great deejay I've already told you about, Dave Garroway, who used to be on WMAQ. He had a program called *The 11:60 Club* that came on at midnight (midnight—11:60 o'clock, get it?). Dave was one of the guys I used to listen to under the covers at night with the portable radio. He was a white disc jockey, but he loved Sarah Vaughan, he loved black jazz, and he would talk about Sarah Vaughan rolling down the street in a white Cadillac and stuff like that. This guy was really good, real smooth.

He'd play records, and the older they were the more scratchy they sounded. But Dave said he loved the scratchy sound; it made the music sound better to him. So when I got on WBEE and played the nice old scratchy records that had been played over and over again, I called them "dusty records," reasoning that it was the dust in the grooves from being around so long that made them crackle.

Actually, to me, if a record's been played so often that it can become a dusty, that means it's good music. To a lot of radio people—managers, program directors, and deejays—the only good place for an old record is the trash can. But one astute radio guy told me when I was young that an old record is like an old movie—it's always good. And I agree. A good song is a good song, from whatever era, and if you find one, it'll be a good song forever. It's timeless.

So those terms, "dusties" and "dusty records," that are used now all over the country to describe oldies records, those terms were invented by yours truly. I've been following a dusties format ever since, at whatever station I've been at, and man, has that been the salvation of my career!

So that was the good part of WBEE. The bad part was that they overworked me. They worked me like seven days a week for maybe a month. One Sunday I was so tired I overslept, and I didn't open up the station on time. They fired me on the spot, despite my ratings and my soaring popularity after being there for four years.

But I was such a well-known jock by that time that the manager of WJOB in Hammond, Indiana, heard I had been let go and hired me immediately. I stayed there for about a year. It was an all-white station, but I was on twice a day. I was their star deejay.

One of my fondest memories at WJOB was covering the Indiana County Fair in Crown Point in 1959. We had just recently purchased a portable tape machine at the station, and it worked really well. Had a rechargeable battery in it and everything, really nice. It just so happened that Duke Ellington was playing at the fair. I was still a young cat, just thirty, but of course I knew who

Sir Duke was. I found him in his trailer on the fairgrounds, and he was eating a Tastee Freeze or something like that. He was sitting behind the wheel of the bus that pulls the trailer.

I explained to him who I was, and he gave me a really, really good interview. We talked about his kind of music, and I mean, Duke Ellington was just a music impresario! We talked about the swing music that he did, and I asked what he thought about doo-wops and R & B. He liked that, he said. "I think it's just great music." I was in the presence of a great guy, but some kind of way I lost that tape, which would be priceless today. I've lost a lot of stuff like that in my lifetime, but that one I truly, truly feel bad about.

I only stayed at WJOB for about a year. WBEE wasn't crazy. They realized the star power I had at the time and that all my star wattage was being used at this little station in little Hammond, Indiana. So they called and asked me to come back. This time I took an offer to come back to a station that had fired me.

I truly felt bad leaving WJOB, though, because they were some very fine people who treated me well and with much respect. They were in tears when I left them—they actually cried. But it was a career decision—WBEE was the bigger station and known as the gateway to Chicago radio, and that was what I needed. So I left WJOB and went back to WBEE.

(ANSWER TO QUESTION ON PAGE 51)

Chuck Berry was previously a beautician; that's why his 'do was always together!

When Doo-Wop Was King

How did the singing group the Spaniels, who had the hit "Goodnight, Sweetheart, Goodnight," get their name?

(ANSWER ON PAGE 61)

Let me digress a bit here before we continue this journey and tell you about some of my favorite all-time music that I asked Duke Ellington about—the doo-wops! Around this time in the 1950s, when I was moving from station to station, soul music was an early art form that was just in its embryonic stage, just getting a foothold. One of the top records of the fifties was a song called "Honky Tonk" by a brother named Bill Doggett. It went number one on the R & B charts and number two on the pop charts, which was really OK. "Honky Tonk" was like a shuffle blues, with an organ and a guitar; it was a little jitterbug-type number that you could bop to. I learned to play it on my guitar recently. (Yeah, I play some, been taking lessons for a while from Pete Cosey, who used to play with Miles Davis. I'm pretty good, too!)

"Honky Tonk" was my favorite song of the fifties before the doo-wops craze just came in and took over. The fifties was the decade of the doo-wops, and the golden era for doo-wop singers occurred between 1955 and 1960. There were definitive doo-wops like "Goodnight, Sweetheart, Goodnight" by the Spaniels, really a great one, and "Earth Angel" by the Penguins—that one, of course, was good for slow-dancing and grinding.

The doo-woppers were singing groups, generally young teenagers you'd find huddled under street lamps, on street corners, or in vestibules, and their trademark sound was harmonizing with a predominant bass and a high falsetto. Before the groups hit the recording studios, they sang a cappella—they couldn't afford instruments, though sometimes a guitar was added. But even when they recorded their songs, they used a minimum of instrumentation, perhaps piano, bass, and drums, because it was the voices that ruled and were the essence of doo-wop. Though most of the groups were black, there were some whites ones, like Sha Na Na. Back in the day, doo-wop groups were the hottest thing going from coast to coast and, as I think about it now, they were probably more popular then than rap is today.

Doo-woppers were sometimes known as "bird groups" because a lot of them were named after birds: the Wrens, the Sparrows, the Flamingos, the Robins. Some were named after cars, like the Cadillacs and the Edsels, and one of the car groups, the El Dorados, even got on the *Ed Sullivan Show.*

Another defining characteristic is that a lot of the doo-woppers were very young, just fourteen or fifteen. Doo-wop was a fad, a craze; everybody wanted to sing in a doo-wop group, and they were found everywhere—schools, gangs, just everywhere. I had my own group for awhile called the Kool Gents, and out of my group came some famous guys like Dee Clark (best known for the song "Raindrops"), guitarist Phil Upchurch, and bluesman Cicero Blake.

There wasn't a lot of choreography in doo-wop in the beginning; the Temptations' type of movement onstage didn't come until a few years later. They just sang. They all just kind of humped around one microphone and sang harmony. Doo-wopping was about singing, pure singing. It was a demonstration of the beauty of the human voice as an instrument, and these guys sang their asses off!

They did have gaudy little uniforms, though. And above all, everybody had their hair straightened, permed, fried, dyed, and laid to the side. Incidentally, many of today's top stars sang in doo-wop groups, like Frankie Beverly and Jerry Butler, just to name a couple. The girl groups were also popular, though they didn't doo-wop as such. But they did have a distinctive sound, like the Chantelles, the Shirelles, and the Bobbettes.

The major record companies quickly honed in on the doo-wop scene. Atlantic Records had the Drifters and the Clovers; Capitol Records had Patti Drew and the Drew-Vels; Chess Records had the Moonglows; Vee-Jay Records were big in doo-wop in Chicago with groups like the El Dorados, the Kool Gents, the Spaniels, and the Magnificents. Heck, some record companies were built just to record the groups. It was a golden era. And it was good being a deejay at the time because the music was so good and harmonious to listen to. I had a solid-gold knack for playing this kind of music—and if there was ever anything in life I understood, it was doo-wop. I loved it!

Doo-wop eventually came to a slow end, and one of the things that led to its demise was the "corruption" of the lead singer. Record companies would offer the lead singer stardom and money to go solo, and more often than not they went for it. If you take a lead singer like Ben E. King away from the Drifters, the rest of the group loses prominence and never enjoys stardom again the way they did before Ben E.'s solo act. The Commodores were not doo-wop, but when Lionel Richie left to go solo and the Commodores still sang as a group, it just wasn't the same. Sometimes when the lead singer leaves, it's a bad deal all the way 'round. For example, J. T. Taylor left Kool and the Gang and couldn't buy a hit record as a solo, while the Gang just faded away. The separation was bad for both of them, I believe, as they were one of the best black groups in history.

Bringing this situation back to the doo-wop groups: Dee Clark left my Kool Gents, and we were dead. Jackie Wilson left his group, the Dominoes, and most people don't even remember the Dominoes, but everybody remembers Jackie. When Curtis Mayfield left the Impressions, Curtis went on to become a super-star, but the Impressions slipped back to start and did not pass go. Gene "Duke of Earl" Chandler left the Dukays and the question became, what's a Dukay?

Technological changes came along that also spelled doom for the doo-wop groups. More orchestration was added, and the Fender bass guitar began replacing the voice of the guy who sang bass. And along came multiple-track recordings, background singers, strings, and keyboards, which evolved the doo-woppers into groups like the Spinners, the Manhattans, the Temptations.

There is always evolution in music as the technology changes and musicians take advantage of the new sounds and the new hardware that are available to them. A lot of music goes in phases, lasting only two or three years. Disco only lasted about that long and it was gone. Doo-wop music lasted a little longer than that, maybe four or five years. Hardly anybody does this kind of music anymore, but the doo-woppers left behind a great legacy, and you can still hear remnants of it in the music today.

I have taken you on a rather quick musical trip here, but for more information, you can read *Doowop: The Chicago Scene* by Robert Pruter or *Du-Wop* by Johnny Keyes.

(ANSWER TO QUESTION ON PAGE 58)

Their girlfriends watched them rehearse one night and said they sounded like a pack of howling dogs. The Spaniels coined the term "doo-wop," by the way. They were singing a song and in the background were going, "doo-wop, doo-wop." The sound, or lyric rather, was simply picked up by other singing groups.

How I Jack Them Jams Like a Big Dog

> Ruth Lee Jones was one of the most popular black female singers in the 1950s. What was her stage name?
>
> *(ANSWER ON PAGE 68)*

Playing doo-wops for five years really helped me get my style down on the radio, and so did the sets I was starting to do around town. I've played club sets, parties, and dances for as long as I can remember, and who knows how many record hops. I did record hops from the late fifties almost to the eighties. I was always doing record hops for high schools in Chicago, and I also traveled all over the states of Illinois and Indiana to do record hops at colleges.

The first record hop I did was while I was working at WBEE and this white dude came over and introduced himself. He said, "there's this new thing, Herb, where people will come listen to you play records and you can charge them to come in and listen." I said, "No, that's unbelievable." He said, "Let's do one." So we did one, out in Chicago Heights, and true enough, people came out and spent a dollar to get in, and we split the money. I remember playing this record by the Fiestas called "So Fine," and this big ol' guy liked it so much he gave me a dollar to play it again, after he had just paid a dollar to get in. That was my first record hop, and I do remember it as a phenomenon that just swept the country.

In addition to hops, I've spent many hours jackin' dusties and steppers records at the clubs. Back when all the club deejays played albums, we found that the LPs fit perfectly in a Martell case. So it was not uncommon to go to these gigs with three or four cases packed with albums. Also, for years some of us would carry our own equipment to these clubs. That would usually consist of a flight case containing two state-of-the-art Technics turntables, a mixer, and various and sundry other items, like earphones, lights, 45 spindles, etc. When this case was closed up and buttoned down, it was five feet long and very heavy. It was made of high-impact plastic, so you could hit it with a sledgehammer and not damage a thing, but you paid for that protection.

The flight case had a handle, but it still was a struggle to carry it from your car to the deejay booth because it was so heavy and bulky. Shoot, nine out of ten deejays couldn't lift that thing over their head, and I have a bad back today from juggling those heavy Martell cases in and out of my car. Sometimes you also had to bring your own amplifier and speakers, so this got to be a major moving job. A lot of guys only got paid thirty-five dollars a night for all that struggling and lugging.

Today, things have changed a lot for the better. The flight case has all but disappeared, unless you're a younger guy mixing. The turntables have been replaced with small, lightweight CD players, and there are some on the market that have a variable speed controls that allow you to mix.

The biggest thing is that wax albums have been replaced with CDs—now six heavy Martell cases full of LPs can be replaced with perhaps one small container of CDs. As far as the other equipment, most clubs have installed their own state-of the-art stuff. So now when I go spin at the 50 Yard Line nightclub, they have everything. I just take my CDs. And you can expect even further reductions in size and weight as high-tech keeps in step with digital technology.

So here we are at the 50 Yard Line, jackin' the music, with folks piling in like crazy. Some lady friends tell me, "Hell, Herb, you just have one big old party don't you!" But this is not true because with both my radio show and in spinning records at the clubs, I have the responsibility of keeping people's head in the music—and that's a job! I'm right at the center of everything and if I screw up, that stops the whole show, the whole flow, at the club and on the radio.

At the club, if your collection of records is poor, your response on the dance floor will be poor. You have to play the right music, in the right order, at the right time. Sometimes little things happen. Like, CDs have their own idiosyncrasies and they can do anything—skip, stop. Or sometimes you may just get tired and hit the wrong button and cause a big mess. You might have a jam-packed dance floor and the music just stops dead. People react differently. Sometimes they just stand there and wait; it's a physical thing. Sometimes people will holler out and say, "Hey man, why don't you get that shit together!"

There are times when someone will come up and ask you for a record they know you don't have. They'll say, "I know you don't have this record," and then they call out four or five more records they know you don't have. Then they'll leave with this strange expression on their face mumbling, "He ain't got no music."

But this is the one I really hate: you're jackin' the music, you got your groove on, the house is rocking, then someone comes up and begs you to play a little off-brand, insignificant record! She (and it's always a she!) will say, "I have to go to work—please, please please play this record." Or, "I have to leave in five minutes because my husband will be home and my baby's sick." So you give in and play this record that no one else has ever heard of, and the dance floor empties. People stop dancing and start milling around. So then it takes you two or three records to get the crowd to start dancing again. Now here's the bad part—the person that begged you for their special song at 9 P.M. is still there at 2 A.M. when the set is over and the lights come up. They're still running around having a good time. That infuriates me!

I cornered a young lady once and asked, "Why did you do that to me?" and she said, "Oh man, you were playing music so good I couldn't leave!" Well, I guess I should be happy that I can still do what I love doing—jacking that music so much the crowd just won't go home. And if you're at the top of your game, you can get folks jammin' to your music all night long.

Then you have to play to the crowd, try to accommodate them as much as possible. Now, steppin' music evolves and changes—it doesn't stay the same. For instance, "Love's Going to Last" by Jeffrey and "Don't Let the Joneses Get You Down" by the Temptations—those are songs that at one time you had to play three or four times a night to keep people satisfied.

Now if I get a request for a song like that, I can tell it's from a person out of touch or who just doesn't get out much. On the steppin' circuit, newer records come along that replace the old ones. But there are classic stepper cuts that still get played from time to time. It's a finely developed art that you have to stay on top of. If you know what you're doing, you can capture an audience and they love it—and you love it.

I've always felt that working the clubs gave me an edge in learning how to play music on the radio. At the sets, you're playing music and watching people react, so you get to know music really well. Not to knock them, but usually to determine what they're going to play, radio station program directors generally take surveys of people sitting down hearing bits and snatches of music. They'll say, I like this song or that one. But I see what they really like, and I play music based on how they react to it and what they ask me for, so I kind of know, too. It means that if a certain piece of music doesn't hit on their survey list, it doesn't mean the record's not good.

I have the street feel because I've been out in the clubs doing it for decades, and I'm still doing it. At these clubs, I'm out practicing my art, playing music, watching reactions and adjusting accordingly. If you do right, you're going to have a good set, people are going to dance. If you play the wrong stuff, they're going to sit down on you and boo you—which you certainly don't want if the club owner or party host is paying you—so you really become part and parcel with the music.

And then, in my case, down through the years, your voice and name become synonymous with the good music that you play, so when these same people catch you on the radio, they automatically think, "I'm going to hear some good music from Herb Kent." When they hear you, they're conditioned to expect good music. I get it all the time that people say to me, "I heard you play such and so, and it really sounded good." It sounds good because they've listened to you for years.

This is not an easy job that we deejays have, but I'll try to explain to you how it goes, what my style is, at least. First of all, I try not to play the same stuff over and over. You can play the same record just once a month and it'll sound redundant to you. I'm always ahead. When I get on the air, I'm always thinking ahead, sometimes maybe a series of three records ahead, thinking of where I want to go.

I usually follow a Sunday morning gospel program, so what I like to do to open up my show is to throw a kind of religious record on early, like an Edwin Hawkins Singers' "Oh, Happy Day." Or Harold Melvin and the Blue Notes' "Prayin'." Or maybe a Staples Singers song, so I kind of hold on to some of the gospel audience and ease into mine. Then I try to play an ear-catching record that I haven't played in a long time.

At that point, my mind starts to run like a computer, and this is the way I think: Suppose I play "Flash Light" by George Clinton and Parliament/Funkadelic. Well, then, let's have some Bootsy and keep on with the funk. After that, bring in some George Duke with "Reach for It," then do some "Backstrokin'" by the Fatback Band—all the while keeping that groove going.

Then I'm into a radio break. I come out of the break saying, "We just had a lot of funk, now let's have a couple of mid-tempo things," or "Now we're going to have a sixties record here. Let me do something by Johnnie Taylor." Johnnie's a guy I really hung out with, so I'll start talking about how we used to girl-watch on Sixty-Third Street and how he was earmarked to replace Otis Redding after Otis died and that's how Johnnie really got his start.

But before I play the record, I might give those little facts without mentioning the name of the artist. As I'm cuing up the record up, I might ask, "Who replaced Otis Redding?" or "What guy replaced Sam Cooke who's a good friend of mine and we used to hang out?"

The audience will be thinking, "Who the hell is he talking about?" Then I come on and play "Who's Making Love (To Your Old Lady)?," and they go, "Oh, Johnnie Taylor!"

Then, since I'm going back so far with Johnnie, in order not to lose any audience I'll jump back up to a nineties record that might have the same beat. Or I may jump from an old Johnnie Taylor to a later Johnnie Taylor like "Disco Lady" and move from there to "Dazz" by Brick, same beat, or go to a Bee Gees thing with a similar sound.

I may not have a particular song I want to play, but a particular artist or group. So I'm thinking to myself, "I'm feeling Luther, but which one? Which Teddy should I play, which Aretha?" There are decisions to be made, even long-term. I may think, you know, I haven't played any Whispers in a while or any Al Green, but they might not fit in with the flow of that day's show, so I'll file it away to play next week.

So I'm thinking that way all the time while I'm spinning. I'm really working the audience so I don't lose anybody, and I listen to what they say when they call in and react to that. I play and I blend and I play and I jam. Try to anyway.

But when people say how good I am at what I do, I never get this sense of, yeah, I am that good, I've got these people out here going! Far from it. I'm fearful that I'm not good enough. I just want to make sure that I'm pleasing everybody and I'm thinking all the time about the audience out there. Are they liking what I'm playing? Can they dig what I'm doing?

It's being an artist. We can be in a room where you get fifty records and I get fifty records. I'm going to play mine differently than you play yours. We can have the same records, and I might get a better response than you because I may know how to play them better. It's how you play these things and what you say that hooks people. It's absolutely like the old basement parties where you had to play the right records in the right order to keep the party moving—if you didn't, the party died.

You're trying to do the same thing on the radio. You want to keep that "dance floor" full all the time, to use the party analogy. But on radio, it's a little more serious. At a party if you play an off-brand record, folks will sit down on you. On the radio, if you play off-brand, people will tune away from you to another station, which can make you lose your job.

If I have some nineteen-year-olds listening to my dusties show, I'm constantly wondering, "Now, what sixties song might they like?" So I try to hook them and make them think, and I'm happy to say that a lot of the youngsters do stick with me. My goal is for there to be something for everybody on my show before I'm through, and pretty much I have fun on every show, which I think comes through to my listeners and has always come through in all the years I've been on radio.

(ANSWER TO QUESTION ON PAGE 62)

Ruth Lee Jones was better known as Dinah Washington.

Shock Jocks, Freedom of Speech, and the N-Word

> Jimi Hendrix is generally regarded as the greatest guitarist of all time, but who was his guitar teacher in Hendrix's early years?
>
> *(ANSWER ON PAGE 77)*

In determining a radio style, yours or mine, there's more involved than just learning what music to play and how to play it. There are some moral and ethical considerations to be made, as well, as to what you'll say or do on the air and what you won't.

One of the more noteworthy trends in the broadcast industry in recent years—for better or worse—has been the development of "shock-jock" radio. Shock-jockism is a unique category where the main purpose is to get on the air and say controversial stuff that is often offensive, occasionally mean-spirited, and usually sex-related. Radio is an informative, entertaining medium, so I guess you could consider shock-jockism an extreme form of entertainment, although I certainly wouldn't call it educational.

Like any "extreme" activity, the goal for shock jocks is to come as close to the edge of what's allowable to talk about on radio as possible. Howard Stern, long the top dog shock jock, is an expert at it. I'm always amazed at how these guys can weave in and out and how near the line they can come without crossing over it.

They'll talk about anal sex, for instance, and while they can't use the exact slang words for the act, "fucked in the ass," they'll talk all around it, and you know exactly what they're suggesting. They can't use words that are pornographic or indecent, but they're right on the verge of it and are extremely talented in how they do it.

You can't say "shit," but you can say "turd," and that's what they do. That's probably why people listen, because the jocks shock them so much by what they say. It's titillating, and a lot of people love that type of radio. Personally, I don't. I don't think the airwaves should support that type of thing; I have enough respect for radio to think that it can bring better stuff to people. I'm obviously in the minority on that, because just look at the ratings some of these shock jocks have. Look at the money Howard Stern makes.

But too many times they step way over the line. In 2007, there were two XM shock jocks—I won't dignify them by calling their names—who were suspended for thirty days for doing a skit about a homeless man having sex with Condoleezza Rice while punching her in the face. Their suspension was remarkable, because you can say damn near anything on XM and satellite radio, which is not FCC-regulated. These same two jocks were fired a few years back by CBS for airing a segment on what they said were two people having sex in St. Patrick's Cathedral in New York.

Then you have Don Imus, also infamously fired by CBS Radio in 2007 for his notorious "nappy-headed hos" remark related to the Rutgers University women's basketball team. Ironically, the "nappy-headed hos" statement was not illegal under FCC regulations. It just so happened that there was a hue and cry raised about it. If nobody had said anything, Imus and his producer might have gotten away with it.

The first thing I think about when I think about shock jocks is the difference between black radio and white radio. Black radio is far more conservative. Black radio might have a lot of the hollering, screaming jocks, but they've never hollered and screamed about sexual things as much as about the music or urging listeners to go out and buy something. They rhyme, stuff like that, but generally they leave the pornography alone. I don't know any black deejays far out enough to be shock jocks.

And it may be racist on my part, but if you just tune into some of these shock shows, they're all so white. You get a chance to see how they feel and think, because they're not pro-black at all. I don't feel that shock jocks lean toward liberalism, toward black people that much, because they don't have many black listeners or viewers. I used to watch Imus's show because I was fascinated by how very few black people they actually had on. They were not very friendly toward New Orleans mayor Ray Nagin, Jesse Jackson, or Al Sharpton. Imus's show just seemed to be not driven toward black people, let me put it like that.

I'm not a shock jock by any means, but in my more than six decades in radio I've been called on the carpet many times about what I said, or didn't say. It happens to everybody if they stay in the profession long enough. One time I said "shit" on the air before I could cut the mike off. This was back in the 1960s, when cursing of any kind wasn't tolerated. Fortunately the bosses didn't hear that one, but my friends did. One of them called into the station and said, "Man, do you know what you just said on the radio?"

Another time, when I first started in the business, I was having trouble with a microphone. I thought it was off and said, "Dammit, I can't get this thing to work!" The boss ran in and said, "Damn it to hell, Herb, you're cussing!" And the microphone was still on!

I've told this story on radio: sometimes when I go to a movie, my butt falls asleep. You know, the movie might be good and you stay in one position, and before you know it your butt falls asleep, then starts itching when it comes back to life. Another lady disc jockey called me when I told that story and said she thought it was funny because her butt goes to sleep, too! That's pretty cool to put on the air, and that's about as far as I would go. That's about the worst for me.

I have said "ass" on the air, but that was almost harmless. It wasn't like, "Look at the ass on that woman." Then it's sexist and will get you standing in the boss's office. That's something a shock jock might say. But you could say the same thing in a positive way, like, "I'd like to have that woman because she's got a great, big butt!" It's still implying that you want to have sex with her, but you don't find anything wrong with it being on the air if you say it that way. James Brown had a song with lyrics that went something like, "Goodness sakes, take a look at them cakes!" talking about a lady's bosom. Sometimes you can play those records and slide those lyrics in where folks don't notice or just kind of look the other way.

The stuff I've been called on the carpet about has been pretty tame, but it still developed in me kind of a built-in policeman as to what's right and what's wrong to say on radio—morally, ethically, and legally. There are things I won't say, things I won't do. I won't use four-letter words, I won't use the n-word. What you say on the radio, what shock jocks say on the air, can similarly influence what their listeners think and say. And if they're spewing out filth, where does that get anybody? And make no mistake—listeners are picking up the messages that are sent out over the airwaves. Radio is a powerful tool, and that's why advertising agencies spend millions of dollars on it, because they can get that message across. If you keep repeating it, keep repeating it, people are going to run out and buy that product or car or whatever it is they want you to go out and get.

So, the sixty-four-dollar question becomes: what's appropriate to say on the radio? That's a wide range there, brother. The airwaves are precious, like the freedoms that we have in America, and personally I think they should be used more respectfully than the way shock jocks use them. You may argue that one of those freedoms is freedom of speech, so you should be able to say anything. If you can say something like "nappy-headed hos" in the privacy of your living room and if you're thinking that, why not be allowed to say it on the air?

Because it's derogatory not only to black women, but to women, period.

Just because we say things among ourselves doesn't make them right, and publicly deriding black women, calling them whores, is definitely derogatory. Just because you have the freedom to, can you, should you, say anything if it's hurtful to someone else? I don't like to say anything on radio that is hurtful to people. When the Imus thing happened, black and white people noted in his defense that he only used a term black people use themselves—*hos*—in music and videos. Why get on Imus when black people are saying far worse stuff, like *bitches* and so on?

Well, I don't think that leading black radio personalities like Tom Joyner or Doug Banks, who would be analogous to Don Imus, would say "bitches" and "hos" on the air. We may say it driving around in the car, and I'm sure that Imus and them drive around in their car, and talk about bitches and hos, and niggers, too. That doesn't mean Imus can get on the air and say "nappy-headed hos," or that *I* can go on the air and say "nappy-headed hos," or say "honkies with long hair that smell bad." It's the same thing. I can't do that and wouldn't do that. You might do it with your friends in private, that's one thing, but when you get on the radio you shouldn't say it, because it's influential to people growing up and it is hurtful and derogatory.

One important point to remember is even if these kinds of things are said by black artists, you have another freedom, in addition to free speech. You have a freedom of choice. If you want to hear rappers say "bitches" and "hos," go out buy those CDs and videos. That's your choice. Richard Pryor would curse like all get out, was funny as hell, and often used his vulgarity to say something very powerful. It was your choice to buy his CDs or pay to watch him perform live, but it wouldn't be your choice to have to listen to him say "motherfucker" on the airwaves.

You know if you go to the video channels that you're going to see that kind of stuff, and that's your choice. But if you're just sitting down eating breakfast, or are in mixed company, and somebody on TV says out of the blue, "That's some nappy-headed hos," that should never fly! It's a matter of choice, and Imus didn't give me a choice. If you just happened to have the TV on, you didn't have any choice—you had to hear him say it.

Personally, I would love to see the lyrics and the images in the videos of that segment of black music cleaned up. It's been getting progressively worse with the permissiveness and the degradation for a couple of decades now, and it's got to stop somewhere. The main thing in the videos is the debasing of black women, with their butts hanging out, low-cut bras, bare midriffs, and it's gone a tad too far. It's like the *Girls Gone Wild* commercials that have gone too far. They were kinda cool when they started, but now they're like soft porn, and you don't want your kids watching that on TV, even if the spots do come on late at night. There are still always a lot of kids up at that time.

Maybe they should just have one big ol' porn radio channel and one big ol' porn TV channel. Funnel all that stuff right there, and if that's what you want, just go watch it or listen to it all day long!

There's freedom of speech, but to what end? The music, images, and messages in some of the music and videos degrade females to the point that young women are actually degrading themselves in real life. Calling themselves bitches and hos. The way they dress, sexually suggestive with no real concept of what they're projecting, because they're shown and told that they're supposed to look like that.

I don't like the way the guys dress either, walking around with the pants bagging down to the knees, and no shirt sometimes. I hate that. I hate that! I don't think it's doing anybody any good.

And the bad thing about the whole thing is that they glorify gangsters, and I think that should be stopped, too. They rap gangsta-this, gangsta-that, thug life and whatnot, and I'm sure it affects the mind-set of a lot of these guys, and ladies, too. But you don't want to come home and find a thug in your driveway, you don't want a gangster in your bedroom shooting you up and raping your wife.

You've got all this music glorifying the gangster life that we allow our young people to listen to, then when thugs are actually in the community killing children in gang crossfire, we condemn that and ask why it happens. And then they fight like crazy, too! You go to some of these teenage functions now—you think they fought bad back in the day, I mean, they have some real fights now, brother! Murderous ones.

It's absolutely true that all generations go through their own little thing in coming of age, their rebellions, but this has gone a little far. You can forgive a lot of stuff, but the way of dress, the guns, the gangsters and the thugs, just seem to be a little far to me.

Of course, along with the use of bitches, hos, gangstas, and thugs in the rap music and videos, is the big word, the n-word. It's a word that makes me cringe, it really does. I think a lot of the problem with public usage of the n-word is peer acceptance, or at least pressure to go along with the usage. I would suggest to anybody of any age that if you're in the company of people who say *nigger*, if you really feel strongly against it, just say, please don't use that word, and nine times out of ten they will stop and say I'm sorry if I offended you. I used to use it, and after enough people asked me not to say it around them, which I never did after they asked, I just stopped saying it.

In many cases, young kids honestly don't know they shouldn't use the word because they hear their mothers say it, their fathers say it, and it has been passed on through generations. And when people get angry, they start spitting out words to the point where you're surprised at just how vile they can be.

That's life, unfortunately, but I don't think we need to listen to it on records and such. The rappers argue that it's real life, and that's why they use it. People also argue that one of the criteria in using the n-word publicly is the skill of the user, like Richard Pryor, as opposed to Michael Richards. Michael used the excuse that he was just trying to be funny onstage and bombed, but it sounded like he really got angry and was downright insulting.

I don't care how so-called brilliantly it's used, I want to abolish the n-word, period, and I've been campaigning to do that since the Imus incident. I don't think I'm going to get far with it, but I'm not going to cease trying. I think if we had a campaign with enough people who have real strong voices to come out against it and we could get it out of the music, we could make real progress in slowing down the use of the n-word.

We talk about it on my show sometimes, and on my Web site. The majority of people who tune in and comment also want the word abolished, by about a 70 to 30 ratio. But that might not be an accurate cross-section because when I talk to young people, I feel resistance right away. They think there's nothing wrong with it. To show you how tangled up and convoluted this n-word situation is, I got one letter from a listener who said it's white people who want blacks to stop using the word. She said it's a white conspiracy to take something away from black people that they own—the n-word—and that therefore she wasn't going to stop using it. Talk about some twisted logic.

I find that many young people don't want to let go because they say it doesn't mean that to us. It means friendship; it's a term of endearment, and we're the only ones who can use it. We put an *a* at the end instead of the *er*, so it's different. They want to turn around and use it as a positive synonym for "my friend"—"my nigga!" You might think it's endearing, but you're not going to get on TV and use that. You're not going to stand up in class and use that. You might think you're changing the meaning of it, but you can't change the meaning of that word—it is what it is.

And nonblack people certainly don't see it that way. I can't explain the concept some people have that white people *can't* say it, but we can. I've heard white people even say it playfully among themselves—"Hey, ma' nigga! What's happening ma' nigga!" But when they say it toward us, they use it in the way it was originally intended.

The original meaning of the word is very derogatory, and the image that goes along with it is not a good one: a Sambo image.

When you have people calling themselves that, it's the ultimate form of brainwashing—they see themselves as inferior and take it as a good thing. That's really when people outside of us can control us. For you to be calling yourselves niggers means you're doing their job for them.

You even have black people who use it indiscriminately in front of white people—they don't care—and it just makes me go, "Oh, God, don't say that!" Then white people just smile and laugh on those occasions, and are probably thinking, "Look at these fools!"

And when black people use it, it's not always a term of endearment; often it's quite the opposite: "These niggers came and left all that shit on my doorstep!" Or they'll see a dirty-looking house, and it's, "There's niggers living there!" They use it the same way white people use it when talking about blacks.

It is so ironic that white people can do *anything* to black people *except* call them niggers. They can redline them with insurance rates, put poor schools and drugs in the neighborhood, put black men in jail, charge higher prices for everything, and not give them access to jobs or economic development. But you can't call them the n-word, because then they want to fight. But then they'll turn right around and say, "Hey, now that's ma' nigga over there!"

(ANSWER TO QUESTION ON PAGE 69)

Johnny "Guitar" Watson tutored Jimi Hendrix.

3

◆◆◆

THE BLACK GIANT

WVON: The World's Greatest Radio Station

> The Supremes had their first hit, "Where Did Our Love Go?," in 1964. Who were the three original members of that group?
>
> *(ANSWER ON PAGE 88)*

W orking at the old WVON was the apex of my career. The station was fun to work for and extremely powerful in what it provided to the community, and I was proud to work there. The most famous jingle went, "WVON, 1450 . . . you ain't heard nothing yet!" The breadth and scope of WVON was immense; that's why it was known as "the Black Giant." Suffice it to say that WVON will be remembered as one of the greatest stations in the history of radio. It was the most magical thing I've ever seen.

WVON in the 1960s became Chicago's first black R & B station, and one of the few of its kind in the country. It was more instrumental than any other station, probably, in ushering in the glory days of soul music. I keep saying that one day there's going to be a movie on this, because WVON was the *baaadest* station in the country—black, white, or whatever. It was just phenomenal. And yours truly was there from the beginning; in fact, I was a key player in the deal that made WVON, WVON.

It was 1960, and I had returned to work at WBEE, the sunup-to-sundown rhythm-and-blues station that had fired me about a year earlier. I went to work at WJOB in Hammond and stayed there for a year or so before WBEE lured me back. But it was like slave labor out there, and almost as soon as I went back, the unions asked the staff if we wanted to unionize. One of the reasons they fired me in the first place was that I couldn't handle the strain of working seven days a week. We said fine, so we struck, and WBEE flew in scabs while the deejays sat outside days on end waiting for the strike to break.

As the strike went on, the union found me another, better job in Chicago at WHFC-AM, which paid a nice salary plus 30 percent commission on any airtime that I sold. That was the first time I made $35,000 a year, and that was *great* money back in those days.

As soon I started there, I took off like a skyrocket. My popularity soared even more than it had during my initial years at WBEE. The whole city started listening to me. WGES was the dominant station that black people in Chicago listened to at the time, but I kicked their ass. I mean, I kicked their ass. I became the most-listened-to disc jockey in the city of Chicago, and I was so strong that Leonard Chess, who was making records at the time with his company Chess Records, got the idea that he might want to buy the station. This rich entrepreneur was considering getting into the radio game based on the strength of what I was doing.

He approached me and asked if WHFC was for sale. I said, "I don't know, Leonard." He said, "Go ask." So I talked to Mr. Hoffman, who owned the station, and he said, "Mr. Kent, I'm willing to sit down and talk." I got them together, they negotiated the sale of the station, and it was done.

Leonard bought WHFC-AM for a flat million dollars, with a little FM station thrown in for free. The AM station alone would sell for a million dollars today; the FM station, I don't know if you could buy it now for seventy or eighty million dollars. But Leonard bought the stations for one million dollars and he made more than that in the first six months.

Leonard's station officially went on the air in March 1963, and he changed the call letters of WHFC to WVON, which eventually came to stand for "Voice of the Negro," but not when he made the change; I can't remember what the call letters originally stood for, but it was something different. The FM station first became WSDM—another historic station for Chicago—an all-female-deejay jazz station. It's call letters stood for "Smack Dab in the Middle," and it launched the career of Yvonne Daniels, who was inducted into the Radio Hall of Fame along with me. WSDM today is known as WLUP, the Loop, and it's a white rock station.

When Leonard bought WHFC the station played R & B music, German music, Spanish music, Lithuanian music, etc. It was known as a family station. Listeners had their favorite ethnic disc jockey, and they would tune in at a certain time to hear their kind of music. Also, on Sunday, black churches broadcast over the station all day long. Because of the strength of my performance and the size of my audience, Leonard came in and wiped the programming slate clean so that there was nothing but R & B music playing 24/7.

Being a man of music, a record producer with a good ear, Leonard knew where to get the best deejays. He went around the country, hired them, and brought them back to Chicago. The genius of WVON as it was created by Leonard Chess—he was so smart and wise—was that every single individual at WVON was an out-and-out personality. Each one had their own theme song, their own little signature—a laugh, a sound, or a saying—and every single one was highly entertaining.

Personalities around the clock. Joe Cobb, the morning jock, would say, "I'm having more fun than a one-legged man in a football-kicking contest." The midday jock, Bill "Butterball" Crane, used to say, "Never be rude to a young dude!" E. Rodney Jones, our program director, used to sign on and say, "This is the Mad

Lad on the scene with the swinging machine," and would sign off with, "I'll see you tomorrow, good lord willing and the creek don't rise." Cecil Hale would sign off with something political, something that would make people think, like, "What would happen if the people only understood and knew the power of the people?"

Of course, I came on from 7 P.M. to 11 P.M. and I'd go, "Yo! Lawd know, I say yo!" I would sign off with, "Good night, Mrs. Livingston, take care of Michelle. And to the rest of you YL's out there, a bunch of 73s," then I'd play "Open Our Eyes" by the Gospel Clef. I've been asked a million times, but I've never ever explained to anyone who Mrs. Livingston and Michelle were. Our all-night deejay was Pervis Spann, the Blues Man, whose claim to fame was saying, "I don't talk to no men!" and he only took women's calls on the air.

There was *Hotline*, Wesley South's nightly hour. It was the first black talk show that I can remember, and it was on this show that I first met and got an autograph from Dr. Martin Luther King Jr. We had Roy Wood doing editorials on current topics, and he would always end with, "Now, run and tell that!"

There were the other deejays and on-air personalities who were part and parcel of our collective soul, including Lucky Cordell, Bernadine C. Washington, Bill "Doc" Lee, the Magnificent Montague, Ed "Nassau Daddy" Cook, Jay Johnson, Isabel Joseph Johnson, James Rowe, our white news guy, McKee Fitzhugh, Franklin "Sugar Daddy" McCarthy, and Richard Pegue.

At first, we were all just helter-skelter, pretty much doing as we pleased at the station until Leonard Chess formatted us. But it was kinda difficult for a bunch of freewheeling deejays to fit into some sort of format, so we only used the parts of the format that benefited us, like the jingles, prerecorded spots, things like that. We launched a number of careers at WVON, including Don Cornelius, who went on to create *Soul Train*, and Don Jackson, head of Central City Productions. This was an exclusive fraternity.

For a long time, there didn't seem to be any jealousy among us, no problems, because we were like a family. We were all working guys, our women didn't clash, everybody had their own style, their own thing, their own following, their own set of nightclubs that they worked. For many years we were all very close until some disruptive influences came along and we weren't quite as close, but for a good while, we were a close-knit bunch of guys. Part of our strength came from that cohesiveness. We were the WVON "Good Guys." It was all for one and one for all. Even though we each had our separate thing, we could count on each other. I loved being with those guys. I loved being part of them.

Even the engineers were great all-around guys. They knew all about electronics and they had jumper cables, so they'd help you get your car started if it died or get it open if you got locked out. They were real handy guys, not just in engineering, but with tools, the whole nine. Most of them were black, a few white, and remember, this was back in the sixties, so having a mostly black technical staff was a big deal in itself.

The engineers would send me out to get these delicious hot dogs from Goldblatt's down in the Little Mexico neighborhood, around Twenty-Sixth Street. I'd bring them back and they'd plug a wire from the electrical outlet and stick them in the hot dogs, and they'd go *zap*! I said, "You guys are all right!" because we didn't have any microwaves or hotplates back then. Put 'em on a little bun—man, those hot dogs were great! Absolutely delicious.

It was just a badass station all around. We hit so hard, we hit immediately, and man, did we have fun! We were allowed to play records three or four times in a row if the record sounded good, and we were jamming. Aw, it just went on and on and on—twenty-four hours a day, we were jamming that radio!

Ed Cook was laying on his white rug. E. Rodney Jones was saying he was "looking finer than a rich man's front porch." I was saying, "Stay in school," and, "I'm so cool I'm froze in my clothes!" And our boss, Leonard Chess, just egged us on. Leonard would say, "Come on, talk shit now, c'mon, talk shit!" He said, "Open up and talk it while the records are going! Talk shit! You're not talking enough!"

The mood was always nonstop, happy good times. There was a great ambience, always people there, hangers-on, females, artists to be interviewed, record promoters in and out coming to see you, guys having fun on the air. The good times started from the get-go, and the good times lasted for a long time.

The WVON Good Guys were heroes in the hood, and one of the primary reasons for our success was our commitment to the community. We were the epitome of a community station. Rodney and Pervis were promoting concerts all over the city. My main thing was encouraging all the kids to stay in school and avoid gangs. In fact, I did a fifteen-minute spot every day telling kids to stay in school. It was sponsored by Lieber Brothers and was probably the most popular thing we had at the time.

I would go to the schools and interview the kids, talk to the teachers, and find out where and what the problems were. I interviewed different people who also told the kids they should stay in school. That ran for a couple of years, and it was phenomenal. The segment was good because it really helped influence a lot of people, because they really listened to me and what I had to say. The sway that I had with my listeners was just astounding, and I got another title as the "Pied Piper" for my teenage listeners.

One of my big fans at that time was Bill Campbell, a long-time broadcaster at the ABC-TV affiliate in Chicago. Bill has long been one of my best buddies, and he's never said it, but I think that he might have had some problems in school back then, and he felt my little segment helped him a lot. Bill went on to become a Rhodes Scholar. I can't even tell you when I met him, we've been friends for so long. But I did influence him with these stay-in-school segments, and I think a thing like that would be just as helpful for the kids today, with all the problems the schools are facing and everything the young students are up against.

The other part of my little education initiative was doing record hops every weekend all over the city. I would broadcast from a different high school every Friday night to give the kids something positive to do. Sometimes if I was bringing in Aretha Franklin or somebody to the hops, they'd occasionally be on the air with us, too. That was kinda cool.

WVON was involved in every worthwhile venture that took place in the black community, and we had our claws into everything that happened in Chicago. The city was just opened up for us, for whatever we were doing. We could tell folks to go sit on the steps of city hall and get five thousand people to show up there. We're the ones who made Jesse Jackson. When Jesse came to town in the sixties, he was truly a country preacher. WVON took him in our arms because we liked what he was saying. We believed in him, we put all the forces we had behind him, and that propelled his Operation Breadbasket, which became Operation PUSH. Rev. Jackson came to us, we had him on the air, and he learned how to manipulate the media through us. I think he would be the first one to say perhaps that WVON was a big part of his history.

What was so phenomenal about WVON is that the station was just one thousand watts during the day, and only two hundred fifty watts during the night, which meant that you had to turn your radio certain ways to pick up the signal. Primarily our audience was the South and West Sides, because Chicago was so segregated at the time. Virtually all the black people in the city lived on the South and West Sides, so we captured pretty much the entire black community. But even though we were a weak AM signal programming to a small geographic area, we came in number one in the city in the ratings!

I remember when that first happened. It came out in the Arbitron ratings that little WVON was number one twenty-four hours a day and beat every station in the city of Chicago. At the time, WLS was a fifty-thousand-watt monster whose signal stretched from coast to coast, when you couldn't even hear us past Ninety-Fifth Street sometimes (about thirty miles from our broadcast facility). When our number one ratings came out, WLS called us and said, "Who are you guys?" They didn't even know we were on the radio!

We were so phenomenal that we "broke" practically all the black hit records from the mid-sixties through the mid-seventies. Breaking a record is being the first one to play a new release, making it popular and causing it to be picked up by other stations around the country—and, of course, to sell at the record stores. If a record didn't break on WVON, sometimes the record labels would forget it. The station was just that strong. I've never seen anything like it.

Motown was just cutting its teeth when WVON was the powerhouse that it was, and I'd say that 90 percent of Motown's songs during that period got broken right there at WVON. We did that for a lot of other labels, too, like Atlantic, Stax, Columbia, Philly International, and Volt.

Back in the day, people would fight to have their song played on WVON because you knew it would hit the national scene. We were that powerful of a station, and just the mention of a record on our playlist would start folks ordering it. We also helped boost many local acts to the national stage, like the Impressions, Curtis Mayfield, Jerry Butler, the Dells, the Chi-Lites, Gene Chandler, Ramsey Lewis, and Alvin Cash's phenomenal hit "Twine Time," just to name a few.

I was a young, hot deejay with a huge audience, and personally broke dozens of records. I got an honorary solid-gold record from Motown for the introduction of the Temptations' top seller "Runaway Child, Running Wild" in 1969. I also broke one by the Vibrations called "The Watusi." You may remember the song and the dance—it became a national phenomenon. How this happened is that the record was manufactured by Leonard Chess at his record label. He made me play the record, and when I did, he called the station and told me to play it again. Then he called again and said play it again. All in all, he had me play that record five times in a row. The next day the record broke and they couldn't keep it in the record shops.

There's one more record I'd like to tell you about, a record that without me would not have been a number one hit. It was written by Raynard Miner and sung by Fontella Bass. It was also manu-factured by Leonard Chess, but he hated the song.

One day we all went over to his office, we played the record, and I told Mr. Chess, "If you don't let this record out, you're crazy because it's a hit." Leonard said, "Mr. Kent, if you say this is going to be a hit, it is going to be a hit, and I will release the record." It *was* a hit, and in 1965, it went number one R & B, and number four pop nationally. The record was "Rescue Me," and it has been in movies, commercials, and is still making money today.

The good times at WVON lasted from 1963 to 1977, when the station was eventually sold and all the Good Guys were "involun-tarily retired." I'll recount that sordid period later in the book, but right now, let me tell you some of the more memorable stories of the Black Giant in more vivid detail in the following pages.

(ANSWER TO QUESTION ON PAGE 80)

Diana Ross, Mary Wilson, and Florence Ballard were the original Supremes.

Thank Goodness
for Pig Ears

In 1967, what group did Cindy Birdsong leave when she joined the Supremes?

(ANSWER ON PAGE 92)

Power steering that goes out. A pig ear sandwich. A one-dollar insurance policy. All these items combined in a weird, lifesaving way in one of the stranger tales from my time at WVON.

It all started with the death of a well-known deejay named Dr. Bop. I first heard of Dr. Bop when I was visiting my uncle in Columbus, Ohio, where Bop worked. He was on the radio all day long—morning, noon, and night. I don't know how he did it! But he was a dynamic, flamboyant soul brother who could really jam.

Rumor has it that one Saturday night Dr. Bop was out on the town with a shapely, blue-eyed blonde. Apparently paying more attention to the blonde than the road, it's said Dr. Bop lost control of his shiny Cadillac and crashed into the house of the chief of police. The car ended up in the chief's living room with the blonde still in Bop's arms. That bit of chicanery ended his radio career in Columbus, Ohio.

I next heard Dr. Bop was in Milwaukee, where he reigned as king of R & B radio for years, until his death around 1975. Sev-

89

eral of us WVON Good Guys attended the funeral. Riding to Milwaukee in our limo was program director E. Rodney Jones, general manager Lucky Cordell, and two record promoters, Kirkland Burke from Warner Bros. and Eddie Holland from Atlantic Records.

It was a great funeral, and after it was over, E. Rodney Jones declared, "I gotta have me a pig ear sandwich." We all said, "No no, let's get back to Chicago, we don't have time." But Rodney was our leader and he had his way. So off we went all over Milwaukee in search of a pig ear sandwich.

We were dressed all slick and cool and attracted the attention of six teenage girls. I guess they had never seen any Chicago guys like us. We couldn't shake 'em and they went everywhere we went like a shadow. This pig ear search got to be nerve-wracking until, after we'd looked everywhere else, one of the girls suggested a place called the Speed Queen.

Mercifully, Rodney got his pig ear sandwich, then it was time to go. We waved bye-bye to our young friends and finally took off for Chicago in our long black limousine. But as we were speeding down the highway, the limo driver said, "Uh-oh, the power steering just went out." I remember he had huge arms and was very strong. He was able to manhandle that limo down to the next gas station where we waited while they put a new belt on the power steering.

We were off again, with no further incident until the WVON parking lot came into view. Then it was the most amazing thing I have ever seen. All our cars, which we had left parked in the lot, were severely damaged. Broken fenders, broken windshields. A yellow Corvette was reduced to powered rubble with only the engine left. We entered the parking lot in stunned silence until one of us yelled, "What the fuck happened?" It seemed like something huge had descended from the sky and hit our cars. What in the world? We scrambled to get out of the limo, and I remember tripping over Eddie Holland. This was a true out-of-body experience. Trauma, trauma, real trauma.

I rushed over to my car, which was a rental. I remember that when I rented the car the lady asked me if I wanted insurance that only cost *a buck*. Just a dollar. Luckily I decided, "Yeah, give me some, I'll take it." The whole front of this rental car was caved in—and there were distinctive tire tracks across the hood! On further inspection, it looked like a missile went straight through Eddie Holland's yellow Corvette, then into Kirkland Burke's white 1974 Sedan deVille and literally destroyed it. The rest of the cars had suffered similar fates in one way or another. Then a bystander who had witnessed the accident told us what happened.

The WVON office is located right under a busy raised street. It seems as though two Mexican dudes were speeding by the station on this raised street, doing at least 100 mph, when they lost control and their car jumped the guard rail and sailed over into the parking lot. The first car they hit was mine, straight across the hood. Then, like a pool ball, they ricocheted and careened off several more cars, which threw them into the Corvette at an even higher rate of speed—which bounced them into the white Cadillac, which was totally destroyed. Matter of fact, the car that went out of control was still there in the middle of all this mass destruction. (I remember saying at the time, "Now, where did *this* car come from?") All its wheels were sheared off and it was sitting flat.

We were told that the two guys jumped out after the impact, obviously but miraculously unhurt, and ran at a high rate of speed before they were apprehended by the police a few yards away. I don't know if they had stolen the car or committed a crime or what.

Now here's where all those weird items I listed up front come into play. On hot summer nights at WVON—as this night was—a lot of the jocks and record promoters loved to stand in the parking lot and talk. That is undoubtedly where we would have been standing that particular hot night had it not been for the pig ear sandwich and the broken-down power steering.

In fact, we calculated the amount of time it took us to find that pig ear sandwich and the down time to fix the power steering. It turned out that if those two events hadn't occurred, we'd have been back at the station—probably standing in the parking lot—at the actual time the car crashed. We would have been killed.

Also, if I hadn't had my little one-dollar insurance policy, I would have had to pay a two-thousand-dollar car repair bill. Isn't it funny how life works? Who would have ever thought a pig ear sandwich would save my life? And that's how I used up the fifth of my nine lives!

◆ ◆ ◆

Just a note to update: E. Rodney Jones passed away in his daughter's arms from lung cancer in January 2004. Many people are put on this earth to leave their mark and change things and he was one of them. Rodney was WVON's program director; he was a gifted musician, a born leader, and someone who could spot trends better than anyone else I know.

He had a golden ear. When Rodney listened to a new record his instincts would tell him whether it would be a hit or not, and almost all the time he was right. He broke white records in the black community like the Rolling Stones' "(I Can't Get No) Satisfaction," and B. J. Thomas's "Raindrops Keep Falling on My Head." It was just unreal to watch—or listen to, rather—Rodney's ability with music. He was an exciting guy to be around. Miss you, buddy.

(ANSWER TO QUESTION ON PAGE 89)

Cindy Birdsong left Patti LaBelle and the Blue Bells.

All About the Promotions

What white group got tired of playing rock music, tried their hand at soul, and became a one-hit wonder with a number one hit on the R & B charts in September 1976?

(ANSWER ON PAGE 97)

Years and years ago, radio stations simply played music and commercials and that was that. As time went by and the competition between stations increased, it became an issue of ratings. So we began to see more personal appearances, in-store visits, and things of that nature. These things are called promotions.

Starting in the 1960s and continuing until today, they are a vital part of the popularity of a radio station. WVON was involved in public service for the city of Chicago and gave away tickets to big shows on the air and T-shirts with the station's logo by the thousands. The thing that really did it for the station was the awesome promotions; there was never a dull moment.

One of the first promotions we did really showed me the power of radio and how strong we were. We buried a small amount of money, say one hundred dollars, in Washington Park, and left clues as to where it could be found. Before you knew it, there were hundreds of people digging up Washington Park. They dug from King Drive to Cottage Grove, from Fifty-First to Sixty-First—almost the entire length of the park. From sunup to sundown, they tore up the park looking for this money. The damage to the park was so bad that we got a censure from the city on that one.

One of our most incredible promotions was when WVON first went on the air as a new station. Before our official debut, we played the same record over and over again for days to announce our arrival. It drove people crazy, but they knew a new station was coming on the air, and the promotion worked like a charm. It made us a force in the radio marketplace from day one. We also had floats in the Bud Billiken and Christmas parades, where we threw out candy and T-shirts. It was an electric atmosphere.

One promotion that sticks out in my mind is when we hid the key to a brand-new Cadillac somewhere in the city of Chicago. I remember this contest because one of our deejays was accused of giving the location away to this girl he was in love with. It was never proven, but I believe he did it. The key was hidden behind a billboard on Twenty-Second and Michigan. To tell you the truth, we didn't really have much time to get that one going because the girlfriend "found" the key right away.

Another great promotion was our Easter egg hunt in Garfield Park on the West Side. We hid Easter eggs and gave away lots of T-shirts. There were so many people that we couldn't move; they had us blocked into the WVON truck, with people everywhere.

While this was going on, this lovely lady managed to work her way to the front and get pressed against me. I would move to the left, she would move to the left. I moved to the right, she would move to the right, all the while pressed against me. Then somebody would yell, "Everybody get back, get back," and she would back up, and I would find her mashed up against me again. Finally, after a long time of this, she let out a low moan and then quickly disappeared. I know that sounds strange, but that's a true thing.

Another time, we had an open house at WVON that I will never forget. We opened the doors to the public and painted footsteps from the parking lot to the lobby, through the station, and out the back door. As folks walked in, the radio personalities were shaking hands and signing autographs. I've never seen so many people go through the little WVON radio station in all my life, just people upon people all day long. The Chicago police had put out a rerouting bulletin because the station's location at Thirty-Third and Kedzie had been cordoned off for couple of blocks to accommodate this huge crowd.

Once we had a promotion giving away free transistor radios. The boss bought thousands of these radios and gave them away for free—all you had to do was come to the station and pick one up. The beauty of this promotion was that our boss pulled some strings to get transistor radios that could only get one station, ours at WVON. I don't know how many we gave away, but we managed to block Kedzie off again in the process. Like I said, physically it was a little place with a small parking lot. We had so many people come down that traffic got snarled all the way back to a nearby expressway's exit ramp.

♦♦♦

Would you believe that I once raced a female professional Roller Derby skater and won? Here's how this unbelievable promotion happened. In the early 1970s, Charles Mootry was the VP and general manager of sales for WVON, and one of our biggest sponsors was the Roller Derby. Chuck approached me one day and said, "Herb, can you skate?"

I said, "Yeah, not so good, but I can." He said, "Great, I'm gonna set it up so you can race 747 in the Roller Derby." It was 1974, and 747 was the hottest skater in the world at the time. Folks just loved her. She had an Olympic silver medal in the shot put and I'm thinking she could probably bench-press better than four hundred pounds.

We advertised this matchup as "The Roller Battle of the Century: 747 vs. Herb Kent." You've got to remember that I was six-foot-two and barely one hundred forty pounds soaking wet. People couldn't wait to see this matchup, which was to be held on a Friday night at the International Amphitheater, one of the largest entertainment venues in Chicago at the time. You would have thought the circus was in town because the place was packed to the rafters.

I was dressed in black tights with a long cape that had my initials on it. 747 was dressed in red, white, and blue American flag colors, and she looked very big and strong. Now, you know we had to fix this thing—no way was I going to be able to beat an Olympic athlete—so the three of us, 747, Mootry, and myself, planned it out. The problem was that I had to obviously win for the station, but on the other hand, 747 wanted to save face and didn't want to look bad in front of her fans.

So here's the dumb thing Mootry and I decided to do. We would skate around a few times, and 747 would always be in the lead with me trying to catch up. On the last lap, however, I was to take my cape and throw it over her head. While she struggled to free herself, I would skate past her and win.

I was led by some other Roller Derby people out to the rink, which was made of some very strong, thin, flexible material. When you fell on it, it didn't hurt at all. Well, we got the race under way and skated around until the last lap when I took my cape off as planned and wrapped it around her head so she couldn't see. I skated right by her and victory was mine.

But the inevitable happened, as it usually does when you can tell an event has been fixed—the whole place erupted into a chorus of deafening boos! So Mootry and I thought it would be best to get the hell out of there quickly. On our way out, the boos got louder so we literally began to run.

About an hour later, we met up with 747 for a bite to eat and a good laugh, then we went to a local roller rink so her fans could meet her. We had a ball that night, and 747 proved to be a truly wonderful person in addition to a great athlete. I don't know what happened to her—I think she's deceased. But that evening didn't hurt my career at all, and Mootry has owned two radio stations and a couple of McDonald's restaurants since.

The promotion of all time that I remember was the WVON window stickers. This was the first time Chicago had seen anything like it. These were white stickers with black lettering that said WVON.

We would announce things like, "See you at Lake Meadows' parking lot at three o'clock. Meet Pervis Spann and get a window sticker."

People would come to the lot and we would jump inside their car, pasting stickers on their windows. Maybe at the same time we'd have Joe Cobb at the Jewel grocery store parking lot on Eighty-Seventh and the Dan Ryan Expressway doing the same thing.

I swear to you, after a week or so, every car I saw had a window sticker, black people's cars and white people's cars. It was phenomenal. It was like a status symbol—if you didn't have a WVON sticker, you were not happening.

My eyes get a little misty thinking about those good old days. Radio stations today still do promotions, though they are a bit more contemporary. For example, for my current station, V103, I occasionally do cruise promotions on a boat in Lake Michigan. Maybe some day for one of my promotions, you'll be the lucky thirteenth caller and I can give you tickets to a really good show.

(ANSWER TO QUESTION ON PAGE 93)

The group was Wild Cherry, the song "Play That Funky Music White Boy."

Meeting the Jacksons at the Airport

The Spinners had a big hit in 1972 with the song "I'll Be Around." The B-side of that 45 was an equally big hit. What was the name of that song?

A. "Could It Be I'm Falling in Love?"
B. "Sadie"
C. "Games People Play"
D. "Rubberband Man"
E. "How Could I Let You Get Away?"

(ANSWER ON PAGE 100)

The Jacksons—Michael and his singing siblings—came to Chicago to play the Amphitheater on Forty-Seventh and Halsted back in the seventies. If it hadn't been for WVON and the station's deejays, the Jacksons' success might not have happened.

We were really their springboard, what with their appearances at the Regal Theater's talent shows, plus several appearances they made for me at my teenage club called the Time Square, and various other deejay affairs. We knew the Jacksons before the fame, money, and cosmetic surgery. Before they made it big, the Jacksons were managed by Marshall Thompson of the Chi-Lites and Pervis Spann. One night, they just left town in an old beat-up station wagon on their way to Detroit and never looked back. And none of us remember any of them ever saying thank you.

On this particular occasion, some of us deejays were assigned to welcome the Jacksons to Chicago for this Amphitheater date. They were arriving at Midway Airport on a bright Saturday morning. I had what I thought was a brilliant idea to buy all the Good Guys some straw Panama hats, so that we could recognize each other in the crowd. Little did I know at the time how prophetic that would be.

That morning, Good Guys Cecil Hale, Jay Johnson, and I got into two big, black, shiny limousines, smiling and laughing, and took off for Midway. When we arrived, the airport was jam-packed, with people coming from everywhere. The crowd immediately surrounded our limos and started beating on them. I can remember seeing hands and faces and hearing thumps of people slapping on the cars as we slowly inched into the airport.

I have never seen a crowd like that, so frenzied they even spilled over onto the tarmac so the Jacksons' plane couldn't land. The police finally cleared the area for the plane and somehow got the Jacksons off and whisked them away somewhere. Disappointed that the Jacksons were out of reach, this big frantic crowd then said, let's go get the WVON Good Guys in them silly Panama hats. Next thing I know, we're running like crazy!

The crowd wasn't trying to hurt us, they just wanted to kill us with love, but it was so many of them that we were fighting for our lives. We would have been crushed. Somehow, I got separated from Jay and Cecil, but I can still see it. I watched two Panama hats being carried away by a huge wave of human beings, hollering and screaming. I found out later that Jay and Cecil had run to the terminal building's baggage carousel, where they found some overalls. It was a great disguise, and they were able to escape.

Meantime, I was running away like a jackrabbit from what seemed like thousands of people in hot pursuit. I saw a door up ahead, ran to it, and breathlessly knocked. No answer, so I banged harder, and *hallelujah* the door slowly opened and a little old man said, "Hello?"

I screamed, "Please, sir, please let me in! This crowd is about to do something to me! Please sir, I'm begging you!" He looked over my shoulder, saw all the people, then slammed the door in my face and locked it!

What followed was truly traumatic. The crowd had me on the ground (my Panama hat was long gone) and was reaching, pulling, and grabbing whatever they could get ahold of. I guess the police must have rescued me, but I really can't remember a lot of what happened. I don't know how I got out of there, don't know how I got back to the radio station, don't remember anything after that. I hated them Jacksons right then and there!

Back at the station a few days later, we looked at pictures taken by helicopter. The whole airport was covered with people, so many people standing everywhere that you couldn't see the two limos, only people shaped like limos. People on top of the hoods, on the sides—it was like people growing out of the limos like sprouts on Chia pets! Then we saw the actual pictures of the cars in the repair shop. Windows gone, bumpers gone, the cars were totaled, crushed, smashed. You couldn't recognize what were once two beautiful, big, black, shiny limousines.

The experience had such a profound effect on me that I have never been able to go to Midway Airport since without looking behind me. But when I think back on it now, I would do it all over again—it was exciting as hell.

(ANSWER TO QUESTION ON PAGE 98)

The flip side Spinners hit was E. "How Could I Let You Get Away?"

Partying at
the Time Square

In 1978, the O'Jays made a popular record called "Brandy." Who or what was Brandy?

A. Wife
B. Girlfriend
C. Old friend
D. Pet dog
E. Liquor

(ANSWER ON PAGE 105)

Today at 4859 South Wabash on the South Side of Chicago, you'll find the Charles A. Hayes Family Investment Center. It's a comprehensive source of welfare-to-work assistance for low-income families that provides one-stop access to employment training, job placement, and supportive social services. The center is a beautiful place, put together with four million dollars' worth of funding. One of the driving forces behind all of this is the president and CEO, Zenobia Johnson-Black.

Zenobia is a dynamic person. She took me to the center and showed me a computer school with fifty stations using the Pentium II system. The center also has daycare, medical examining facilities with doctors and nurses, conference rooms with walnut furniture, an elevator, and a dance hall with a stage. Everything is state-of-the-art. As we strolled through the place, Zenobia reminded me that this was my home, the home of Herb Kent— and indeed it was. It was at one time a teen nightclub that I called the Time Square.

Many years ago, the place was known as Bacon's Casino. Then it was a wooden-and-brick structure that you could rent out for parties. It was also a home for labor organizations, mainly the United Packinghouse Workers of America, and it eventually took the name the Packing House. In 1957, the union moved to this building when it had outgrown its previous space.

The head man was the late Charles Hayes, a black guy who negotiated for the union to get their workers more money. Charlie was awesome and was ultimately elected to the United States Congress to fill Harold Washington's seat when Harold became Chicago's first black mayor.

Declining union membership forced the Packing House to close in the early 1980s. Ownership of the center was turned over to Charles Hayes, and it was renamed the Hayes Center. But the building began to decline and came close to being demolished. The Chicago Housing Authority bought the building for one dollar, and today the Hayes Family Center continues the tradition of helping those who are most vulnerable and empowering those without a voice.

Here's how it became a teenage club. In 1965, when I was one of the biggest disc jockeys in the world for teenagers, I was giving these record hops and dances everywhere, all over Chicago. That got to be kind of cumbersome, and eventually I thought it would be great to localize in one place.

I approached Charlie Hayes and negotiated terms to take over the ballroom of his center on a monthly lease. He agreed, and I was in business. One of the first things I did was paint the entire ballroom black. I installed some of the newer lights that changed in time to the beat of the music and gave a brilliant display in the dark.

Then I built a soundproof booth on the north wall. Underneath the booth I built a little bar, and the whole thing was very functional. I installed what at that time was state-of-the-art equipment: an RCA board, a tape machine, and a cart machine, which were used by all the radio stations. I also put six big fifteen-inch Altec speakers around the ballroom for intensified sound. I installed turntables and jacks, and it was really slick.

After I trained jocks on how to work in my special little booth room, they started really jammin'. One of the jocks who trained in there was Loretta Kraft, known as the Boss Lady, who was bad! My longtime friend Jerry Simmons was my right-hand guy. He did everything from tend bar to spin records, and without him it probably never would have happened the way it did and as big as it did. This had to be the most creative period of my life. With Jerry at the Time Square, we pioneered so many firsts.

We were the first to use two turntables for continuous sound at these record hops. We were the first to have a booth for the disc jockeys to spin in. We were the first to use fog and big flashing lights and a strobe in the party hall.

For my fog, I discovered this stuff that the navy used to use to create smoke screens, and I bought some of that equipment. You got this can of oily stuff that you poured into a black container that was plugged into a wall. In about five minutes it heated up and you'd press this plunger down and big thick fog just rolled out. In less than a minute you could obliterate a hall of a thousand people, and the kids just loved it. The only thing was that it had a peculiar odor. I'll never forget this one guy danced by and he said, "Herb, it smells like you have a giant can of Fly Dead in here." I told him I called it "Romantic Atmosphere."

I bought a powerful airplane strobe light that emitted powerful flashes of light for short durations. I hung it in the center of the ceiling with the controls in my specially constructed booth. On a signal, we turned all the lights off, making it pitch black. When we played some music and turned that strobe on, the effect was like freeze-framed movies—it was awesome.

The first time I did that and we turned the house lights back on, the crowd gave me a rousing ovation. Some nights I couldn't walk straight or see straight after using the strobe so much. I called this effect "the skunch," but you won't find that term in your dictionary.

Since I catered to the teenage kids, we only charged a dollar to get in. We had teen hops on Fridays and Sundays, and college kids on Saturday nights. We only served pop and ice cream, but on the occasions when we would cater to adults or did shows, the bar would be in use.

The Time Square was very popular. One of my radio creations—the Wahoo Man—did his thing in there, and at least twenty couples met there and got married. I think the most amazing thing about the Time Square was the people who performed for us, some for free, some that we paid for.

I booked Little Richard and Junior Walker, and both of those shows were packed. For the Little Richard show, Martha Reeves of the Vandellas came by with a cheetah on a leash. Acts that performed free to promote their records included the Temptations, Smokey Robinson and the Miracles, Sam and Dave, the Impressions, Gene Chandler, the Five Stairsteps, JoAnne Garrett, even Ernie Terrell and the Heavyweights with Jean Terrell, who later became a Supreme.

The kids got a big show for their dollar. I even had the Jackson 5 there twice with a young Michael Jackson, but ironically, both times I missed actually catching the show because I was too busy pitching some woo to some female friends on the couch in my booth. I also installed a drum machine and used it to record my first hit record called *The Tea Box*.

As I toured the Charles Hayes Family Center with Zenobia, all of that flashed in my mind and I got choked up. That was over forty years ago.

I thought about my manager, Don Robinson, who has since departed. I thought about Ira Murchinson, who sold me my ice cream freeze. And this is one of the places where walkin' and boppin' really got shaped up into steppin'. My, what memories.

(ANSWER TO QUESTION ON PAGE 101)

Brandy was the dog of one of the O'Jays.

Kickin' It at the Kappa Karnival

> What was the smash hit by James Ingram and Patti Austin that the TV soap opera *General Hospital* just played to death?
>
> *(ANSWER ON PAGE 110)*

'll bet the mere mention of Kappa Karnival unleashes a flood of memories for some of you. Others of you might be saying, yeah, I heard about it from my mom or dad. The rest of you are going, what's a Kappa Karnival? Well, it was just one of the most exciting things you'd ever want to be at!

The Kappa Karnival was in existence between 1961 and 1979 and started as a homecoming dance for the brothers in the Kappa Alpha Psi Fraternity who attended Southern Illinois University (SIU) in Carbondale, Illinois. I got involved in 1967, when two of the frat brothers paid me a visit at my teenage nightclub the Time Square. I wish I could remember their names; perhaps they or someone who knows them will read this and get in touch with me. I think they were grad students at SIU.

Anyway, they said that since I was the biggest teen deejay in Chicago, I had an opportunity here to lead a lot of kids on the right path. They spoke of educating our kids, school dropouts, and gangs. They thought it would be a wonderful thing if some of the younger folks could attend this event down in Carbondale that was held once a year. They wanted me to get kids to see what college life was like, which would hopefully motivate them to stay in school, go to college, and eventually have great careers.

We talked for a long time, and I remember their sincerity; they were terrific guys. They asked me to pump the Karnival on the air, then come down and spin records at the actual party. I was excited because I've already told you that talking to kids about staying in school was my thing. I got on the radio and talked about the Kappa Karnival every night, but none of us knew how huge this was going to turn out to be.

The whole body of events lasted about a week in the first part of April. We developed a whole array of events, so that some people could just go over the weekend for two days or stay however long they could. We had activities like campus tours and meet-and-greets for people from around the country.

At that time, I had such a loyal following that I knew we would have a nice crowd. If the Cool Gent said, "Let's go," then it was let's go! I grabbed a couple of my friends, packed my bags, and took off for Carbondale.

The I-57 expressway that you take to get there eventually runs out and leads you to Route 55, which is a two-lane highway, but we finally made it. Upon arrival, we went to the motel where the Kappas had me staying. A sign said, "Welcome Herb Kent from WVON!" That was the first time I ever saw my name in lights.

We got out of the car and immediately began to party, starting at the motel. We proceeded from there to the Kappa fraternity house and partied some more. We partied on the main thorough-fare called Illinois Street. We partied in dormitories. We partied all night long into the next day and nobody slept.

That next day, the party grew even more as people arrived from Chicago, St. Louis, and East St. Louis. Students from other colleges in other states came because they heard about this thing.

The Kappas had me set up my equipment and I would spin records here, spin records there; hell, I spun records everywhere! The Saturday night party was at a place called the Hippodrome, and half the records I played there were by James Brown because everyone loved him and the Kappas could step to that music—the college fraternity stepping, not the nightclub steppin'.

It was a fabulous promotion, and little did I know at the time that I would be making history, a lifetime of good friendships, and enhancing my career. And that was just the beginning. That first Karnival I attended was so much fun and so well attended that I talked the station into letting me broadcast live from there the next year. The second year we did it, this thing just went through the roof!

We were a little lucky because the Karnival is held the first week in April when it's generally a little cool, but this year it was warm and sunny. I have never seen so many people attending a function in my life. They came from everywhere. Before the event, I plugged it on the air once a day for an hour for weeks on end. I would describe the beautiful drive down and the wonderful landscape. I especially talked about the many evergreen trees you see on the drive, from the little ones to the big ones. I was as descriptive as I could be and really painted a picture.

As a result of me talking about this thing, and the fact that WVON was the number one black station in the nation, the response was overwhelming. In Chicago, high school teachers organized groups of students and went down. Two junior college clubs, the Travelers and the Sweepers, competed with each other to see who would bring the most people down. Every side of the city was well represented, plenty of single guys and gals showed up, and the party was on. The Kappas themselves traveled to many colleges to plug the event in person. As a result, college students from every major university in the country showed up, especially from the Historically Black Colleges and Universities.

The week of the event, car upon car homed in on Carbondale. If you were on the road, you could tell who was on the way to Kappa Karnival because everybody had an Afro hairstyle. You could see six people in a car with six big round naturals. Another way to get to Carbondale was by train. I have visited the station as the train arrived, and my God, the doors opened to just an outpouring of people. Thank goodness the weather was so nice because there were so many people and not enough accommodations.

People piled into the dorms as best they could, but when room ran out, they slept in their cars or on lawns with blankets. Or they didn't sleep at all, they just partied—you know how young people are! And there was never any violence at all. It was very peaceful, which is pretty remarkable for a group that size.

During our years there, there was only one thing that came close to being a "situation," and that was when Dr. Martin Luther King Jr. was assassinated. The city had the national guard strategically located all over the campus and around the hotels. They didn't bother us, but their presence was there. After a while, though, it was like you didn't even see them.

The amazing thing about the Kappa Karnival was that the university actually turned the whole campus over to the Kappas for the week and allowed them to organize and coordinate everything. The entire university was being run by students between nineteen and twenty-four years of age, and they did a great job of keeping everything together.

I must tell you about one crazy, really scary incident that I was involved in. The motel I stayed at was run by a manager who was not very tolerant. He was a mean one with a big belly and a white shirt with buttons pulling too tight; you know the type.

I had a white friend who went to school there, and he told me not to venture out of Carbondale into the small surrounding towns late at night. He said, and I quote, "Herb, down here is Down South just as much as Alabama or Mississippi is Down South." He told me there were two things that they absolutely did not like in these little surrounding towns—"niggers, and honkies with long hair." That got my attention, all right, and I always stayed in Carbondale, where it was cool.

Anyway, we had a party one night in my room at this motel, maybe fifteen or so of us, including some girls that attended the college. This intolerant manager found out about it and was furious! He demanded that we stop the party and said he was going to turn the young ladies in to the university. The girls were afraid to leave the room, figuring they could be expelled if the manager identified them and fingered them to school officials. So he called the Carbondale police and insisted that they come and empty the room.

Well, the Carbondale cops came, crashed the door down, and rushed into the room. I can still see their shiny batons waving around—I think they were intent on doing some damage. But I had brought along two Chicago police officers who were acting as my bodyguards. My guys immediately pulled their guns and shouted, "Stop, we're Chicago police!"

Things got real tense at that moment. It became like the irresistible force and the immovable object. Our police began quoting the innkeeper some rules, and the Carbondale police were quoting some other rules. It became a true impasse. For about what seemed like an hour nothing happened, with neither side giving an inch, until a young guy who came with us—Rudolph Williamson, who was about twenty years old at the time—had the bright idea of calling the mayor of Carbondale. The mayor got out of his bed in the middle of the night, came over to the motel, and defused the situation.

He called the university and got the female students out of trouble, then asked the Carbondale police to leave, and the standoff was over. But it got really hot there for a minute.

(ANSWER TO QUESTION ON PAGE 106)

General Hospital played "Baby Come to Me" to death.

The Big Bike Rides

What was the first R & B single to go platinum?

(ANSWER ON PAGE 113)

In my radio career I've been responsible for a lot of firsts that I bet you didn't know about. Among them, I was the first to organize a monstrous bike ride in the city of Chicago.

By 1970, the ten-speed bike was all the rage in this country, and everybody wanted to get one—the skinny-tired bike with the gear shift on it. You could just ride for days and not get tired like on the big balloon-tire bikes. I got the idea of having a huge bike ride with celebrities, listeners, fans, everybody. I went to city hall for a parade permit, and surprisingly, they gave it to me with no problem. I knew then that I had a name that could open doors.

The route was as follows: we'd assemble at Thirty-Fourth and King Drive in Lake Meadows, head down King Drive to Twenty-Second Street, from Twenty-Second over to Michigan Avenue, through downtown, through Lincoln Park, through a tunnel to the bike path in Lincoln Park. The final destination was not far from Sandburg Village apartments, two blocks of pavement surrounded by a little valley of grass on both sides with a ribbon of concrete pavement in the middle. It was a gorgeous area.

We had police cars all along the way to direct traffic, and I was able to get a few policemen off for the day to be my personal assistants. One was Tyrone Foster, a tough West Side cop who was assigned to assist a promoter named Sam Chapman. Once word got out about the bike ride, this thing started to grow exponentially—people wanted to help, and celebrities wanted to ride.

There was Pervis Staples of the Staple Singers, Gene Chandler, and record companies sent their promotion guys like Frank Chaplin, Kirkland Burke, and Jerome Simmons. There were so many folks I honestly cannot remember them all. I promoted the ride on the radio, talking about how we would ride down Michigan Avenue into the great expanse of Lincoln Park. Nobody can describe things like I can after I really get going.

That Saturday morning, wow! Bikes came from everywhere—and, oh my gosh, all kinds of bikes. The crowd was predominately black, but there were a number of whites, Asians, Hispanics; you name it, we were all there. This was the first bike rally that the city of Chicago had ever had. I can't give figures, but there were thousands of us. I think it was the granddaddy of all bike rides. It was so exciting, but quiet excitement, because, you know, ten-speed bikes don't make a lot of noise. We were quiet like silent assassins.

By the time these thousands of ninja bikes made it downtown to Michigan Avenue, all the major news media were there. The TV stations didn't know what was happening—and thousands of black people riding around on bikes together during the 1960s certainly captured the attention of the TV stations, and a lot of other concerned white people as well. So I got interviewed by the stations, and we were all over TV, partly because the bike ride was such a phenomenon in itself and partly because the media wanted to let white people know: *It's OK, you can come out of your houses—they're not on the warpath.* A black TV reporter named Bob Petty was my first big mainstream media interview. And you know, I was young and handsome—I looked almost as good on TV then as I look now.

The riders descended into Lincoln Park, to our little place, and we had a two-block bike race. Gene Chandler shifted into a low gear right at the end and shot in front of everyone else to come in as number one. The second-place winner used to manage Marvin

Gaye, but I cannot recall his name. I barely managed to beat this guy, Eddie Thomas, who used to manage the Impressions. Then we all headed for the long ride home, but it was OK because it was a beautiful, simply gorgeous day and turned out to be a wonderful promotion for both myself and WVON.

After the race, Sam Chapman and his policeman assistant Tyrone Foster arranged a big afterset at the Keyman Club. Hundreds of bikers rode over there to party, and we were entertained by Billy Butler and Lalah Hathaway, Donny Hathaway's daughter. It was a tremendous success, and we split the money from that three ways. Sam and Tyrone became promotional partners and have been very successful from that day to this, throwing the biggest steppers' sets ever.

I did the Big Bike Ride every year for three years, but after the first year, the power structure in the Lincoln Park area, which was a mostly white, uppercrust neighborhood, would never let us ride into that area again. They fought it, and the police department moved us to the planetarium instead, in downtown Chicago along the lake, which was not the same. But we had later bike rides to Fun Town Amusement Park on Ninety-Fifth and Stony, which were really fun.

After I got fired from WVON a couple of years later, they tried to duplicate the event but didn't have the heart nor the touch. They gave a watered-down version of the Herb Kent Bike Rides. Now that I've got that off my chest, we can move on to the next topic.

(ANSWER TO QUESTION ON PAGE 111)

"Disco Lady" by Johnnie Taylor was the first platinum R & B single.

Staying Awake for Black Power

> How many records do you have to sell before you get a diamond record?
>
> *(ANSWER ON PAGE 118)*

One of the most interesting things that has happened to me in my career was my involvement with the black power movement of the 1960s. At WVON, we crusaded and collected money for a lot of the groups involved in civil rights and black power, including some of the then-controversial ones, like Angela Davis and H. Rap Brown.

When we were trying to collect money, we would often broadcast our shows from a trailer located in Lake Meadows Shopping Center at Thirty-Fifth and King Drive. We would come up with all types of antics to get people to come and see us and drop off donations. It was hard work, but we raised lots of money back in the day. Our midday deejay, Bill "Butterball" Crane, was a pro at it; he was a champion money-getter. Butterball would preach, holler, and scream. He'd say stuff like, "If you want us black folks to get our rights quicker, you have to drop off that iron, baby!"

As a matter of fact, we all shifted to a higher gear when it came to raising money in the name of black power. We'd go round-the-clock, twenty-four hours a day, and the money poured in. We would, in turn, give the money to organizations like the NAACP and Rev. Jesse Jackson and his group, which back then was Operation Breadbasket.

We created all kinds of stunts to get people to donate their money to us—to "drop that iron." One that comes to mind was the time we convinced a shapely young lady to come to the trailer in Lake Meadows on a blustery winter night at midnight dressed only in a bikini. You should have seen the folks running over to see that sight and to drop off their money.

The culmination of these fundraising activities was a contest between the station's deejays to see who could stay awake the longest. It was a dangerous thing to do and proved to be physically damaging to some of us. Even so, it was a dilly of an idea, though I never knew whose idea it was.

All the money we collected was designated to go to several groups, including Breadbasket, the Urban League, NAACP, SNCC, CORE, and several others. The year was 1965. We were in the Lake Meadows Shopping Center, in front of the old Benson-Rixon clothing store, and this trailer had a giant picture window in front so everyone could watch the stunt and make sure we weren't cheating.

The rules were that once we entered the trailer, we were really locked in. No one was allowed to leave until after they went to sleep, meaning, of course, that they would have lost the contest and were booted out. So, bright and early one morning, we all said good-bye to our families or significant others and trooped off to our trailer.

We were greeted there by a doctor and four nurses and suddenly it hit us how serious this thing was that we were about to do—to stay awake for as long as possible and not go to sleep. Think about it. It's certainly not a natural thing to do. In fact, Dr. Albert Spalding, the attending physician, was really against it. He said it could cause permanent damage to us. But we went for it. We were the WVON Good Guys—station deejays who all loved each other more than brothers. It was an unbelievable kinship.

The participating lineup in this stunt as best I can remember included: Ed Cook, the Magnificent Montague, Lucky Cordell, Butterball Crane, E. Rodney Jones, Pervis Spann the Blues Man, Bill "Doc" Lee, our religious announcer, and me. So now the show is about to begin. Dr. Spalding checked us out as we went into the trailer, and we were all in pretty decent condition. The first day was fun. We took turns playing records and begging for money and it was just a gas!

But that first night, E. Rodney Jones was pulling up bottles of whiskey through the window on a string. By morning he had passed out, so he was gone. We were one down, but the money continued to pour in.

The four nurses came in to take our blood pressure readings after we had been awake all the first night. Sure enough, our pressures had started to drop slightly, even though we were consuming buckets of Kentucky Fried Chicken. Sometime the second day, deejay Ed Cook fell out, and they were extremely worried about him, so they took him home. By the end of that second day, we knew this was not going to be a cake walk. It was gonna be a sho-nuff fight!

But the people continued to come from everywhere to see us and pledge money for the cause. They shouted encouragements at us, like "C'mon, you can do it. Stay awake, baby!" About this time, somebody slipped me a little energy pill. Shortly after I took it, I started to sing and dance, to do the Twist all over the trailer. The other guys were zooming right along with me. I felt like I was charged with twenty thousand volts of electricity. I just knew I was going to win this thing. But after the stuff wore off, I was really ready to go home and crash.

A little while later, Bill "Doc" Lee, our religious disc jockey, went unconscious, and they took him to the hospital, where he stayed for a week. By now we were into the third day. The crowd had kept coming, cheering us on, and the money was growing and growing.

After a while, though, the flow of people coming by slowed to a trickle. So to stimulate the crowd again, I requested the fire department come and put me on the roof of Goldblatt's Department Store in the Lake Meadows shopping complex. We heard sirens in the distance and knew the fire department was responding to my call. With a hook and ladder, they put me up on the roof. You have no idea how long that ladder was or how high that roof was. I hadn't had any sleep and was scared to death—especially when the fire engine left me up there alone. The worst, however, was yet to come.

The guys down in the trailer were continuously broadcasting over the air, "Come see Herb Kent on the roof!" And it worked; the crowds came back. But then it happened—the world's worst thunderstorm! Piece of advice: never be on the roof of a tall building when a thunderstorm hits. My God, it is the scariest thing, something you'll never forget.

The rain came in torrents, lightning danced on the roof, and I was terrified. Where was the fire department? Help, help! After what seemed like hours, they came and took my tired, six-foot-two, one-hundred-forty-pound, sogging wet body off the roof.

But they took me right back to the trailer for me to continue with this crazy contest and be punished some more. I made *Jet* magazine because of the roof incident. Well, back in the trailer, the nurses came and took our blood pressures, and we had all dropped dangerously low.

I remember saying on the air for people to come and see me because I was from the Ida B. Wells projects and I used to shoot pool in the pool room on the second floor on Thirty-Ninth Street. This was the third day and I was beginning to fade. Fast. I remember telling a friend of mine who came to look at me through the glass, in a hoarse whisper, "My legs are gone, my legs are gone." I seemed to be in a dream world somewhere. I remember people saying, "Come on, Herbie Baby. Don't go to sleep, you can win, come on."

But I couldn't hold out any longer and I just crashed! I believe they carried me out on a stretcher. The next thing I knew, I was at home in bed, but I could still hear the music and it seemed to me that while I was in bed, I was still back in the trailer at the same time. It was wild, but it was also a dangerously bad condition for me to be in.

I couldn't remember anything, I couldn't concentrate, and as a result of this experience, to this day, I sometimes have very short memory lapses. They come and go quickly and don't happen very often. But that's my contribution to the freedom movement.

So who did win, you ask? I don't know how he did it, but of all the deejays left, some of whom also ended up in the hospital, Pervis Spann managed to last an entire week and was the winner. We raised an enormous amount of money and most of the deejays said they'd do it again. Maybe I would, too. Then again, I don't know.

(ANSWER TO QUESTION ON PAGE 114)

You have to sell five hundred thousand units to get a gold record and one million to get a platinum record. But to get a diamond record, you have to sell ten million copies of your album—in the United States alone, not worldwide. And if you do that, man, you've got a monster hit and are set for life!

4
♦♦♦

THEATER OF THE MIND ON RADIO

Ivy Leaguers Versus
Those Evil Gousters

What piano-pounding star was banished from radio
for marrying his thirteen-year-old cousin?

(ANSWER ON PAGE 123)

I have the reputation of being maybe one of the most creative
disc jockeys ever. Instead of just talking smack on the radio, I
created situations, characters, running gags, and that kind of thing
to entertain my listeners and keep them coming back to find out
what was going to happen in the latest installment of their favorite
gimmick. I called it Theater of the Mind on Radio, and my ability
to successfully engage my listeners in this fashion came from my
background of doing plays and drama with the Hyde Park Radio
Club, the WBEZ radio workshops, at NBC, and with the Skyloft
Players. So I brought not only a good voice and the ability to play
music but also skills in writing and acting. I drew upon all of these
abilities.

One of the things I think people liked about me was the creation of these characters. They just came out of my mind, just stuff
that I thought of, but I also reflected off the audience. I listened
very carefully to what folks said to me, then I'd create a character,
bring it to life, and put it on the air. When one character died, I'd
come up with another one.

One of the earliest bits I did on radio when I was big-time popular in the early 1960s dealt with the "battle" between Ivy Leaguers and gousters. We had big fun with that, and the teens and young adults went crazy over it because it went directly to their lifestyle and sense of identity. I've heard over the past decade that a lot of sweet young things who have heard about old school radio and me in particular have been trying to figure out just what exactly is meant by the term "gouster."

My, my, that brings back so many memories. Well, being the musical and lifestyle historicologist that I am, let me open up my *Herb Kent's Unabridged Dictionary of All Things Black and Cool* and try to explain to you young 'uns what this was all about. Step into the Way Back Machine with me and set the levers to five decades ago. In 1960, there were two types of teenagers—gousters and Ivy Leaguers. I believe the term "gouster" originated somewhere in England, but I'm not sure.

Gousters and Ivy Leaguers were diametrically opposed opposites, but they weren't gangs as we know them today. Not like the Bloods versus the Crips, or the Stones versus the Disciples. They were more like greasers and preppies. Greasers wore leather jackets and slicked-back ducktail hairstyles. Kinda like the Fonz from *Happy Days*, but they were rougher-looking. Preppies wore polo shirts and pullover sweaters and were generally from the nice side of town.

Our Ivies and gousters affected similarly particular ways of dressing, and each group copped its own specific attitude. Gouster guys wore wide-brimmed beaver hats that they often put Vaseline on and swirled the hairs; wide-legged pants with cuffs and triple pleats; long-collared shirts with big Windsor-knotted ties; suits with long jackets; top coats; and pointed-toe shoes with white stitching on the soles, known as knob triple A's. The toes of these shoes were so pointed, some guys said they could kill roaches in the corner! Sometimes a handkerchief was stuffed in the suit pocket to be removed and used for styling while dancing. Think

Morris Day and the Time—he would have been a gouster (*I know dat's right!*). The gouster girls wore plain dresses and were not as fashioned as the guys.

Ivy League dudes wore Brooks Brothers–style suits, with skinny-legged floods hiked maybe a couple of inches above their shoes; button-down collars; and ties with skinny knots. Their shoes had thick soles, wing tips, were sometimes oxblood in color, and their hats had teeny-tiny brims. Ivy League girls wore peppermint-striped shirts with button-down collars and pleated skirts or poodle skirts, with saddle shoes.

As you can tell, the styles were absolutely opposite, to stress the individual identity of the two groups, and at dances, more than occasionally, fights broke out for this very reason—with the gousters winning most of the time. Gousters were a more aggressive group and more prone to rumble. Then again, some Ivy Leaguers were pretty good at fisticuffs, and nobody messed with them. But by-and-large, to categorize, gousters were more outspoken, and Ivy Leaguers were more laid back.

I don't know how all of this happened or got started in the first place, but it was pretty big among black teens and young adults, especially when it came to the parties. At the dance you were either Ivy League or gouster—there was no in-between. But it was all pretty harmless, not like gangs competing at parties today with people getting killed. Gousters just tried to always outdo the Ivies in everything. The competition was there in the form of dressing, dancing, even getting the girls.

And for some damn reason, all those cute Ivy League girls always fell real hard for those big, rough, tough, smooth-talking gousters. This type of thing still happens today and probably always has—a beautiful young lady told me recently that she prefers her man to have a slight "edge" to him. Why is that, ladies? 'Splain that one to me, please!

So, back in the day, the gousters had all the ladies, even though the Ivy League guys were the better dressers and dancers. However, around 1961, gouster jackets arrived on the scene. They were casual jackets in many colors—red, green, plaid even—with brass buttons. But above all, they had collars that reached down to your knees. These jackets were smoking, and they were so popular that even the Ivies had to buy them. They sold for between thirty-five and one hundred dollars, which was a helluva lot of money in the early sixties.

Only one guy in Chicago made them, Jerry the Tailor, who kept a crew of women forever busy sewing up batches of jackets. One Easter Sunday morning, he had a sea of people stretching around the corner to pick up their gouster jackets to strut around in as their Easter finest. Some of the high fashion stores tried to copy this famous jacket as knock-offs, but by then the trend was dying out.

Like most of the amazing trends—pet rocks, Beanie Babies, etc.—the gouster/Ivy League thing had a short shelf life. By the mid-sixties, it had faded out. One final note about this whole thing: I will never forget one particular cutie pie with beautiful long hair and button-down collars. Man, she was cute, but she fell for a gouster, and I was chagrined, because as you have probably guessed by now—I was an Ivy Leaguer!

I look around today at these young cats with their pants hanging down past their ass, underwear showing, gym shoes, baseball caps cocked to the side, do-rags, stocking caps, sports jerseys, and it makes me long for the old days.

So what about you, new schoolers? Answer me this: If you were back in the day or could bring the trend up to the present, what would you be—Ivy League, or an evil, evil gouster?

(ANSWER TO QUESTION ON PAGE 120)

Rocker Jerry Lee Lewis married his thirteen-year-old cousin.

Grunchions, the Gym Shoe Creeper, and a New Teenage Language

What was Chubby Checker's real name?

(ANSWER ON PAGE 126)

For this section, I think back fondly on the daughters of veteran black deejay Sid McCoy. I used to look up to Sid McCoy—I still look up to Sid McCoy. I listened to him when I was in high school. I thought he had a great voice and I wanted to sound like him; I wanted to be like him. Sid, of course, went on to be the longtime announcer for *Soul Train.*

In the long run, he kind of admired me as I was establishing myself, but we had a falling out. Sid was a golf nut—I mean, a fanatic. I saw him someplace once, some event, and he had this hand-tooled golf bag where you could smell the leather on it from across the room. Had all these fancy clubs with little wool jackets and tassels on them. I told Sid, "Man, where'd you get that stupid-looking bag? What do you need all that shit for?" He did not speak to me for two years!

But Sid's daughters were fans of mine and liked the language that I used on the air. Really, I just took citizens band (CB) terminology stuff and used it. "Y.L." meant "young lady," "20" was your location. "73s" meant greetings, salutations, and love, while "83" meant you're drunk and you get put out. So when I would sign off the air by saying, "A bunch of 73s to you Y.L.s out there," people would say, Wow, he's invented a new language. A lot of people—most people at the time probably—weren't into citizens band, so they had no idea where I was getting this stuff. I suppose I just used it in all kinds of creative ways back then, with my earphones on my head and buoyed up by the music, jamming and popping my fingers—all that stuff would just flow out of my mouth like water.

I had a cousin who walked somewhat on the wild side and her nickname was "Hammer." That led me to using the term on the air for females, especially the ones who had a little kick to them—"hammers" were the girls, "nails" were the guys. Years and years ago, I remember talking to a guy at two or three in the morning. He had been in the army, but had come out and fallen on hard times and turned into a gangster. He said that when he was young, they use to call young women "fesneckies." I searched around for the word and the closest I could come was some kind of flower—a fesnecky. I started using it on the air, and then for obvious reasons, "dikneckies" came up from there for the guys!

I guess I did make up a language. I took words and just made up phrases—a fesnecky was a girl; a "fern" was whatever you wanted it to be, so I'd be on the air talking about "a fine fesnecky with a mellow fern!" You figure it out.

Then I invented the grunchions—I don't know where I got that name from, but they were little tiny people, smaller than half a grain of rice, who lived in your hair. They weren't head lice, now, but they were people who lived there. There were orange grunchions and green grunchions. The green grunchions were black folks and the orange ones represented white people. These microscopic people lived on my head in my hair, and they were always at odds with each other.

So I'd tell stories like how the green grunchions would be standing in line at the cafeteria and the orange grunchions would just step right in front of them and get fed first! It was just crazy, man. But people loved it, so I made some green and orange grunchion neckpieces that we gave away. Wish I still had one today. Anyway, that's how I got tagged with the creative language moniker.

People would tell me about real creeps in the neighborhood, and I fashioned the Gym Shoe Creeper after this real-life guy whose thing was to go around and find a pretty woman, then take off his shoe and whine, "Sniff my sneaker!"

But now, turn the page, and let me tell you about my greatest creation of all.

(ANSWER TO QUESTION ON PAGE 124)

The real name of Chubby Checker—the man who introduced the world to the Twist—was Ernest Evans.

The Wahoo Man

What male singer cross-dressed and sang with a group called the Cockettes?

(ANSWER ON PAGE 132)

The Wahoo Man was the most popular thing I have ever done and is a part of radio history. Let me tell you this dark tale of a character who roamed the landscape—making little kids pee on themselves, and ladies afraid to look under their beds at night out of fear!

Here is how it all began, and this is a true story. In the Year of Our Lord 1964, after deejaying one of my sets at the Time Square, I went for a midnight snack. I took a guy named Nitro and a girl named Brenda with me to a place called Chili Mac's, a legendary restaurant in the hood for chili and tamales. We drove there in the gray Cadillac Eldorado I was sporting at the time, which had been previously owned by Muhammad Ali. As we exited the Caddie, we observed two beautiful women running diagonally across the street and screaming in terror.

They were being chased by a muscular man with a broomstick who, rather oddly it seemed, was accompanied by a little black dog. Upon seeing us, the guy ducked into a doorway while the women scampered away. We had stopped frozen in our tracks watching this play out, and Nitro, who was very vocal and excitable, exclaimed, "Boy, dat sho' was sump'n!"

At that point, we went into Chili Mac's and got seated. As the three of us prepared to feast on the eatery's most popular dish— chili with tamales at the bottom—the man with the broomstick suddenly burst into the restaurant. Chili Mac's was a small diner with a counter and stools on one side, several booths on the other, and was fairly crowded that night when this strange guy came in, walked down the aisle, and glared at everyone.

When he got to me, he shrunk down and stared into my chili. He was so close that I could easily see the puss-filled sores that covered his face. It seemed as though those sores were about to drip something icky into my chili, so I told him he had to move on. He left me, went straight to the cashier, and said in a loud voice, "I'll kill you!" The cashier, who was a rough dude, replied, "You better get outta here 'fore I mess you up." Hearing that, he took off and ran out the restaurant.

As we downed our chili and made conversation, Brenda and Nitro agreed that the man was crazy. We finished our meal, paid the bill, and as soon as we got outside, there he was again. With a broomstick in his hand and the little dog by his side, he was sing- ing the blues. We quickly jumped into the Caddie and slammed the doors. Then he rushed us, broomstick held high, ready to strike the car. I hollered, "Oh man, don't you hit this car!" But he came on anyway.

So I reached for my car theft alarm and quickly flicked it off and on. It made a sound like wah, wah, wah, which froze the guy in his tracks. Then he hollered, "Wahoo, wahoo, that don't scare nobody!" and ran away into the night. Nitro said, "Dat man oughta be called the Wahoo Man!" I said, "You're right, we could make a character out of him."

The Wahoo Man character we eventually created catapulted me into a famous place in history that still exists today. I started off the whole gimmick by just talking on the radio, describing this crazy guy with the scarred-up face who terrorized people and chased them with a broken broomstick. I told spooky stories about him on the air that scared people pretty good, like it was something from Vincent Price or Boris Karloff. Mothers called in to the station and complained that I was making their kids wet themselves.

One lady called in complaining that she was frightened because she lived by herself and begged me to stop talking about the Wahoo Man on the radio. I replied to her on the air, "Don't you dare look under your bed because he might be there," followed that with a villainous laugh, then hung up on her while she was still protesting.

People would tune into my show every night just to hear what the Wahoo Man was going to do next, and mothers would get their kids to behave by threatening to sic him on them if they weren't good. It got to be like Orson Welles's famous *War of the Worlds* radio broadcast, but on a smaller scale. People began to call in from all over the listening area, claiming to have spotted the Wahoo Man getting on a bus, running down an alley, climbing trees outside their houses, wherever.

My ratings were going sky high, so we decided it was time to take it to the streets. There was a young fellow working for me at the time named Robert Stallworth, who was very talented. He thought it would be a good idea for us to transform him into the Wahoo Man for promotional purposes. So we went to the Goodman Theatre in downtown Chicago and found their head makeup artist, Patrick Henry (yes, that was his real name!), who also had done makeup work for a few people in Hollywood.

We told him what we wanted to do, and he agreed to work with us. For a fee of about $250, Patrick made Robert a new face. He fashioned it out of some kind of rubbery material. As I talked and described from memory what I had seen of the demented dude at Chili Mac's that night, Patrick created the face right in front of my eyes. It was the most amazing thing I had ever seen. It included the runny sores and looked exactly like the man.

We then went to a thrift store and bought an old worn coat, an old man's fedora, a faded plaid shirt, and some old gym shoes. We picked up a broken broomstick and even found a little black dog that had seen better days. The transformation was now complete and it was frightening to look at—"the Wahoo Man." Robert even taught himself to speak the way a person who looked like this would probably speak: "I-am-the-Wahoo-Man!" With this setup and stunt, I was about to become one of the hottest disc jockeys in the country.

We went to the A. R. Leak Funeral Home where the owner, Spencer Leak, gave me a real casket. Spencer and I became life-long friends after that. I bought a copy of Bach's *Toccata and Fugue*, which is an eerie, ethereal organ selection. I got an American flag, dressed six of my helpers in Keystone cops outfits, and had a lady friend pretend to be a widow in a long black dress and veil.

Then my man Robert Stallworth suited up as the Wahoo Man in the old raggedy outfit we got for him, and he climbed into the casket. We were set to go out and terrify Chicago. Our first stop was at a popular nightclub called the Green Bunny. We parked about a block away and my six Keystone Kops carried the casket down the street. People gave us some very strange looks, but they got the hell out the way.

In this very bizarre scenario, we solemnly marched into the nightclub, which was packed that night, and set the casket on the stage, playing it totally straight-faced, totally serious. I had worked the Green Bunny many times, so I knew they had a piano onstage. We starting playing the organ music, then the supposed widow began to weep and mourn. We draped the flag over the casket and set six burning candles around it.

Picture this scene: this was totally out of the blue and no one in the place knew what to make of it (except the manager, who was in on the joke). It was spooky even for us—the people had gone absolutely silent, stopped in their tracks, mouths hanging slack and eyes wide open. After a while, as the music played, a black-gloved hand very slowly began to emerge from the casket. The fingers grasped the lid and slowly pulled it open. Then Robert even more slowly sat upright, and then his leg, with the old tennis shoe, came over the side of the casket.

People in the audience started to scream, and at this point, Robert raised his broken broomstick, quickly hopped out of the casket, and howled, "I am the Wahoo Man and *I will kill all of you!*" Pandemonium. Yelling. Screaming. Hiding. Some people ran out. The Wahoo Man himself dashed out the back door to a waiting car parked in a predetermined spot and was whisked away.

After that first success, we pulled this act all over the listening area. We even built a cage and carried the Wahoo Man around in it. But he would break out of the cage with broomstick in hand and run through the crowd. He would always get away because a car was always there waiting and no one knew when he would leave or where he would go.

One woman once didn't get out of the way in time as Robert was making his escape and he accidentally ran right into her. This woman got hysterical, turned gray, and fainted. We had to call an ambulance to take her to the hospital. We tried to avoid situations like that thereafter.

One time, we laid the Wahoo Man out in state at a local high school and let the students take a look at him. Robert was good at holding his breath to appear dead, and many of the students thought he actually was. At an appearance in front of almost two thousand people at the old Capitol Theatre on South Halsted Street, Robert did such a spooky job of easing out of the casket that some real Chicago policemen who were on the stage at the time for security almost pulled their guns.

One said, "Herb, I know this is just a gimmick, but tell him to keep away from us." Then, when Robert leaped off the stage down the center aisle to make his escape, it was like Moses had parted the Red Sea, and folks got out of the way.

At another high school's homecoming dance, we snuck the Wahoo Man in the balcony, and he pretended to go after one of the prettiest girls at the school. Not knowing what was going on, members of the football team took off after Robert, but once again he got away through a previously planned escape route.

We did this so many times, always with success—sometimes people would jump on Robert's back and he'd just shake them off—and my ratings continued to go sky high. But finally, the Wahoo Man's image grew too strong. A whole lot of parents were calling WVON about their little kids being traumatized and scared out of their wits. Because of that and some other side issues, concerning liability, I think, the radio station one day left me a note saying: "Herb Kent, as of tomorrow night, you will kill off the Wahoo Man. Period!"

So the following night, the Wahoo Man disappeared forever from the airwaves of Chicago. The real Wahoo Man just flat out disappeared and no one I know ever saw him again. But you know what? You still better not look under your bed. Sleep well, friends. Ha, ha!

Robert Stallworth went on to become the head of radiology at a hospital in Macomb, Illinois. He's got property in Hawaii and is filthy rich, but he's still got the mask. I'd have to give him enough time, but if I called, he'd hop in a cab and come do that Wahoo Man thing all over again!

(ANSWER TO QUESTION ON PAGE 127)

Sylvester made 'em feel real as a cross-dressing Cockette!

The Electric
Craaazzzy People!

What Motown recording artist/musician became famous after the scheduled singer for his session failed to show up and he had to sing the song himself?

(ANSWER ON PAGE 136)

"My name is Rudolph! *Eldorado-driving, suede-shoe-wearing, downtown-building-owning, rings and thangs upon my fingers!*"

That was a signature line from the one of the funniest comedy groups in the history of radio—the Electric Crazy People, a stand-up comedy group that I created in the seventies. We had a cult following in Chicago and almost made it to the big time a couple of times.

The group consisted of Ben Sexton, who was big in Chicago as the mechanical man in store windows; the late Orlando Reyes, a comedian who died in August 2006; Carolyn LeBlanc, an actress and a comedienne; Woody Henderson, an actor and a comedian; Emmanuel Arrington, a comedian and blues singer; Larry Langford, our announcer and narrator; Rudolph Browner, the funniest man alive; and yours truly, creator and founder of the group, Herb Kent.

I can't tell you how much I love these wonderful, talented people. To give you an idea of how crazy we were, our nicknames went by our complexions. Emmanuel was the darkest, and Woody was the lightest. Woody was #1 and Emmanuel was #8; the rest of us were 3, 4, 5, and 6 depending on our shades. We did skits about everything under the sun, mostly life experiences in the 'hood.

For instance, we did a skit about a guy receiving a gold watch for being a good worker at a corporation, and during the ceremony, his wife accuses him of making eyes at a woman in the audience. His wife embarrasses him by yelling loud, and the company takes her side, takes back the watch, and fires him. We did a skit about the Snatch-It-Back Corporation trying to repossess a refrigerator in the projects, whereupon the occupants sic their snarling pet wolf on the repo man and he never returns. In another one, a lady hails a cab in the pouring rain and takes a long time to enter. The cabbie eventually says, "Lady, what is taking you so long?" She hollers, "Can't you see I only have one leg?" And he goes, "Well, hop on in then!"

Everybody in the group could do comedy and we all wrote the skits together. Rudolph Browner was the funniest person in the group and I did a lot of special skits with him as a solo. He was the legendary Rudolph, Eldorado-driving, downtown-building-owning man.

We did these skits on a daily basis on WVON radio, and then people began to love us so much, they booked us and we would do gigs on the side and made a little money. We also made money by doing commercials for a barbecue restaurant called Rib Supreme. We took this average rib house and made it the number one rib joint in Chicago by using funny, innovative, appealing ideas—simple but funny stuff like the guy asking, "Miss, do bread come wid dis order?" The people just flocked to Rib Supreme. I could get all the free ribs I wanted, but I couldn't even get in sometimes. It was amazing.

We created most of our ideas on Tuesday nights in the basement of my house. I had a miniature studio in my basement, and we'd get Coca-Cola and giant hot dogs or clams, oysters—we munched on all sorts of stuff. And man, it was big fun! We would do all kinds of things, make funny noises, say silly things, and laugh at the top of our lungs. Premeditated, riotous silliness.

I remember my mother saying that we woke her up at night and that there really were crazy people in the house—and she wasn't laughing when she said it. At the end of the session, which often lasted into the wee hours of the morning, we would have a skit or something that was about a minute or a minute and a half, something that could play on the air.

Everybody had day jobs and we would just come together when we needed to tape for my show, a commercial, or if we had a gig. We were a tight group, very close friends. I'd give the tapes to E. Rodney Jones or Butterball Crane and they would play us during their shows, and we became very popular that way.

We played everywhere—McCormick Place, theaters, night-clubs, everybody loved us. One time at the Arie Crown Theatre, Al Johnson, the car dealer, gave us a brand-spanking-new Cadillac Eldorado. We put the car backstage, dressed Rudolph in all white with a big fake diamond ring about the size of an egg. We put five gorgeous women in the car with him, darkened the theater, turned the car lights on, honked the horn, and he parked that thing right in the middle of the stage. First the women got out, then Rudolph emerged to howls and thunderous applause. The he delivered his famous line: "My name is Rudolph, Eldo driving," etc., etc. My man, mack daddy!

We did so well that a syndicator heard us and made a deal to tape us for possible coast-to-coast network syndication. We worked very hard in preparation and the syndicator reviewed it, but said he didn't like it. We had another offer to go to L.A. with round-trip airfare paid, but we couldn't get hotel rooms because some of us couldn't afford it. I think if we could have done the Hollywood circuit, we could have made it big.

We did record a successful album that should be rereleased. I've talked it over with Rick Williams, who was the producer of the LP, but he cannot find the master tape. I've got tapes of the Electric Crazy People I never played that I'm starting to use on my current weekend shows on V103 radio, and I'm trying to re-create the group to do new material.

I've been in touch with all of the group members and we're definitely going to at least have a reunion—we've even discussed future projects. So let's get the giant hot dogs, oysters, and Coca-Cola together once again, and just maybe this time we'll make it.

(ANSWER TO QUESTION ON PAGE 133)

Junior Walker sang "Shotgun" himself when his lead singer didn't show at the recording session, and the record became a hit!

5

•••

TALES FROM
THE COOL SCHOOL

Jeez, the Experiences a Deejay Can Have

> What physical characteristic do I share with all the original members of the Temptations?
>
> *(ANSWER ON PAGE 148)*

Being a top jock in the radio and TV business for years, man, I've really done some stuff. This section is devoted to some of the things, incidents, and people that stand out in my mind. For instance, I introduced Johnny "Guitar" Watson to steppin' music, and he just loved it. And once, out of sheer curiosity, I slept in a casket one night. It's an overrated experience.

Still another time, on the way to a soul boat cruise I was deejaying, I was on a jet leaving out of Chicago. Most of the people on the plane knew me, so the flight attendants let me take over the microphone and I just put on an impromptu performance for the whole flight. We had a ball.

Recently, beautiful actresses Jasmine Guy and Holly Robinson Peete saw a picture of me on the wall at V103 as they were visiting the station and mentioned that they thought I was cute. I wish I had been there in person, but then again maybe not, because Vanity—remember Prince's beautiful girlfriend-singer-actress?—once flirted with me in real life and I was too bashful to do anything about it.

In my career, I've interviewed many, many artists. I have quite a collection of tapes of these interviews and many memorable recollections of these entertainers. People always ask me, what is this person like, what is that person like. I can't give a definitive answer, but I can tell you what my impressions were of some folks right off the top of my head.

Let's start with Oprah Winfrey (does she even need a last name anymore?). I didn't interview Oprah, but I did deejay a set for her. I was with her and her production staff, and my impressions of her were of power and kindness. When she came into the room, she just took it over, but she made me sit down while I was eating barbecue on her set. She was a very impressive woman.

James Brown was very proud of an older deejay like me. He was strictly an old school guy and gave you your props and encouragement. At the same time, he would let you know that he could talk to the president of the United States anytime he felt like, and no matter who the president was!

The worst interview I ever had was Major Harris, who sang "Love Won't Let Me Wait." He was half asleep and never woke up, didn't even try.

Gladys Knight was private, and minded her own business.

Bobby Womack started off an interview normally, then every other word was a curse word, which was a challenge being on the air live. But once he gets going, he doesn't want to stop, and he knows what he's talking about.

Tyrone Davis is a real romantic type of guy. Very stylish and dresses real sharp, whether for his performances or just walking around.

Nancy Wilson is a super cool jazz singer, but lacking in some other niceties.

Jerry Springer is a genius.

Dionne Warwick is nicer than people said she would be, surprisingly nice. Not too long ago, she bought me breakfast and we talked for over an hour. It was historic and great; I'm glad I met her.

Martha Reeves is an intelligent, dyed-in-the-wool Motown artist who makes a lot of friends and loves to reach her audience.

George Clinton is an extremely intelligent, gifted man, who can adjust to any level you wish to interview him on.

Sugarfoot (of the Ohio Players) did not speak until he had his cognac.

Minnie Riperton was a ray of sunshine; her personality was as sweet as her voice sounded, and she was beautiful inside and out.

Years ago, Chicago mayor Richard Daley didn't know I was on radio. He had seen my TV dance shows and thought I was a great TV performer, but then started listening to my radio shows, and now he's one of my biggest fans.

Mitty Collier was a popular singer who turned minister and a provider of food for the homeless. She seemed like a serious person.

Melba Moore, very cute, lots of guts, still hanging in there, is the comeback kid.

Teena Marie, sexy in the morning, fell asleep during the interview.

Gino Vanelli, the Canadian heartthrob, is his own boss.

Tim Reid told me he based his Venus Flytrap radio deejay character on WKRP *in Cincinnati* on a combination of me and famous disc jockey Frankie Crocker. Tim's an outstanding businessman in the industry, in addition to being funny and a fine actor.

Johnnie Taylor was hard to find and hard to get to, but gave excellent interviews once you got him.

Little Richard seemed like he had found God.

Millie Jackson, as you would guess, is not a soft-spoken lady, and what you see is what you get.

Al Hudson ("Lost Inside of You") is the kindest, most soft-spoken artist I've ever met, and a genius to boot.

Michael Jackson, very feminine and soft-spoken. A soft interview.

Ron Banks, excellent singer, tough Detroit type, talks a lot in an interview.

Tommy "Hitman" Hearns talked slow, like he took too many hits in the boxing ring.

Dennis Edwards should be on the Walk of Fame; he was as real a Temptation as any of the others. He paid his dues.

J. T. Taylor (Kool & the Gang) was real smart and knew his business inside out.

Curtis Mayfield was a great storyteller and a very good businessman.

Frankie Beverly really knows how to win over an audience.

Chubby Checker, who created the national dance craze the Twist, was quite a historian.

Eddie Levert is always on. He has a magnificent personality, and speaks with a loud, clear, commanding voice.

Motown sent the Supremes to WVON when they were just starting out. They spent the day with us and each girl partnered up with a deejay she liked. Diana Ross took Rodney Jones, and Mary Wilson took me. We had a ball! They were just girls from the projects then and were innocent and fun; they were cool. I interviewed Mary many years later and she didn't even remember me, when I thought at one time she liked me. Oh, well!

◆◆◆

Now how about some quick little stories! I've never been one for playing basketball. I did it as a kid but I was never good at it. Even though I was a tall six foot two, basketball has never been my thing. But I did have a wonderful opportunity while working with WVON to play basketball against the Harlem Globetrotters.

WVON had a basketball team made up of the Good Guys and some other folks on our staff that played against high schools in the area. We mostly clowned around, but didn't do too bad.

We had this great promotion once of playing the Globetrotters on their annual trip through town. My teammates passed me the ball, and I don't even know how to dribble, so you can just imagine what this scene looked like. I screamed, "Harlem Globetrotters or not, I'm going to run right through you!" and ran straight at them. They caught me, picked me up, and stuffed me through the basket!

Another time I'm on the air at WVON and guess who comes in? Muhammad Ali. He just loved the radio station and would drop in from time to time unannounced. He came by one evening and I took him back into the studio. We were on the air talking and all of a sudden, he asked, "Can you box, man?"

"Can I box?" I echoed. "Naw, I can't box." Then Muhammad told me to get up. He went into his crouch and started shadowboxing, throwing punches at me—left hooks, right crosses, and that famous jab. He never hit me, of course, but my heart just stopped beating. Can you imagine standing in front of Muhammad Ali in his prime and he goes into a boxing stance? Especially when you're trying to talk on the air?

One time, I needed to get to Milwaukee to interview James Brown, so I decided to rent a plane to get me there. In the course of trying to find a plane, I ran into a helicopter pilot—a black guy—and he asked me if I wanted to go for a ride. I said, "No, not really." He said, "Well, that means you do; get in that helicopter!"

This is always happening to me. So, I got in and we took off. He explained to me that when you see that dramatic shot of helicopters leaping off the ground, that's not good for them. He said it puts so much wear and tear on the helicopter and that it's much better for them to ease off gently. But like in the movies where they just jump off the ground, we jumped off the ground, too!

We flew around for a while until he said, "You know something, I believe you'd make a good helicopter pilot," then just took his hands off the control. He said, "Here," and gave me the stick. I lurched around like a big ol' dragonfly; I had that helicopter all over the sky! They are so sensitive; with every little move of the stick, they go left, they go right, up, down. But I was scared to death. Evel Knievel can have that kind of lifestyle.

Then he said, "Let me show you something else." We went way, way, way up, then he cut off the engine, and we just started dropping! I said, "Aw man, aw man, what are you doing?" And he waited until we were just about to hit the ground, then he turned the engine on and we flared out. Vroom! I was too shocked to even *think* about soiling my pants!

So, I'm still trying to get to Milwaukee for James Brown's interview. I knew a gentleman named Emmett Stovall. He was a premiere black pilot who flew everything from 747s to Piper Cubs. I rented his twin-engine Beechcraft (and him, too!) and we were on our way to interview James Brown in Milwaukee. The Beechcraft had a pilot and copilot and could carry four or five other people, so I brought four friends with me, including a photographer.

Before we took off, Emmett went through a check-off list. He handed me this piece of paper and on it were all kinds of directions. I would read stuff, he'd say, check, OK, and as I read, his hands were flying all over the instrument panel. We did that while the plane was warming up.

Shortly after we took off and stabilized, Emmett said he was very tired and had just had a flight that morning, so he handed me the wheel and said, just keep the arrow on the line. And that's what I did. I kept the arrow on the line and I flew that plane the whole way to Milwaukee. Then Emmett woke up and said, OK, I'll take over, and he landed the plane.

We met James Brown at the airport, where he had a Learjet with two pilots. He showed us around inside, we took pictures, and it was just wonderful. Then we went to his concert, and there was a big fight that night. Those guys in Milwaukee, they got it on! But there were some police ladies who waded into the crowd with their nightsticks and that fight was over.

One night, I was with Eddie Levert of the O'Jays. This had to be in the mid-sixties. We went out and stayed up all night in some diner. The O'Jays had done this record, *Lonely Drifter*, which was a hit. But Eddie was so tired of doing gigs—they were on the chitlin' circuit, many times they didn't get paid, and it was just not any kind of life for him anymore.

All night long he talked about it, and he said I'm going to quit this game. I remember talking to Eddie and I said, "You know what, man? You just have something special in your music, honest to God, just a special something that I hear, and I'm sure that if you just can hang in there, it's going to be good for you."

I believe I actually talked that man out of breaking up the O'Jays that night. Seriously! I talked him out of breaking up. Wow, if they had broken up, think of all the fantastic music they later made that we'd have never had. Eddie halfway remembers that night now when we run into each other. He doesn't remember all of it, but . . .

We also had a séance at my house. The O'Jays did a record hop with me, so I said, "Let's go to my house and have a séance." I don't know what made me even think of that. But there were the guys and some girls that had come along with us. We all joined hands and got to mumbling and asking for ghosts to come appear—and one came!

It was like kind of an ectoplasmic thing, and it was child-shaped. We were down in my basement, and it came down the steps and flitted about the room. It was made out of smoke and stuff and you could see right through it. One of the ladies with us screamed and started to cry out, which made it disappear. Every time I see Eddie I say, You remember the ghost? And he says, "Yeah, man, the ghost came." No mass illusion, the ghost really came!

The late beautiful Minnie Riperton was a real fan and friend of mine. She would go out of town and she'd always call me when I was on the air. She'd tell me where she was and we had great interviews.

Before she got really big, she used to sing in a group called the Gems. The piano player was a blind guy and personal friend of mine named Raynard Miner. I've been in Raynard's corner for a long time. I played his first record, and he wrote "Selfish One,"

"Rescue Me," and all kinds of stuff like that. So we're friends from all the way back.

Raynard told me this story once, where he and Minnie were real hungry after a hard recording session at Chess Records. Remember, Raynard is blind. So, he and Minnie were walking down the street and approached another blind man on the corner with a cup. While Minnie got his attention, my other blind man, Raynard, slid his hand into the cup and stole the man's money!

I said, Why'd you do that? What did you do with the money? Raynard said, "Man, we were starving and broke. We went around the corner and bought a bunch of greasy hamburgers!" I asked if they were good. He said, "They were just delicious!"

I once emceed a rally for Dr. Martin Luther King Jr. at Soldier Field. It was his last Chicago appearance, and Stevie Wonder performed. This was history making.

Dr. King made a statement, if you remember, that he had seen racism everywhere in the world, but nowhere like he saw it on the South Side of Chicago. His voice was shaking when he said it. Mayor Daley turned Dr. King away at City Hall—they wouldn't let him in. Then his entourage came to Soldier Field, where there were thirty thousand people waiting. King's right-hand people had something to say. Then Stevie sang. Then Dr. King spoke.

It wasn't until then that I realized Stevie was six feet tall and skinny. We were both skinny together. And when he sang, he just jumped so high. I asked him why and he said, "Well, I don't know. I just didn't want to jump off the stage, Herb."

My impression of Dr. King was that he was a very powerful man of peace, and very, very dedicated. He had an unreal dedication that you could feel just exuding from him. I didn't realize how many white people liked him, but when he died, that morning everybody had their headlights on. Not just black folks—everybody had their lights on. It struck me then that Dr. King had reached and convinced a lot of white people that we should all live and work together. It was just numbing to have been around him.

Stevie and I go back a long way. We have a friend in common, Raynard Miner, the blind guy. I'm the one who got Raynard started and he knew Stevie. Raynard told me one day he was going to get a little electronic gadget that would let him see again. He had read or heard that they had invented this electronic thing that you could stick in your eyes and carry a battery and you could see. This was about ten years ago. Stevie and I got on the phone and Stevie said, "That's just not true." Then he added, "And I need to be the one to tell him that it ain't gonna work!" Stevie and I are cool. Stevie is all about his music and blackness.

When Dr. Martin Luther King was assassinated, we at WVON got on the air twenty-four hours a day and all we did was talk to the listeners and beg them, "Please, please, stop burning and looting and destroying. This is not the way to do it!" I feel we were really successful, myself and the other WVON Good Guys. I think we were more successful than anybody who was trying to calm things down. We had the gang leaders call in—it was just really something.

Very quickly, I got a call from the ABC-TV affiliate in Chicago (WLS/Channel 7) and they had me host an emergency ninety-minute TV special. We had all the civil rights leaders on, and they came and talked, and we certainly tried to do what we could to discourage the rioting and the looting. It was a terrible time in the city of Chicago, but it was also the first time I was on TV hosting a show. In that sense, it was a wonderful experience at a really bad time. I've never even seen a tape of it myself, but I remember one of the producers from out of town really liked me and he said, "You're a special guy and you're going to go a long way in TV." I should have followed his advice.

◆◆◆

Being a celebrity deejay, I had so many things happen. Once at six o'clock in the morning, there was a knock on my door. I answered and there was a guy out there named Maurice. He was a motor-cycle rider, and he said, Come on and ride on my bike because you're famous and I want to be famous, too.

I said, "Oh no, man, it's too early." Well, he kinda coerced me, so I got on that bike and we went on a very famous expressway in Chicago called the Dan Ryan. We did a wheelie for about forty blocks—just rode on one wheel. Thank goodness it was so early on a Sunday morning that almost no one else was out driving at the time.

Maurice was a great guy and motorcycle rider. He's since passed, but was on his way to becoming famous. He would put obstacles over the railroad tracks on Ninety-Fifth Street and jump his bike. The police loved him—they would hold the traffic back while he was jumping. Maurice, I certainly will always remember him.

One thing happened more recently. My car was in the shop and they gave me a white four-door Cadillac rental until my car was fixed. I had an affair to go to that night. It was a rainy night and when I came out the valet brought the Caddy. As I was sitting in it, a lady who always comes out to these different things—she's a PhD—she was trying to talk to me, saying something through the window.

She was real animated and I thought she maybe had too much to drink, so I just said, Yeah, sure, OK, whatever, now will you please get off the window, please. And I pulled off. But what had happened was that I was given the wrong Cadillac. This lady also had a white Cadillac that looked just like mine. And she was try-ing to tell us that. I had pulled off, was driving along, and noticed that my black umbrella had turned into a flowered umbrella, and that the keys in the ignition looked a damn sight different than mine.

I looked around and said, Oh my gosh, this is a different car. I looked in the rearview mirror and saw that another white car was frantically trying to chase me down, and it was the PhD lady driving my car. We got out and swapped rides and she called into my radio show a few months later to discuss the incident. That was the strangest thing, but fortunately, it ended really nice.

> (ANSWER TO QUESTION ON PAGE 138)
>
> The Temptations and I are all over six feet tall.

Grand Ballrooms and a Whodunit

Who is credited for the choreography of the
Temptations?

A. Honey Cole
B. Cholly Atkins
C. Gregory Hines

(ANSWER ON PAGE 154)

Here are two of my favorite tales from the Cool School. The first involves a fabulous fight, the second combines intrigue and romance.

I was driving my big, long, red Cadillac down Sixty-Third Street one day and it got me to thinking about the old Pershing Hotel Ballroom at Sixty-Fourth and Cottage. The Pershing in its heyday was very elegant. It had a bowling alley in the basement, a nice lounge on the main floor, and a huge, ornate ballroom on the second floor. In that first-floor lounge, world-famous jazz pianist Ahmad Jamal recorded a fantastic album that is still being played today. The album included songs like "Poinciana." It was beautiful.

The bowling alley was converted into a plush nightclub called the Beige Room—I remember partying there in my younger days when I was underage, and once I got drunk and threw up all over my gabardine pants. They carried me in the back and stretched me out on a wooden plank until I came to.

When I was semiconscious, this nice-looking lady came by. I had kinda curly hair back then, too, and she lifted my head up and said, "Nice looking, too bad," then let my head plop back down on the wooden board. She was too fine, I was too drunk.

The second-floor ballroom hosted jazz greats like Woody Herman, Stan Kenton, Dizzy Gillespie, and Lester Young. It was a gas! And most of the audience were white guys in blue suits just digging all that jazz.

Down the street from the Pershing was a great theater called the Tivoli, where you could see a stage show and great movies—generally all in one day, for one low admission price. A block farther down was the Trianon, which was the sister club of the Aragon Ballroom on the North Side, but the Trianon was twice as big—there's never been anything like it.

When white folks went there, it was the host for great ballroom dancing and shows. When it turned black, we saw LaVern Baker, Frankie Lymon and the Teenagers, Esther Phillips, Bill Doggett, Roy Hamilton, and many more. Changing times forced that beautiful ballroom to be torn down and replaced by public housing.

During its height, that whole area up and down Sixty-Third Street was littered with swank nightclubs of every conceivable kind. There was the fabulous Crown Propeller, which had a huge tank of water surrounded by seats for spectators. Every few minutes, a well-endowed female would swim in the tank and turn some very seductive underwater flips. White male customers bombed out of their skulls would look at these brown beauties gyrating in the water with great amazement and supplication.

When I started promoting dances it was for the Pershing, even though the glitz and glamour nightclubs in the area were going down. The Beige Room, for instance, was replaced by the legendary Budland, which was one of the greatest nightclubs of all time, although it was a bit run-down.

But I was promoting teen record hops at the Pershing Ballroom, which was still quite usable. Now, back then when we did teen hops, there were always a lot of fights, but the fights generally ended with guys having busted lips and that sort of thing. I always hired several policemen to control these hops as best they could because the fights could really be quite awesome. Here's an example.

I was having this dance at the Pershing once and this fight broke out. Before we knew it, these guys had fought down the stairs from the second floor all the way out into the street. Then, still fighting like mad, they turned north and fought a whole block down the left side of the street toward Sixty-Third and Cottage.

The traffic light turned green—they had actually stopped while it was red!—and they resumed fighting across the street to the east side of Cottage. Then they turned north and fought down to the Tivoli Theater. They fought *into* the Tivoli—I swear this is true!—through the lobby, up to the ticket booth, back out the door, and headed back up north on Cottage Grove.

They fought up to Sixty-Fourth Street, recrossed the street, and fought back to the entrance of the Pershing Ballroom. Then they fought back up the steps into the ballroom where the dancing was still going on. By then, all the fight participants were tired, so they just stopped, just like that. They all proclaimed that it was a good fight, and then they danced the night away.

This is an absolutely true story—you had to be there to believe it—and there were no serious injuries, just a couple of arrests for disturbing the peace. I saw quite a few fights doing teen hops, but never anything like that.

As the years passed, the Pershing continued to decline. The top three floors lost their windows, and hundreds of pigeons flew in and made the place home. The lounge closed, then the whole hotel closed. The Budland club remained open for a few years before it, too, closed.

Then came the wrecking ball and the whole thing was reduced to a pile of bricks and rubble. Today, there is nothing but a big vacant lot, and sometimes as I drive by, my eyes get moist as I think about back in the day.

The second incident happened about fifty years ago, when I used to work at WGES selling airtime to make a living. I would broker radio time for a couple of hours a night five days a week. I don't remember how much I brokered the time for—maybe five hundred to one thousand dollars a week—I'm not quite sure. Then I would go out and hustle up sponsors who would pay me to broadcast their products over my shows.

Hopefully, I would make enough to meet my weekly bill at the radio station, and anything over my brokerage fees I could keep. I would get up early every morning knocking on doors to get sponsors, and I got to be pretty good at it. I sold time to restaurants, beauty shops, nightclubs, a shoe store, a custom hat shop—I even sold time to singer Little Richard, who came to town to do an evangelist show.

I had all sorts of sponsors. I had a gypsy who could read your palm and tell the future. I had a root doctor who used magic roots that could cure anything. I had a record shop that sold imports—the owner made a name for himself through advertising with me.

Another of my sponsors had a product that killed roaches. The can had a spray nozzle so that if a roach climbed up on the wall, you could spray it. The roach would fall off the wall, do a death dance in the air, and be dead by the time it hit the floor. It was the most deadly insect killer I have ever seen—the stuff was phenomenal.

But let's talk about my barbecue house sponsor. The owner— we'll call him Red—had a secret recipe for making hotlinks—hotlinks to die for. I'm sure they were 100 percent cholesterol, and you literally might die from them, but they were so damn good!

I used to collect my sponsorship money from Red late every Saturday night. One hot Saturday evening when I went to collect my dough, I took a young lady with me. I had just met her, and man she was fine. She was built so good she was turning heads and stopping traffic even though I was walking with her.

Let's called her Shaqwanda. When we arrived at the 'que shack, Red told us to sit tight until he returned from running an errand. So we went into the back, where we were all alone, and had a seat. We talked for a few, then held hands. Her perfume made me giddy. When Shaqwanda looked deep into my eyes, I didn't need no further invitation—I knew it was time to get busy!

Suddenly, we were locked into an embrace, kissing like mad, feeling, rubbing, and groping, only to be interrupted by a loud noise at the back door. As we looked up and tried to get recomposed—adjusting our clothes and all—a young man walked in and said, "Good evening."

We said hello. As he walked toward the front of the store, he had noticed what we were doing, and as he passed by, he said, "Y'all are OK, don't worry." Then he strolled over to the cash register, opened it, and took some money out. He walked back past us, said, "Have a nice night," went out the back, and closed the door.

Cool guy, we thought. After he left, me and Shaqwanda started doing our thing again, wrestling all over the place, damn near falling out our chairs trying to grind and whatnot. Shaqwanda could kiss like crazy, and we were about to get right down to the real thing when we were interrupted once again, only this time by Red.

As we scrambled to get recomposed a second time, Red said, "Sorry it took so long," and went to the cash register to pay me. He stared into the drawer for a long time, then said, "Oh my God, all my money is gone!" I said, "No, don't worry, your partner came in and took it." And Red says, "I don't have no partner. I've been robbed!" Then he looked at me and said, "Did you take my money?" And I said, "No, I was gettin' my groove on with Shaqwanda." Then Red said, "Well, what the hell happened?"

I told him about the noise in the back and the friendly gentleman that walked in. It turned out that the sound we heard was an old rusty lock being broken off. Red asked what the guy looked like. I told him he was hard to describe because he was an average-looking guy—kinda short, kinda tall, kinda light, kinda dark. The only thing I could be sure about was that he was an average-looking guy who was neatly dressed. Red was reluctant to believe me, but he finally did, I think.

Red reached into his pocket and paid his radio fee from out of his walking-around money, but that was the last time he broadcast with me. We stayed friends for a while, but then drifted apart. I don't know what happened to him.

Shaqwanda and I got our thang on that very night; that robbery didn't stop nothin'! We were together for a good length of time, but eventually, we, too, drifted apart. She was really, really nice and I miss her today. In fact, I miss them both.

As far as I know, Red never found out who robbed his store. I guess it was the perfect crime. This is a true story—I just changed the names to protect the innocent. In this case, the innocent were Shaqwanda and me!

(ANSWER TO QUESTION ON PAGE 149)

B. Cholly Atkins created the Temptation Walk and their other steps.

My Friend,
Smokey Robinson

How old is Smokey Robinson?

(ANSWER ON PAGE 161)

My business involves music—playing it, hosting concerts, interviewing artists on the air, attending music conventions—so it's only natural that disc jockeys and musicians end up spending lots of time together. It's just a business dynamic: when an entertainer has a new record, of course the record companies want it to be played on the radio, so they cultivate meetings and relationships between deejays and the artists, so that the jock will promote the new record or the upcoming concert on the air.

When the record companies send these artists in, it's like anything else—you're always pleasant, of course, but sometimes that time spent blossoms into friendships. During the decades, I've been fortunate enough to have met more entertainers than I can even count, and the most striking thing I've found out is that basically, they're like us. Some of them are very protective, but once you get to know them, it's just like talking to your buddies.

You don't hit it off with everybody, but some you do and sometimes you end up hanging out. Here are some of the folks I've ended up spending time with, and some of the names might surprise you, like Stanley Turrentine. He's a jazz saxophonist and

I've never really played too much jazz on the air, but Stanley and I bonded pretty well—and you don't want to know some of the things we did!

The earliest hanging out I did was with a guy from the singing group the Moonglows; he and I dated sisters on the West Side of Chicago. I used to go nightclubbing a lot with Garland Green, Bobby Womack, and Tyrone Davis. I met Johnnie Taylor when he was a teenager, and we used to go on the corner of Sixty-Third and Cottage Grove and not only girl-watched, but we brought my camera along and took pictures of them, too!

My regular fellas also included Chuck Barksdale of the Dells, who is the world's most dedicated spokesman for a group; Marshall Thompson, undisputed leader of the Chi-Lites, who has the drive of three men and will keep his group working forever; and Ron Banks of the Dramatics, who wants me to come spend a week at his house in Detroit, and whenever I get some time I will do that. There was also Eddie Levert, Curtis Mayfield, Major Lance, Walter Jackson, Jerry Butler, Casper the Slide Man, and my buddy Gene "Duke of Earl" Chandler. Gene and I spent New Year's Eve 2008 partying in Miami.

All these guys and I used to hang out, which usually meant going someplace, maybe sitting up having a drink, or sitting around all night long talking about our respective careers. What we were going to do, problems we faced. We'd also go to parties together, hunt women together, all the stuff that red-blooded American guys do.

But I hung out with the ladies, too. There was Holly Maxwell, who used to sing with Jimmy Smith and made a couple of records. I was tight with Martha Reeves and Patti LaBelle. The great girl group, the Emotions, was like family to me, especially Wanda. Aretha Franklin came and stood on a table and did record hops for me.

Bill Withers came over to my house once. Back in the day it was a much more personable thing. The record labels would not only send the artists to the radio station, but they'd bring them by your house, too, and play their records. At the time, I had a fish in my tank that weighed almost ten pounds. Bill was just a big ol' country boy and he never got over that! This fish could do tricks. You could feed the fish popcorn and meat and he'd come up and let me pet him. It was a fish from South America that I think they don't even let them ship here anymore because of quarantines, stuff like that. In the correct kind of tank, it can grow up to five hundred pounds; the fish will grow as big as the tank will let it. Mine was gigantic, and so tame. I loved that fish. Named him Mr. Lovett. Bill never forgot that fish.

It was all much fun, being close to a lot of the guys. I'm pretty conservative and my mother raised me to be a pretty tame guy, but we had some wild times, sure. I went to Motown Records a couple of years ago in L.A. I went upstairs and the guy announced, "Herb Kent!" and they all got up and shut the doors and started telling all these stories about what we did. I said, Jesus, I must have really been something wild back then! But wait a minute, hold down, I'm cool now. That was then.

During the hanging out with entertainers, there were a lot of offers of bona fide friendship, but sometimes you just didn't have time to take it up because of the nature of everybody's schedules. But several of the stars and I became really close. Eddie Kendricks and I hung out all night on a couple of occasions, and our personalities just totally jibed with each other. Eddie and I would have been great friends, I think, but he was always on the road and I was always busy, so there weren't a lot of times that our paths crossed.

One of the genuine good friends that I have is Smokey Robinson. You might have heard of him. Smokey Robinson and I are cool and have been friends since the beginning. Smokey and I met back in the 1960s when he was with the Miracles. Back in the day, Motown Records had groups like the Temps, the Miracles, the Four Tops, the Supremes, and the Marvelettes.

The record companies would decide what disc jockey in what cities they wanted their acts to get to know so that their records could get more airtime. At the time, I was the hottest teenage disc jockey that Chicago had ever seen. So I got to meet everybody, all the acts.

Smokey was the first Motown artist I really hooked up with. When we met, he was doing the early stuff in his career—"Shop Around," "Mickey's Monkey," "She's Not a Bad Girl," stuff like that. We actually became friends quickly. He used to come over to the house and shoot pool on my pool table. He came to the radio station often and did numerous interviews.

I met all the Miracles, but when Smokey came over to the house, he didn't bring them, just a couple of his other friends. That's the way it is with groups. In the early days all the group members usually hang together and suffer together, but as time moves on, and with technology and travel the way it is, sometimes guys in groups live in different states and just get together to record or do the concerts. It's like a sports team—they don't all have to be best buddies, it's business, so they don't necessarily hang out together in their free time.

Smokey has a very pleasant personality. He's available, doesn't try to hide, and loves his public. Very worldly and knowledgable. Smokey is an old-school type who prefers to do one-take, first-take records with everybody in the same studio at the same time. I think the most amazing thing about him is the absolute control Smokey has over his voice as an instrument.

There was a club on Rush Street years ago, maybe in the mid-sixties, that featured a lot of R & B and Motown artists—the real artists, not the imitators—and they had dynamite stars come perform. At this club, they'd hustle you in, get you to pay for drinks before, during, and after the show, then they'd put you out and bring the next group of folks in. It was always packed. They would have one artist, the Four Tops, the Temptations, whoever, who would do three to four shows a night. It was very intimate, maybe seated one hundred people at a time. The format was marvelous and it was a great concept.

Smokey appeared one time that I recall in this intimate atmosphere, and sang with this kind of subdued silky voice. Because he didn't have to belt out his songs, he was able to be a song stylist on that little stage, and it was just incredible for the audiences to listen to. They went wild!

Smokey Robinson is a very loyal person. During the time when people were lambasting Motown founder Berry Gordy, talking about him, calling him unfair, saying he cheated people, Smokey would have none of that. He would let everybody know instantly that Berry Gordy was the most innovative record producer that ever walked the face of the earth. Berry taught all those young Detroit kids on his talent roster choreography, bought them uniforms, made them really big stars.

You cannot talk to Smokey and say anything bad about Berry Gordy. He considers it sour grapes by people who may have had bad experiences with him. On the other hand, Eddie Kendricks felt the total opposite way about Berry Gordy!

Smokey would always give me an interview, come to the radio station. We just got to be good ol' boys, no question about that. I went to his house recently—such a house you wouldn't believe—out in California. He's doing great. He's written who knows how many songs, so he must get a residual check for a few hundred thousand dollars every three months or so, for all the songs he wrote from way back when. That's a pretty good deal.

I asked Smokey once how many songs he wrote for Motown. He said, "Most of them!" And he did, for all the acts. He writes most of his songs along with Marv Tarplin, his guitar player, and has been referred to as the world's greatest living poet.

He plays golf constantly. In fact, the weekend before the 2008 United Negro College Fund telecast that honored Smokey for his life achievements, he called into my show to say hello. It was a Saturday morning and you know where he was calling from? A golf course, of course. I asked him how his game was and he said, "Actually, it's pretty good, but ssshhh, don't tell golf I said that!"

And he's just as friendly as ever; Smokey is one guy who just never changed. Whenever he's seen me, he's always, "Hey Herb, how you doing? What's new?" And he's asking out of sincerity and interest. Just a nice guy. Some people have a way of *not* being friendly anymore, due to the pressures of stardom and stuff like that. They just rise up there and rise straight out of your life. It's hard to reach them, you know.

One day back when, for some reason I had a camera crew working with me on some project and we happened to film Smokey in Grant Park. It was a special kite-flying day in downtown Chicago and there were hundreds of these colorful kites in the skies. Smokey was just relaxing and grooving to the whole thing. It was a marvelous day. But alas, my camera people were not too reliable and somehow they lost the film. Those images would be priceless today, to see Smokey in Grant Park with hundreds of colorful kites in the air—people would pay good money to see that.

Today, Smokey continues to tour, and that's something he told me he'll always continue to do because he loves to interact with his fans so much and just gets such a joy out of performing. Smokey still makes personal appearances, makes time for people. It's incredible how he still works that hard. He's the consummate pro.

He's also a pretty good businessman and has introduced Smokey Robinson gumbo, red beans, and pot roast dishes that you can find in retail grocery stores. That gumbo is absolutely delicious.

Smokey has cohosted with me on the radio several times, and we've posted tapes of that on YouTube. The last time was a couple of years ago. Leon Isaac Kennedy, who was married to fine Jayne Kennedy back in the day and was in the *Penitentiary* movies, was Smokey's real good friend. The three of us were together on the air on V103 one day and had so much fun.

During this visit, I played Smokey's song "My Girl" on the air on my guitar. After I stumbled through it, he said it reminded him of another one of his songs, "The Tracks of My Tears"! He said he'd by come another time to see if I could mess that song up, too. That's OK, I'm still his number one fan.

I have certainly just enjoyed my life with Smokey and all these entertainers that I've been fortunate enough to be able to hang out with through the years.

(ANSWER TO QUESTION ON PAGE 155)

William "Smokey" Robinson was born February 19, 1940. You do the math!

Visiting "the Godfather" James Brown in Jail

> James Brown's name was mixed up on his birth certificate. What was his original first name supposed to be?
>
> A. Richard
> B. Joseph
> C. Charles
>
> *(ANSWER ON PAGE 169)*

Another cat I became very friendly with through the years was the late great James Brown. I've told you earlier about my attempts to get to Milwaukee to interview him on his private Learjet. That was in happier times. Now, let's talk about James Brown and the time he was incarcerated.

I knew James for a good many years and helped break a few of his records in Chicago at WVON. James was always very talented, forceful, dynamic, full of energy, and devastatingly creative, the most off-the-cuff artist I have ever met. By that I mean his best songs were created right on the spot while he was recording. For instance, on the song "Get on the Good Foot," he introduces the record by saying, "Que pasa, people, que pasa," then "Stop it now, come on get it, stop *bass!*" He was sitting at the organ playing and arranging that song right at the moment it was being recorded.

James Brown worked so hard onstage. After a real strenuous show at the Regal Theater once, I went backstage to visit him. He was lying flat on a table with a doctor administering a saline solution to replace the fluids he had just sweated out.

James and I became very friendly, and he considered me to be the top soul deejay in the world. On national TV, he has jumped up and down and embraced me and called me brother. Needless to say, *I love me some James Brown!*

In the late 1980s, James was involved in a police chase in South Carolina, and they shot out his tires to stop him. I was at my current station, V103, and the management was aware that I knew James, so they asked me, "How would you like to go and visit him in jail on these current charges?" Of course I said yes. We went through a few changes trying to contact James, and the answer finally came back that Mr. Brown would be glad to see me. So we made the arrangements.

Now you have to understand, I had been to Atlanta and Miami, even out of the country down to the Caribbean islands, but I had never been down south, or what's called the Deep South. The farthest south I had ever been at that point that was comparable to Down South was Carbondale, Illinois, when I used to do the Kappa Karnival. I've already told you what the feelings of whites were toward blacks in places like that.

And my boy James was locked up in Aiken, South Carolina, which was about as Deep South as you could be. Like a lot of northerners, I was flat out scared of going to that part of the country for the first time, even though I was a grown man.

As we were preparing the trip, I expressed on my radio show that I had no desire to go Down South, to places like Mississippi, and the phone jumped off the hook with people saying they didn't want to go to Mississippi either. And some of them were white people! Matter of fact, this one white dude said he drives all around the state of Mississippi to get where he has to go if he does have to travel to the South.

Keep in mind, these statements were all made almost twenty years ago. I know things are different today, but I still get a funny feeling thinking about Down South. Because remember, James was sentenced to six years in prison, only served three of them, and it came out in 2007 that the version of events the white police officers arrested him for was far from the truth. So that was another reason for my fear. According to stories, things could happen to a black person in the South that might not be based on right or wrong, and you might never be heard from again, no matter who you were.

But I quelled my fears and hopped a jet to Atlanta, then caught an airbus to Augusta, G-A, as James would say. I'm sure this airbus was the same type of propeller plane that has crashed so many times before, and, man, those propellers vibrated me right down to my teeth. Mine didn't crash, fortunately, but that sucker shook like an egg-beater.

I was sitting next to this white lady and I was really scared. There I was, over sixty years old, and I wanted to talk to this white lady, who was going to Raleigh, South Carolina, but I said no, this is the South. Remember Emmett Till. But when we got off she was real friendly and said, "You're such a nice man, I wanted to talk to you and all, but you wouldn't say anything to me!"

After we landed, I had to catch a cab the last thirty miles. The white cabdriver excitedly told me that he had been to James Brown's house, and as he talked, I began to realize that everybody—white and black—loved James Brown. We finally got to my destination and it was pitch black, midnight. He let me out and just—zoom!—went away. Up the hill sat a ritzy country club on a golf course. This was where I was supposed to stay. I have a fertile imagination and, unfortunately, it kicked in.

Was this where all those gallant black soldiers from the 54th Regiment died in the Civil War? I thought I could see crosses burning somewhere. I thought I could see hooded horsemen riding toward me with ropes and burning torches and shit. I was so scared, I almost messed my pants. I'm standing out there by myself thinking, "Maybe the radio station didn't know where they sent me!" I'm serious, man.

But I took a deep breath and said, "Well, I can't just stand here, or sleep in the road, so here goes!" I knew I had to go up and register at this golf course. So I went to the front desk and asked if they had a room for me, Herb Kent. The white lady clerk said, "Yes we do, sir, and we hope you have a pleasant stay." I knew then that my fears were unfounded. But the hotel rooms just had doors, no double locks or anything, so I was thinking, "Shit, they can still come and get my ass!" I fell asleep awaiting my interview with James Brown in the morning.

After the long trip and a good night's sleep, when I woke up, it was beautiful outside—sun shining, golfers golfing, just a great scenario. James Brown's manager at the time was a black judge. He picked me up for the drive to the jail in a brand-new Mercedes-Benz with windshield wipers on the headlights. On the way, the judge explained to me that James was on work release at a community center. This judge was well educated, forceful, and just what James needed at that time, because everybody was after him. When we finally got to the community center, James was standing outside.

He looked good—his hair was *whupped,* and he had on a little short jacket with a few little rhinestones. Just a little fat around the middle and a great big smile on his face! Wow, the real James Brown! It was a wonderful feeling being with him again.

We went to a restaurant to eat and have the interview. He didn't talk much about his days behind bars except to say some of the guards gave him a hard time, but he overcame it. We talked about the old days at the Regal and the old WVON. We talked about what kind of car he drove. And he was just overwhelmed that those white people loved him.

I asked him if he knew what steppin' was and he said, "Oh yeah, sure, I know," but as the conversation continued, it turned out his definition was quite different from what we consider steppin' in Chicago.

We talked a bit about his music. I said James, why don't you record a real sexy song, about a woman with big legs. A white woman at a nearby table burst out laughing. I hadn't been aware that everybody in the place was looking at us and listening, because this was James Brown, after all. But the way James looked at me after the lady laughed made me sorry I asked the question. James told me he'd be released in a week or so and was a little hush-mouthed about the direction his music would take once he got out. The publicity over him coming out made the time ripe for a brand-new fresh record, but there seemed to be a musical dilemma.

In his later years he was trying to find himself and his music. He was a strong-minded person, and he was trying to figure out what he wanted to do musically when he got out. But he didn't want to hear me suggesting anything about what he should write. I was trying to tell him that everybody I talked to in the business and among my listeners felt he should get back into the "Payback" beat, the "Monorail" beat, "Body Heat," "Pass the Peas"—a more laid-back tempo.

But he didn't seem to be of that mind, and after he got out, you could see why. James's hero was MC Hammer, which is not a bad hero, but because of Hammer's influence, James speeded up a lot of his songs. When he was on the stage, everything was up-tempo. He felt, I think, that music was so fast at that point in time that that was what he had to do. He was strongly influenced by Hammer's song "Can't Touch This," so he wanted to do what the rappers were doing, because he felt that was what the audience wanted.

Even his "Please, please, please" bit with the cape that he did when he performed, he speeded that up, too. I enjoyed it with the slow tempo, but James was the Godfather of Soul and had the right to make his own musical decisions. Who are we to say what's right?

I talked to him about Fred Wesley and Maceo Parker, and maybe getting back with them, and again, it was uh uh, naw, that ain't gonna be. He did do a thing on TV with them one time that

I saw, and I often said, why can't they all just go into the studio one time, do a jam-up record, and then go their separate ways.

I asked him about all these young rappers sampling his stuff and he said, "I think I'm the most sampled individual in the world!" He also said, "Whenever I get a chance, I try to help some of those young guys with some musical advice and I haven't sued any of them." But I'm sure he could, because right about the time he got out of jail, they had started sampling him so bad it was incredible. He had a love/hate thing about that, "Yeah, I like it, it's great they did that, but yeah, I don't like it."

You know something about Down South—when you're talking to somebody, people will just come right up and butt into the conversation. They don't say excuse me, they just walk on up and start talking, man! As James and I were chatting, the white owner of the restaurant came over with a jar of mustard and explained that he and James were going to market this mustard worldwide and call it James Brown Mustard. I still have a jar, but I don't think anything ever happened with the business.

We concluded the interview and James invited me back to the community center, where he made me sign a release. I had no problem doing that. While we were sitting there, James said, "Hey brother, can I show you something?" He reached in his pocket and pulled out a gold card and explained that this was an official card that enabled him to call the president of the United States whenever he wanted! James also said he got several calls from various people who wanted to book him when he got out of jail.

Once he got out, James gave a bunch of wonderful high-energy shows. He still managed to get up on one foot and dance across the stage, and that still drove folks crazy. James tried to come back several times on several levels—he had "Living in America," and that was good—but the death of his wife had a profound effect on him, and I never talked to him again after that happened. But the comeback trail is a hard one, especially as you get older.

All that being said, however, James Brown was the Godfather of black music; he truly was. He was the absolute Godfather of black music for people out here dancing, and for musicians, writers, the whole thing. He's like the basis of modern black music since his time. He took blues and put an extra beat into it, and made it a funk thing that people still use today. I learned that from taking guitar lessons. You play regular blues, and put that extra beat into it, and that changes the whole thing—and you wind up with James Brown!

I can tell you this—James Brown loved music more, I believe, than life itself. He'd rather do music than anything. And he drove his people the same way. He drove you. You could not, better not, make a mistake with him. That's what kept his music sharp, and I guess you would learn from a guy like that, too. His band wouldn't sit down sometimes when they were performing, and he would carry three drummers for one show. He would just run through them, insisting on that driving beat, and one man couldn't keep that up—except James. He'd exhaust one and put another one in there. He had the dance troupe going, too. He just loved music like that.

This story is not over yet. After interviewing James, I went back to the hotel and one of the waitresses asked if I wanted to go to a nightclub. She had a brand-new car and we drove to the club. Someone played the "Electric Slide" and everybody got on the floor.

They had a buffet full of gigantic seafood fresh from the ocean, which was nearby. We were sitting there chillin' when twenty or thirty white chicks came into this all-black club. My eyes got as big as a saucers because I'm still Down South!

My waitress friend informed me that was nothing. She said, "Down here we have these big wild orgies and everybody comes," and that, as a matter of fact, a white dude gave her that new car. When we left and went back to the hotel, she drove like a crazy woman. I never saw anything like it—the white lines in the road were just something to put in between her tires and zoom over!

The next morning at breakfast I saw my waitress. She came to my table with a black eye, limping and bruised, with little Band-

Aids and stuff all over her. She explained that she totaled her car on the way to work that morning. Then to top it off, she said that ten minutes after we left the club, some local gang members came in and shot the ceiling out. So I bid her and South Carolina farewell and returned home to Chicago.

The South wasn't as bad as I thought. It was a great adventure and I would do it again. Mostly though, I felt lucky that I did what many people wanted to do—have a heart-to-heart talk with the hardest-working man in show business, Mr. James Brown. He was a wonderful man, a genius, and I truly loved him.

(ANSWER TO QUESTION ON PAGE 162)

B. The birth certificate was supposed to read Joseph James Brown, but they switched the order. Do you think he would have been as dynamic as *Joe* Brown?

Swimming with
Mean Sharks

The Business Side of the Music Game

> Name the five record labels Berry Gordy owned
> between 1960 and 1975.
>
> *(ANSWER ON PAGE 181)*

N ow that we've talked about some of the artists that I've befriended, let me tell you about the tremendous tolls entertainers sometimes suffer on the business end of what they do. And these are all situations that I know of firsthand.

The artsy creative side is fine—the pretty songs, the jamming concerts—but when it comes to business and how that dough is divvied up, brother, it's a whole different ballgame. For every artist like Smokey Robinson who can live a king's life off of royalties he's earned, there are ten entertainers who have been screwed just as badly in their careers on the money that they, too, have earned.

First of all, basically, all these people are pretty young when they become stars. Anybody past eighteen just starting out in the industry doesn't have much of a chance to make it, because the record companies want them eighteen or younger if they can get them. That's where you get these Hannah Montanas and Lindsay Lohans and Britney Spearses—they're all groomed for stardom in their early teens. Mary J. Blige was very young when she started. Look at Beyoncé. It seems like she's been around for years with all she's done, but she's only like what, not even in her late twenties yet? Hell, when the Dramatics—who made "I Want to Go Outside in the Rain" and "What You See Is What You Get"—started singing in 1963, their average age was only thirteen!

The record companies want them young because they have a better career, and this is a business in which there is very little longevity. Tyrone Davis told me that when he turned fifty, he couldn't get a deal with a major label to save his life because of his age. But he said, "Herb, I'm better than ever!" I saw him perform recently and he really does a hellfire show, but major labels don't look at that. Curtis Mayfield told me, "Man, this is a young people's game," and Curtis knew music inside and out. He said the majority of records are sold to young people, that the whole thing is centered around youth.

Of course, these kids burn out fast and their careers usually don't last long, but record companies really don't care, they just find somebody else. I imagine they *do care* . . . until they find that somebody else. Then, they don't care! That's just Big Business.

I guess if you continue to come in and make hit records, it's fine no matter how old you get, but when your records no longer sell— no matter what your age is—then somebody else comes along and you're yesterday's news. That's when that question comes up, "Whatever happened to so-and-so?" In reality, so-and-so, who may not have been heard from in years, might only be in his early thirties.

That's just the nature of that part of the game, like being a broken-down, has-been tennis player at the age of twenty-eight. But then there's the other, much worse part of the business, and that's the outright cheating. You probably don't know it, but there is so much that goes on behind the scenes of most of the hit records that you hear. I'm talking about backstabbing, power plays, brown-nosing, jealousy, those kinds of things, but what can I say, it's the American way.

Without going into too many details, let me tell you how twisted the road to fame and fortune can be in the music industry by talking about some folks that you do know, and, simply because of how things worked out, some folks that you don't know. How you take a group of unknown people and turn them into world-renowned stars is a tall order, but I'll try to explain.

Ah, the world famous Dells! Through the years, their records, CDs, and tapes have sold to the tune of millions of dollars—but a big portion of that money the Dells never saw! Group member Chuck Barksdale told me that not only did it happen to the old school artists, it's still happening today at record companies. The music business is like any other business—you have to watch your rear end because it's all about the ducats. You have to read the small print and hire good accountants and attorneys; you have to work it.

If you remember, my radio nemesis, I guess you could call her, Vivian Carter, got me fired at my first radio job at WGRY, then went on to help found Vee-Jay Records. Well, back in the day, a lot of the Vee-Jay recording artists never got the money they earned and deserved. Groups like the El Dorados, the Spaniels, the Magnificents, and my doo-wop group, the Kool Gents (yeah, I signed with Vivian at Vee-Jay; never learned my lesson!) all got shot though the grease. Meanwhile, down the street in Chicago, a lot of the same things were happening to Chess recording artists. Leonard Chess told me several times that he didn't want his blues singers to make a lot of money because then they wouldn't work as hard or sing as good. Guess he wanted to make sure they really had the blues.

This type of conflict hasn't stopped. Everyone knows what happened to Toni Braxton, who went bankrupt after making millions.

What's up with that? Florence Ballard, an original member of the Supremes, died broke. I think the most depressing case was Jackie Wilson, who vegetated in the hospital with all kinds of suits swirling around about his money.

I was good friends with Jackie and was fortunate enough to know him. Jackie was one of the greatest entertainers of all time, and there's not a male singer today who is better than Jackie was. Maybe as good, but none better. Jackie was Jody Watley's godfather, by the way.

Jackie was a nice guy, but didn't have much business sense. He wanted to succeed so much that he gave up far too much to the people who managed him. They made more than he did, and he had virtually no voice in calling his own shots about his career. In his early forties, Jackie suffered a heart attack onstage while performing a concert in New Jersey in 1975. I can't say I was surprised. I paid Jackie four hundred dollars to perform at one of my record hops years earlier and he put on such a great show that he literally fell out in exhaustion.

After Jackie had his heart attack, he was in the hospital for almost ten years. *Ebony* or *Jet* had a picture of him with his head swollen, unable to take care of himself, utterly broke. And that's how he died, as a pauper, in 1984. A man whose records and performances brought in millions and millions during his career died broke and penniless. If the famous deejay Jack "the Rapper" Gibson didn't raise money for a beautiful memorial for Jackie Wilson, he might have died without anyone to care.

But let's get back to the Dells. The members from the group are all from Harvey, Illinois. They got together at Thornton Township High School in Harvey. The lineup went like this: Johnny Funches, lead; Marvin Junior, baritone-lead; Verne Allison, tenor; Mickey McGill, baritone; and Chuck Barksdale, bass.

They first recorded as the El-Rays for Checker in 1953, then signed with Vee-Jay in 1955. The Dells can bring tears to your eyes singing hits like "Oh, What a Night," "Stay in My Corner," and "Always Together." They are really an awesome group. When they do "The Love We Had (Stays on My Mind)," everybody goes crazy.

I met the Dells in the early fifties when I worked at WBEE in Harvey. The station is out in the boondocks, and one day I took my collie to the station with me and he got lost. Well, the Dells knew the area, and they went in the woods and found my dog. We became fast friends and even more; I'm like a big brother to them.

They had just started with Vee-Jay. I would play their records on the station and the Dells began to get popular coast to coast. They were making some good records, but then a problem arose. Johnny Funches, who cowrote "Oh, What a Night" with Marvin Junior, got married. He really wasn't the kind of guy who liked to travel around the country like the Dells often had to do, and his wife gave him the ultimatum of "my way or the highway." So he left the group one day after an audition with Dinah Washington.

She hired them to travel with her and be on the roster as her opening act. So, as you can imagine, Funches's departure left them in a lurch, him being the lead singer and all. Johnny got a job in a steel mill and became a happily married man who never looked back. As the years passed, he reaffirmed his love for music by becoming an oldies deejay in some nightclub. Johnny Funches died several years ago.

When he left the group, the Dells were without a lead singer, which they had to have, and Johnny was replaced the next day. All of the Dells went to Simmons Night Club on Ninety-Fifth near the Dan Ryan and waited for a guy, who was a plasterer, to come to work. They physically grabbed this guy, whose name is Johnny Carter, and told him, "You are now a Dell." Johnny never got a chance to say no. He was a former singer with the Flamingos. That group of Dells, now with Johnny, made a pact never to break up, and they haven't to this day. The Dells have been in the business for over fifty years, and they're still the same guys they were back when.

With Johnny, they began touring with the Dinah Washington revue, but she required them to sing jazz; they were not allowed to sing doo-wop and songs like "Oh, What a Night." Dinah was a loving, caring person, but she was also possessive and a control freak.

She had her vices, too. It's rumored that she once caught one of the Dells in a compromising position and she admonished the whole group about sexual encounters with wanton women and such. But the next day, Dinah felt bad about chastising them, so she bought each member an expensive silk shirt. They stayed with Dinah for two years and made about $750 a week, which worked out to about $150 per guy, but they had no expenses, so it wasn't too bad.

The Dells were also schooled musically by Quincy Jones, Thad Jones, Milt Buckner, and Charlie Atkins. From 1961 to 1963, they played all over the states. Have you ever noticed the similarities of Teddy Pendergrass's and Marvin Junior's voices? They sound the same, but who was first? Who copied whom? That comparison is where the plot thickens on some unscrupulous business happenings.

The Dells disbanded temporarily in 1958 because of an auto accident in which singer Mickey McGill was hurt and out for a year. The four remaining Dells had to take other jobs to eat and feed their families.

Vern Allison worked at a hospital, Marvin Junior and Johnny Funches got jobs at the steel mill, and Chuck Barksdale sang with the Moonglows, where he met Marvin Gaye, who also sang with the group at the time, and they became good friends. The Dells ultimately reunited and started singing again.

In 1969, the Dells opened an office in Harvey, Illinois. They were tired of being cheated by so many different people in the music business, so they became the Original Dells Incorporated. They did their own paperwork and made several phone calls before finally hiring an attorney out of New York. They became businessmen, and Chuck became the spokesman for the group in 1971. Mickey does the paperwork, Vern does the scheduling and transportation—limos, planes, buses, etc.—and Marvin and Johnny have their hands full singing, which is another kind of job. At one time they had a manager, but he also tricked them out of some money, so since then they have managed themselves.

Chuck told me that no matter what you might think about the glamour, being a member of a group can be total hell. Although being in a group causes the members to grow closer than brothers and become each other's families, many problems arise because of the power the large record companies have over a lot of groups.

For instance, lead singers from vocal groups often leave for solo careers, like Diana Ross, Jackie Wilson, Teddy Pendergrass, Jerry Butler, Luther Vandross, George Michael, Wilson Pickett, Michael Jackson—they are so many of them—and that spells trauma for the remaining members of the group. Ironically, these newly solo lead singers usually end up with other backup singers behind them anyway.

Let me give you the Teddy Pendergrass scenario. Leonard Chess wanted Kenny Gamble to produce the Dells and, allegedly, Leonard owed Kenny some royalty money that he didn't pay. Kenny had written a song for the Dells called "I Miss You." Because Kenny was mad at Leonard, Kenny gave the song to the Blue Notes, whose lead singer was Harold Melvin and featured drummer Teddy Pendergrass. To further piss Leonard Chess off, Kenny had Teddy sing lead because he sounded like Marvin Junior of the Dells. So just to spite Leonard Chess, Kenny made a Dells song in the Dells style, but without the Dells.

And wonder of wonders, Teddy's voice hit like a ton of bricks. The song "I Miss You" became one of Harold Melvin and the Blue Notes' biggest hits and launched the career of Teddy Pendergrass. Teddy became unbelievably large—women went into a frenzy at the sound of his voice. They threw their panties onstage at him and renamed him "the Hunk." In the meantime, Marvin Junior of the Dells had to endure another man succeeding real big using his style. He was hurt and disgusted, but the Dells, with showmanship and poise, continued on with their careers.

The years have bought them many awards. The city of Harvey has Dells Day every Labor Day, and the group has three miles of street named after them in Harvey called Dells Way, along with a park called Dells Park.

They were also the inspiration for the comedy movie *The Five Heartbeats*. Director Robert Townsend asked the Dells if he could use "Stay in My Corner" and "Oh, What a Night" for vocals in the movie and Marvin Junior at first said no, because there is no humor in black groups; he was still mad about the Teddy Pendergrass incident. But he changed his mind and *The Five Heartbeats* brought the Dells back into the consciousness of mainstream America. The movie was 75 percent about the Dells' life stories, but their voices were really not used in the movie, only on "Oh, What a Night" and "Stay in My Corner," which were already recorded.

The CD version of "A Heart Is a House for Love" was recorded by the Dells after the movie and became a national hit. The movie got more work and more money for the Dells and that still continues, so they didn't end up too bad.

◆◆◆

Now, let's talk about the Impressions and Curtis Mayfield. Let me give you an example of how I worked with a group to help make them number one. In 1956, a young man named Eddie Thomas, who was a really dynamic creative force, hooked up a group of singers known as the Roosters. The group consisted of Jerry Butler and Curtis Mayfield, both out of Chicago's Cabrini-Green housing development, and Arthur and Richard Brooks, from Chattanooga, Tennessee.

Arthur and Richard were fair skinned with good hair, so naturally the girls were crazy about them. Also in the group was Sam Gooden, who had a dazzling smile that left many women weak in the knees.

Eddie and I became very good friends while he was managing the group and I was king of the deejays, and I developed a burning desire to see this group, the Roosters, become a huge success. I played the hell out of their records. I didn't get any money for playing them, but the Roosters performed for every record hop I did, in and out of town. They were very loyal. Eddie told me that other jocks were demanding money to play the Roosters' songs. They said no pay, no play.

This situation brought Eddie and I even closer together and I was even more determined to help this group make it. It was just the little things that made me want to be on their side. Like, these guys were so poor that Curtis Mayfield's guitar didn't even have a back to it; that's how struggling they were. Curtis would always face me when he played so I wouldn't see that the guitar didn't have a back, and in fact, I didn't find out about that until sometime much later.

Also, I was driving a white, fuel-injected Corvette at the time—I always had a bad ride with a pretty girl back in the day—and this car was so cool that it inspired the Roosters to work to make hit records because they wanted sports cars, too.

Eventually, they did all get Corvettes, with the exception of Curtis Mayfield, who got a super-expensive Ford Cobra that could go from zero to sixty in four seconds. Curtis told me later he had to sell the car after he almost killed himself in it several times.

This was a good-time fun-loving group, and after a relatively quick start of two years, in 1958, the group changed its name to the Impressions, because they were such an "impressive" group. After the Impressions' first record in 1958, "Your Precious Love" on the Vee-Jay label, reached number three on the R & B charts and number eleven on the pop charts, it was clear they had arrived.

At that point, Jerry Butler left for a solo career, and Eddie Thomas had his hands full behind the scenes trying to keep the group together after Jerry bolted. Eddie always said Vee-Jay was at fault in convincing Jerry to leave, and it was his understanding that Jerry had two thousand dollars in his pockets when he drove away in a white Mercury with gangster whitewall tires—all courtesy of Vee-Jay.

Vee-Jay Records did not play the game straight. They did the same thing to me. In my group, the Kool Gents, the lead singer was Delecta Clark; well Vee-Jay just snatched him away. He became very big as a solo artist with a hit called "Raindrops."

Of all the record companies that weren't straight, Vee-Jay led the pack. They were a black-owned company that taught even the white companies new tricks on how to screw their artists. Vee-Jay had blues, jazz, and R & B artists, and it's safe to say that they fucked over just about every one of them, making millions of dollars in that sordid little process. But ultimately, they choked on it all and went under. The original founders are deceased, and thankfully, the company is no more. But back to this story.

After Jerry Butler left to pursue his solo career, he was replaced by Fred Cash, Curtis Mayfield stepped up as lead singer, and the group moved to the ABC-Paramount label. Curtis was, of course, an unbelievably gifted singer and writer, and the Impressions made bigger hits and bigger money. "It's All Right," "Gypsy Woman," "I'm So Proud"—can't you just hear those wonderful tunes in your mind?

I gave a concert at Hyde Park High School shortly after Jerry left, with tons of doo-wop groups performing, like my Kool Gents, the Spaniels, the Impressions, and more; it was a tremendous concert. This was the first time the Impressions performed without Jerry Butler. But Jerry came and stood in the wings and watched them perform without him. It was a sad moment. But it was a happy moment over thirty years later when Jerry, Curtis, and I were together onstage talking about old times at the Luster Products Heritage Awards.

Ironically, even while the Impressions were making their big records, Eddie Thomas took a job as a valet for Jerry Butler, whose solo career was also going very well. But Eddie took the job to meet deejays around the country. He'd surreptitiously wine and dine them, and get them to play Impressions records.

Now it gets even deeper. Jerry Butler's guitar player was Phil Upchurch, who used to be in the Kool Gents with Delecta Clark. Clark's career was also hot, and he stole Phil Upchurch from Jerry Butler. Jerry now needs a guitarist, so he reaches out to Curtis Mayfield and they start touring and writing together. So the Impressions are singing and Curtis is singing with them, while still touring with Jerry. Eddie is working for Jerry, but still managing the Impressions.

In the meantime, Arthur and Richard Brooks got disenchanted with their roles, left the group in 1962, and went back to Chattanooga to form another version of the Impressions. They were fairly successful, but many court battles were fought over who could do what under the Impressions name.

In 1968, Curtis and Eddie formed their own production company called Curtom, and produced Donny Hathaway. Eddie left to form Thomas Associates with Paramount, where he produced Barry White. In 1970, Curtis left the Impressions to go solo, replaced by Leroy Hudson. In 1994, Eddie did a TV documentary called *The Rise and Fall of Vee-Jay Records*, for which he won a Peabody Award. The Impressions now are Chattanooga-based with Fred Cash and Sam Gooden. The Brooks Brothers' Impressions no longer exist. Jerry Butler still sings nationally and has been a successful Chicago politician—a Cook County board commissioner—for many years.

As you know, in a tragic accident, a light pole fell on Curtis while he was preparing for a concert in 1990, which left him a quadriplegic. A few years after that incident, I flew to Atlanta to visit Curtis. When I walked in the door, he told his very beautiful wife, "Get Herb a steak, baby." We talked about old times and then about how he became paralyzed.

He said the act before him failed to show, so the promoter asked Curtis if he would go on instead. Curtis said, "No problem," and walked onstage to hook up his guitar. At that precise moment, the stage's lighting tower fell over and struck him. Curtis said he just remembered being on the ground and unable to move and that it was raining and people stood over him with newspapers so he wouldn't get wet. He was never able to move after that day and died the day after Christmas in 1999.

Finally, neither Eddie Thomas nor I were versed enough in contract negotiations, and even though we helped write songs, managed, and everything, when the dust settled, we didn't get a dime from the Roosters, the Impressions, Curtis Mayfield, or Jerry Butler—while the record companies made millions!

But you know what? Despite all the stuff that happened, everyone I just wrote about stayed friends through thick and thin and loved each other dearly.

(ANSWER TO QUESTION ON PAGE 170)

Berry owned the Motown, Tamla, Gordy, Soul, and VIP record labels.

6

◆◆◆

ABOUT FAME
AND CELEBRITY

The Price of Fame

What did Jackie Wilson and Berry Gordy have in common before they got in the music business?

(ANSWER ON PAGE 190)

Throughout my career as a top-rated disc jockey, I've enjoyed fame and national celebrity, always had a bad crib, a fly car, and even flyer women. But that's a two-way street. Fame and celebrity can bring you great perks but also offer some tremendous challenges.

One of the prices you pay for being well-known is the loss of some degree of your anonymity and privacy. It's been that way especially in the past few years as radio station owners have made an effort to make their deejays more recognizable physically to the public by putting them on TV, billboards, what have you. They want the public to know the faces of the personalities—that's now part of the appeal.

It used to be that only your voice was immediately identifiable, but now the general public knows your face, as well. I think I liked it better, it was easier anyway, when my kisser was less known. There's not a lot of privacy, and I like privacy, but can't really get as much of it as I'd like. I went to Toronto not too long ago, and it was somewhat of a relief to walk around where nobody knew me. When somebody said good morning there, it was a genuine thing, one human being to another.

As soon as I got back and got off the plane though, it was, "Hey Herb, how ya doing? Where ya been, man," and that goes on all the time. I can go in a store and somebody will shout, "Hey everybody, Herb Kent is in here!" You wish it didn't happen as much, but you can't be ungracious about it. Smokey is another person like that. If you catch him, he'll smile, give autographs, unless his bodyguard says he can't do it or something like that. But if you catch him, he's really gracious.

On the other hand, some of my own people haven't heard of me, though I'm known coast to coast. When I went into the Radio Hall of Fame, I told some of my distant relatives and they didn't even know what I did for a living! But that was fun.

You'd think that's part and parcel of being a top radio deejay, but you're never exactly sure what's going to come with that territory. You enjoy having lots of listeners, playing records, and making people happy—they're calling on the phone during your show, you're doing record hops, emceeing concerts, and stuff like that.

But you have no idea this other kind of thing is going to come, to the point that guys will just come right up and kiss you. It's not an effeminate thing, they just love you! Guys just grab you and kiss you on the cheek—"Herb, I love you, man, love you, man!" And to be fair, on the other hand, because you're well-known, women kiss you on the cheek and other places, too; they do that too, and I'll talk about that in a minute.

But sometimes fans and the public see you as huge and everything else around you as huge, a little larger than life. A neighbor of mine came into my house and saw my cat, which is a medium-sized cat, but to her, she said, Oh my gosh, that's a huge cat. Sometimes they get carried away.

Sometimes when the police stop you for a relatively innocent traffic violation, if they know you they'll give you a break nine times out of ten. Sometimes they won't. I was a bit on the wild side in my early days of being at the top. I lost my driver's license for going the wrong way down a one-way street, and I drove for a long time without that license. I will never do that again.

I remember one time I was taking this girl home. I was paying more attention to her than the road and did something, and this rookie black cop stopped me. He came up to the car and said, "Let me see your license." I said a little arrogantly, "Man, I'm Herb Kent!" He said, "I don't care who you are!" That broke me up from that and today I am a licensed driver, I have insurance, I don't run lights, and I don't speed, although I have a fast car!

Then you get what I'll just call overzealous fans. I don't want to call them stalkers, but they can be a bit unnerving. I lived at Sixty-Eighth and Prairie, and I pulled up to my house one day and this car pulled up behind me with three girls in it. The one behind the wheel said, "You know, I've been following you for a week." That one kind of scared me. I didn't engage in any more conversation with them; I just excused myself because I thought that was kind of irrational. In fact, I kept looking over my shoulder for the next few days to spot her car, but maybe she got the message, and I don't think I saw her anywhere anymore after that.

This one girl came to one of my gigs. She had nice legs and I mentioned to her that she had nice legs. After that, I started to see her every now and then at my sets or just in different places, which made me suspect that she was following me. It was too frequent to be coincidental that we'd just happen to be at the same place at the same time.

I was at a club with some of my friends, and she came in and came up to our table. The guys I was with found that to be really distasteful. She started to turn up every now and then like a bad penny. One day I went to work at the station and she's sitting up there typing on the typewriter. I guess she got a job as a temp or something, but I gave her one long hard look, and that look said, "If I see you here tomorrow, I'm going to have to tell somebody." The next day she wasn't there.

I was at another club once and there was a phone on the wall in one section of the place in an area that was partially blocked off. A lady was on the phone, and the way the she was positioned I was the only one who could see her from where I was sitting. After she hung up the phone, she turned toward me, caught my eye, and pulled her dress all the way up over her head. She had on a dirty red bikini with little dirty strings crossing her breasts. I guess my eyes must have popped out because she pulled it down. But as she was about to come out of the phone room, she did it again, because evidently, the look on my face was what she wanted.

When she passed by, she told me, "I'm a dentist," and just walked away. That's not nice. You don't want stuff like that to happen. It's scary. It's not pleasant and not the kind of alliances you want to be hooked up in.

They somehow get your number and call you on the phone. I had a female police officer who was a stalker. I'd go eat and she would follow me. That eventually worked itself out and she eased off, but these little things are hard to talk about because your mind wants to push stuff like that away. You know, when women talk about being stalked by men, and how horrible it is, they're not lying! It doesn't happen to men as often as it does to females, but it's not a good thing, to be invaded or scoped out like that. It's not natural.

That kind of leads us to the topic of groupies. You could look at girls as perks, I guess. As a celebrated deejay, you have more females giving you rhythm than the average guy, but if you have like fifty screaming females coming at you, there's just nothing you can do—that's not sexual at all, that's just scary. You feel flattered, but it's scary. It's hard to explain, but you really don't want to lay down with somebody like that.

I remember working at the Red Top Lounge on the West Side in the sixties. There was a lady who had a little blue car and she'd be there every Tuesday when I did my set. Every week this lady with the blue car—a Dodge, I think—would ask me if I needed a ride home. For weeks I told her no, I didn't need a ride home. Little did I know that she was really after me.

One day my car happened to be in the shop when she asked again, Do you want a ride home? I had gotten fairly intoxicated that night and said, What the hell, alrighty. I got in the car. She told me she was a flight attendant and asked, "Where do you live?" I told her and we rode for a while until she stopped and said here we are. I looked up and we're at a hotel.

She said to go in and get a room. I said I can't do that. She said, You better. I went and got the room, we went into the room, and she said take off your clothes and do what I want you to do. I said, No, I'm too drunk. Let me rest a little bit, then I'll do anything you want. So I fell asleep for about half an hour, then she woke me up and made me do what she wanted me to do.

I screwed the hell out of her—mostly out of anger. It wasn't great because I didn't want to do that. I didn't have any intentions of being with that lady when I met her at the set. After we finished, she put me in the car and dropped me off at home, but I really felt violated.

Ten years later, the mysterious lady in the blue car showed up again. I was working another set at the Godfather Lounge and she walked in. I cannot describe the fear I had when I saw that lady again, even after ten years. She just sat there and stared me down, didn't smile or anything. But this time, I hadn't been drinking and didn't approach her, and nothing happened. Not a word was exchanged. You don't want stuff like that happening to you.

You may think this is strange, but I've never liked the idea of groupies, no parts of it. I like fans in the normal way, but some of them just go too far.

I was married for a while—it was a terrible marriage and the one thing I won't discuss in this book—but one year I got home and there was a beautiful valentine made out of roses. Prettiest thing I ever saw. My wife came home and I said, Hey, thanks for the valentine. She said, I didn't send it. I never found who did.

Something else scary that happened: I did a set in the Mexican part of town—I had a bunch of Hispanic listeners. They invited me over to one of their dances once and I felt obligated to go.

While I was there, I ran into a beautiful woman. She had coal-black hair and was just absolutely pretty.

I was the only black person there and she came over and said, will you dance with me? I said I'd love to, but I really don't know how to dance. She left, but came back again a while later and a little tipsy this time. She said, "Nigger, you better dance with me or I'll cut your motherfucking throat!" and she had a knife. *Boy, we danced away!*

She was not joking, absolutely not; she was deadly serious. She was so beautiful, you'd never think something like that could happen, but there was something wrong with her, man.

So, you have to be real careful in those situations, because these women may be beautiful, but they can also be unbalanced. I mean, this lady was with a bunch of other Mexicans. If I would have refused to dance with her again, she might have hollered out, "Hey, he's trying to fuck me; he touched me!" Then it's oh shit, I might get my throat slit for real! I had a few incidents like that happen when I was young. As I got older, I learned to avoid those situations, but they can still happen.

Then you get guys and they feel threatened by you sometimes. One night I was at a club in Harvey, and all of a sudden this guy wants to beat me up, and I don't even know who he is. Turns out his girl liked me, or said something, or something like that, and they had to hold this guy back from jumping me. I didn't even know who the girl was, I never saw her.

The exact same thing happened another time. A lot of people are just crazy, not just now, they always have been, and they carry guns. I was doing a set and a guy came up and faced me down. He said, "Are you Herb Kent?" He had just got out of the army and it seemed like he was going to attack me. I said, "Yeah, I'm Herb Kent," but he didn't do anything at all. A couple of his buddies kind of eased him away.

This guy was big, fit, and looked cock strong; he could have beat the hell out of me. Turned out his girl I guess was also liking me and I didn't know that and didn't know her either.

Then there was this little gangster guy—he's dead now. He had a beautiful wife and she used to come to these different clubs where I did sets. I think she kind of liked me, but I knew her situation—I knew this dude was a real gangster—and totally stayed away from her.

But we were at the Peppermint Lounge one time and this little gangster guy came up to me and said, "Mr. Kent, can you shoot straight?" I said very seriously, "Sorry, I have no idea what you're talking about," and quickly turned and walked away. I don't know. He might have known she liked me, but I don't know. You never know.

All these incidents are scary, mostly because you're not doing anything. You're not crazy enough to go after anybody's girl because you're a celebrity and just rub it in a guy's face. That's a sure ticket to the grave.

(ANSWER TO QUESTION ON PAGE 184)

Jackie Wilson and Berry Gordy were both amateur boxers.

Gangsters, Molls, and Friends

A female singer did a song with Ray Charles that included the lyric, "Momma, he treats your daughter mean." What was her name?

(ANSWER ON PAGE 197)

Speaking of gangsters, I've hung with people from all walks of life and on both sides of the law. One of my good friends and advertising sponsors was a Jewish gangster who owned a food store.

He wanted me to go into the meat business with him. I said, "Whadya mean?" He said, "We just go get meat and we make 'em buy it! We'll make money, man. We'll make money!" I said, "Naw man." We remained friends forever, but I just couldn't handle that part of it.

Once, my girlfriend at the time came over and we went to his store. He said, "Herbie, let her pick what she wants, it'll be on me!" That's all this girl needed to hear. She got a grocery basket and packed turkeys and hams and peanut butter and bread and sugar, whatever wasn't nailed down. Man, she packed that basket so full that I got scared!

Then she took it up to the counter and, boy, was my little Jewish gangster friend mad! Know what he said? He said, "Herbie, she ain't nuttin', she just ain't nuttin'!" But he still honored the agreement and let her carry all those goodies home.

He had given her the basket in the first place and turned her loose after all. He had said, "Fill this and everything that don't fall out, you can have." But he wasn't expecting that! And the baskets they had, they stole from other stores, anyway.

One time a guy came in there to hold them up. Know what they did to him? Took his gun away and threw that motherfucker in traffic, in front of some oncoming cars. Then they shut the doors and said they didn't know what happened to him. After that, nobody ever came in to bother them again.

◆◆◆

One of my favorite folks from the other side of the law was Nitro, from the Wahoo Man story I told you earlier. Nitro was a member of the Blackstone Rangers street gang. He kind of attached himself to me, and would go different places with me. He was a lot of fun. Nitro looked at life a little differently than a lot of us did.

I remember one time I had this girlfriend who was half-black and half-Chinese; she was the most gorgeous thing you ever saw in your life. Nitro came up and looked at her, and just stared at her. Then he said out loud, "What kind of girl is that?"

He made many, many friends, and many of my friends just loved and adored Nitro. When he was with us, my group, he was very good, but I guess he did his little thing. Sometimes he'd go out at night and whatever he did, I have no idea.

Nitro had a thing for robbing airline ticket offices. Back in the day, there were a lot of them along Wabash Avenue in downtown Chicago. That's where you'd go pick up your tickets instead of at the airport. Well, Nitro would go in those little ticket offices and rob them, and in every case, every case, he'd get caught and go to jail. I think he did it because he wanted to get caught. I think life was easier for Nitro inside the joint than on the outside.

He robbed these ticket offices two or three times, and I think the last time he did it, the next morning the police were at his house. He had all the tickets and the money and everything there, and he went to jail again, this time for a long time, and sadly, he passed away in jail. That was my guy Nitro.

◆◆◆

I never had a problem with the street gangs of Chicago. In fact, I had a rapport with them. At the time, in the mid-1960s, the main gangs were the Blackstone Rangers and the Gangster Disciples. I tried to bring them together on a couple of occasions, but it was to no avail.

It was the mid-sixties and the problem was that their warfare had escalated. They had killed each other's people, and that was one hump they couldn't get over. They got over all the rest, but not that. People seem to forget that what's going on today with gangs was going on forty years ago. Drive-bys and stuff may be fairly recent, but the gangs were doing their thing back then, too.

We had a lot of gang fights, and as someone in the public eye and a leader in the community I felt it was my duty to try to do something about it. I was able to keep them cool when they were at my sets; I told them if there was trouble, there'd be no more fun, no more good music. They said OK, but then they'd go three blocks away and fight.

◆◆◆

In addition to gangsters, I hung out with crooked cops. One of them—he's dead now—took me with him to a whorehouse on Dixie Highway in Harvey, Illinois, to collect his payoff. I didn't know that was where we were going, and I was so embarrassed when we got there, but he had to get paid. The whorehouse had all kinds of girls and you could get any kind you wanted. I think I went there twice with him, but I didn't like the way they looked at me and just wanted to get out of there, and I wasn't interested in coming back.

I was at WVON at the time, and this guy was always a friend. Years later, he started hitting on my daughter, Robin, and she said,

"Dad, this guy's crazy." But she was old enough and smart enough at the time to handle herself, over the age of consent, so I didn't have to intervene.

I also hired this guy to act as my bodyguard and do security work at a dance. These little gangbangers came in and started fighting and he chased one of them. A block away he shot the guy and around a year later the guy he shot died. But back in the day, my cop friend never got into trouble for it or anything like that.

Of course, I've had what you might call normal friends. Earlier in the book I told you about Bill Harvey, who has been my friend the longest, and I've had tons of other friends. But nobody has been there for all the significant things that have happened throughout my life.

One of the closest is Jerry Simmons, a music and entertainment photographer. We were pretty close for a long time, then kind of fell out, but we have since pulled back together. Working with me is where Jerry got his inspiration to get into the record business. Jerry's an aggressive guy. He was a postman at one time. He left that and was an air marshal, carrying a gun. He got out of that and started taking pictures, and he was gifted. From the word go his photos were magnificent, and from there he went to working with people in the music business. He does an annual convention where they give out a lot of awards and he has a Herb Kent Award he presents to an outstanding personality. That will probably continue long after I'm gone.

Jerry and I met around 1959 and were pretty close until maybe 1970. After we fell out and then got back together again, I told him, "There's no need of us not talking for anything I've ever done to you. If you felt that I was taking advantage of you or anything—I have no idea what it is, but I do apologize." I had a very rough marriage for one thing around that time that caused me to do a lot that I'm not too happy about now. In fact, Jerry was my best man.

Another really good friend, I'll call him Joe, was head of the Drug Enforcement Agency (DEA) in Chicago, and he's like a brother. We've been close friends since the late 1950s. At that time

Joe was a police cadet, and I interviewed him on my radio show. He was a very tough drug enforcement officer who first ran Chicago, then ran Houston. He retired a few years ago, but went back to work to head up security in Saipan, the Japanese island where the United States has airbases.

And you'd be surprised by what he does if you met him because he's such a nice guy, and one of the best friends I ever had. Then again, we weren't always up under each other like that. But we never had a cross word and managed to stay friends. Joe introduced me to the head of the FBI in Chicago, and we all had dinner together.

I've gone into the bottom of the Federal Building in Chicago with Joe, which is quite impressive as you swipe yourself in there through all these different checkpoints. On the walls you see memorials to people from the Secret Service, DEA, federal judges, and what these people are and have achieved. That's where Joe's office was, and there was also a lockup down there. I told Joe once, "I bet this is the last thing a lot of these guys ever see!" The lockup is for people who are involved big-time in drugs and other federal offenses and they stay in there until they go to court to get sentenced. And the feds don't play. Joe would whip out his wallet with the gold badge, and when you see a gold badge from a federal officer, that is intimidating.

Joe and I partied; he'd never flash his badge, of course, but always told me, "If anybody comes up with any drugs, man, I'm going to be gone!" But that never happened, thank goodness.

I think you don't really have that many friends in life. You go through areas of your life, you go through your changes, and oftentimes your associations change right along with your situations. Sometimes a guy gets married, and obviously that changes stuff. At different stages you do different things and hang with different people, and I think the older you get, the less inclined you are to make friends.

I'd say with William Harvey, Joe, and Seth McCormick—aka Cadillac Seth, who's a more recent friend—one of the main reasons we're still friends is that we're not close enough to get in each other's way. Some of these good friends of yours, if they had to live with you . . . well, I once lived with a good friend, and we just couldn't hack it. Too much togetherness can kill a friendship.

But three of my closest friends, who really grew up with me, are dead—of drugs and alcohol. We were inseparable. Lawrence, Charles, and Herman. Lawrence turned into a complete alcoholic and drank himself to death. Charles started hanging with the wrong people and became a cocaine and heroin addict. He shot heroin and cocaine straight, and he was found in a gangway, dead of an overdose. And Herman died of an overdose as well.

Lawrence stole his ass off! He planned the robbery of a movie house after he graduated from high school. He orchestrated it with some younger guys, and those guys all got caught, but they never ratted him out. Lawrence also worked at Allied Radio, which is where I got my supplies to build radios as a young teenager. But we did the five-finger-discount thing. We'd buy one speaker cabinet, then Lawrence would go around and pull stuff from the shelves that we needed. He filled that cabinet with tubes, wires, soldering guns, turntables—all illegally, of course—then brought everything home, and we'd just have a field day.

We were all so very close—went to our first dances together, slow-danced together—not with each other, but with different girls. No, the gay thing's never happened in my life! We were high school, neighborhood buddies. I think about them from time to time and really miss them.

Two other high school friends were Darwin Evans and a guy named Donald, who moved to L.A. and drank himself to death. I drank with them in high school—a little paper cup of wine, or something like that, to get a little *woooo*. And they smoked reefer, but they would never let me see that because they knew I didn't want to see it.

They were smoking reefer and going to the hotel on Saturday night with girls, while I had never had sex and was at home sitting on the toilet reading *Reader's Digest* and practicing to make my voice right. They talked about me like I was a crazy guy while they were out beating the bushes, smoking joints, and getting laid. Little did they know that I not only was about to catch up to them but also to outrace them—like the Road Runner.

(ANSWER TO QUESTION ON PAGE 191)

The lyric was sung by Ruth Brown.

Sex: What's Love Got to Do with It? And, Well, *Love*

> Which female vocalist of French, Cuban, and Puerto Rican extraction was featured with Arthur Mitchell's Dance Theatre of Harlem and had a hit about six years later with "Tonight I Give In"?
>
> *(ANSWER ON PAGE 205)*

In his autobiography, basketball great Wilt Chamberlain said he'd had sex with more than twenty thousand women in his lifetime. I take the brother at his word, but if you do the math, his days would have had to be forty hours long, instead of twenty-four, and he would have had to have sex two or three times during halftime of all his games. How can you do that and still go out and score one hundred points? You're a better man than me, Wilt Chamberlain. Maybe that's why they called him Wilt, the *Stilt*!

People often wonder if high-flying radio jocks do get laid often as a perk of the job and their celebrity. I have to say that's true, and though I haven't had as much action as Wilt, I've had my share of ladies. But let's start at the beginning of this subject, which promises to get a little raunchy as we go along.

I stayed a virgin until I was nineteen years old in 1947. I met a girl in Gary who was really built. She was cleaning my clothes for free, and I didn't know what was wrong with her; it didn't dawn on me that she liked me. One day, finally, she asked me out. She said, "Let's go to the Sand Dunes"—they're called the Indiana Dunes more commonly now—"because that's where you have your fun." I didn't know what she was talking about, but I said, OK, we'll go and have our fun.

The dunes were about a thirty-minute ride from Gary, and you could stay out there on the beach all night long. You may not believe it, but we saw a flying saucer that night—these three lights in the shape of a kite streaked across the sky, danced around, and we just watched and watched and watched for about ten minutes, then they just twirled and went off in the distance.

So she said, "Let's go to the car." We got in the car, and I was finally catching on to the idea. I said, "Let's get in the backseat." She said, "Why?" I said, "Come back here and you'll find out why!" She hopped in the back, man, and it was just automatic. She hollered, "Aaooohhh!"

On the way home, she said, "You never said a word." I was pretty much embarrassed, but it was really good. I was so surprised that it just all happened so fast without me planning anything. But from that point on, I was on my way.

Shortly after that, somebody set me up on a blind date, and I really didn't like this girl. I took her to the drive-in, and I sat there thinking to myself, "Oh man, this girl, I *really* don't want to be with her." If there's anything I hate in this life, it's to be with a woman that I *don't* want to be with.

When the movie was over, I stepped on the gas and pulled off as fast as I could—but the speaker was still hooked up to the car, and I tore my whole window out! It made the most horrible sound as it came out. The way they built those things—those speakers were bound in concrete and attached to these thick metal posts with a big chain. You weren't going away with that speaker. Then I really didn't want to be with this girl—made it twice as bad.

I got her home as quickly as I could. I don't know if she enjoyed herself, but I don't think she liked that window coming out. She was real quiet and sullen all the way home, with her lips poked out. But they weren't out any farther than mine, because she knew that I didn't want to be with her. I never liked blind dates, and still don't like 'em.

When I was younger I wasn't a bad-looking guy, and I was very popular. In fact, I was a very attractive young guy at the time and attracted a lot of ladies. When I first started going out clubbing, every new nightclub I went around to I wanted to get a new woman, and one particularly unique to that club. I met some very nice women like that, and I mean, that's just normal, given my line of work, which means that a lot of my time is spent in clubs.

When you're twenty-six or twenty-seven years old, good looking, red blooded, with a lot of energy, you're always going to walk out of the club with somebody. But what you have to do is not let her come back to that same club or you won't be able to get any more women from that spot.

My friends Charles, Lawrence, and Herman hipped me to these hotel rooms that you could rent for two dollars for two hours. If you wanted to spend the night, it would cost you four dollars. You could put a quarter in the bed and the bed would shake, another quarter and the radio would play.

You had the Garfield, the S&S Hotel, the Spencer Hotel—they were very famous. These weren't motels; you'd actually go inside and get a room. They were kind of sleazy, but they weren't too bad. But what'd you care? You were horny! There was a bed and a room and no one worried about folks breaking in. I took plenty of ladies to the hotels in my twenties. I was just a young, healthy kid, and my late-arriving interest in sex was pretty high.

As far as my interaction with fans, I'm pretty straight-up with my female fans and listeners. When they approach me for an autograph, sometimes they're very beautiful, and you just want to say, Baby, what's your name? Most of the time I won't say anything because they're not looking at it that way—they just want an autograph, so you don't want to get all predator on them. I'm fortunate to be able to entertain them and want to be able to live up to the type of image that they think I have from the radio.

That having been said, let me say this: the deejays at WVON were having sex all over that radio station! I personally screwed ladies on Rodney Jones's desk, on Bernadine Washington's desk, on the floor of Rodney Jones's office. But it wasn't just me; it was most of the Good Guys. This one lady came in to see one of the jocks who was on the air at the time—I won't embarrass him by calling his name—and this woman was drop dead gorgeous. She pulled me aside and said, 'Tell him to come in the room because I just want to suck his dick. That's all I want to do."

So I went into the studio and while he was playing a record I told him, "This lady is here, man, and she is really fine. She says all she wants to do is suck your dick." He couldn't wait to get off the air and he ran in that room and slammed that door shut, in the middle of the afternoon.

I had this white girl, she had really nice legs. It was so funny; I had her on the floor and I said, "You know, every time you open up your purse, I smell the lovely perfume." She said, "And every time you open your wallet, I smell your whiskey!" And we just got it on. *Bim, bam, boom.* And she was serious because this stuff was turning her on. Ooh, that girl had pretty legs. Umh, umh, umh.

It was quieter in the evening at WVON because most of the people were gone and I could do my thing better. We'd go out in the car and do it; one lady didn't want to do it in the car so we went into Rodney's office and did it. You could get away with doing this on the air because the engineers cooperated with us. They gave us little breaks. We'd give the engineers some records, and they'd say, "Go 'head on," and they'd sit up and play them for you for half an hour or so while you did what you needed to do.

I guess I started getting with my female fans around 1952 to 1953, when I was at WGES. My first one was a Polish girl named Nancy. I met her at the Tremont. Some big artist was playing there, we met, and we started dating. She used Royal Crown hairdressing in her hair just like the black girls did, and she just liked black guys.

During this time, there were females who wanted me just because I was Herb Kent and I was hot on the radio. I think the next time I took advantage of a situation involving a fan was with this one lady who said she was married. I really didn't want her, even though she had nice legs. But she just kept on, kept on, and she finally got me over to her girlfriend's house. We went to bed, and the sex was really sensational, but I never called her and she got mad as hell; ooh, she got mad.

But hey, she was married. I was a young single guy and didn't want to get wrapped up in that. I just probably didn't like her. You know, when you're a young guy, you don't have to like 'em to have 'em. I mean, you can like them, but you don't have to be in love with them.

Other deejays have the same experience, and it basically comes down to human nature. Some deejays are dogs, some are religious—just like regular people. Some may not have been as famous as me and didn't have the same type of opportunities. I don't know. Basically, you're just a guy. You see a fine lady, and you'd like to have this lady, so you're going to hit on her. It might be a bonus if she's a listener, maybe you get an in you wouldn't get if you were just John Doe. I liked women to know who I was because if it was a pretty lady who didn't know and wouldn't give me any play at first, I could say I was Herb Kent, and right away she would get with the program. So I liked the leverage involved with that.

Once I got hot at WBEE, the floodgates just opened with my lady listeners. A lot of white girls made themselves available, and this was in the mid-1950s, around the same time that Emmett Till was being lynched in the South for whistling at a white woman.

I found that ironic, but it didn't stop me from sleeping with these white girls, who more often than not approached me and who were more than willing to drop their knickers.

When I went to WHFC in 1960, girls would call up to the station while I was on the air, and if I liked the way they talked, after I signed off at 11 P.M., by midnight they'd be coming down the hall of the station or over to my place. They'd give me a blowjob and then leave! Never saw them before, never met them before, usually didn't see them anymore. That happened plenty of times. I never let them spend the night. They had to get up and go, but they had as much fun as I did. Some of them were persistent, and I kept them around and they would just come and do this particular oral thing. Sometimes I had full sex with them but mostly I'd just get blown. I could generally call them up and they'd just rush right over.

At this point, I was thinking that I had two different kinds of girls here. I have the really nice girls that I would meet and date, and I have the radio girls who I would hook up with after I got off the air. But by the time I was at WVON, they just all blended and there was no difference. They all became just girls. I would meet them at dances, clubs, over the air, wherever, and we'd just start having sex. This was way before HIV and AIDS, thank God.

More recently, I had a girlfriend who worked at Walgreens. She would leave the store and come see me, bringing just one rubber and one Viagra that she took from the pharmacy. Another girl-friend counted some rubbers on me one time, and when the tally didn't add up right, she pulled a knife. Ah, the old count game.

I had this one girl who I was after for a long time and she finally came around. She was really, really pretty and indicated that she did cocaine. She was going to come by the house, but she said, "Wait a minute, I'm going to go see this dealer I know." I drove her there, she went and stayed about an hour, and I was sitting there going, damn. But when she came out, she had a whole lot of cocaine, so I said OK! You can only imagine what she had done because she didn't have any money. But it was all right because

I was her guy of choice that night. So we went to my house. She went in the bathroom and a few minutes later she came out without a stitch on, butt naked, shaking this test tube because she was going to smoke the cocaine in the pipe. I will never forget that. I mean she had nothing on and plopped down on the couch. She said, "Oh, just look at that pussy, look at that pussy, look at that pussy!" I said, "I see it, I see it!"

It wasn't all just mindless sex, although most of it was. I also met some women that I ended up having substantial relationships with. One of the best was a girl who had just won a modeling contest. She heard me on the air and called me up, and, man, was she a knockout. Prettiest woman I ever had in my life, and we dated for a long time.

But probably the most intense relationship I developed was with this gorgeous woman I met when I was deejaying at WBEE. They were doing some kind of remote and called me from location and said this nice woman wants to meet you. So I went to the spot and met her. We eventually had sex, but it took me a while to find out that she was a lesbian, or at least bisexual. She'd disappear for a week, then she'd be back with me. I couldn't figure out what it was until somebody told me, "Man, she's got a girl on the side."

She finally brought her girl to my house and put all three of us in bed. But she got in the middle and said, "Don't you dare climb over me to get to her!" That was way back in the late 1950s, early 1960s, before those kinds of alternative lifestyles became as acceptable as they are today. She was what we used to call a butch, but she was absolutely one of the most beautiful women I have ever seen—even to this day. She had long pretty hair and great legs. She was also very helpful to me as a person, in grooming and teaching me about life.

I fell in love with her, and that was very hard for me to face in the long run, sharing her with another woman. I asked her once, "How do you think that makes me feel?" She thought about that for a long time, then turned to me and said, "How do you think I feel?" And I got a real insight into how conflicted she was about all that shit, too.

It was more taboo back then; today anybody can freak, but you still can feel all the negative emotions that can come with being gay. She liked women, said she didn't want to, but also said she couldn't help herself and felt trapped. She was in love with me and in love with this woman.

How did this end, Chuck, you ask. Well, we broke up. It was just too emotional. And a few years later, she told me that she and the girl had also broken up. A few years after that, I found out that she had married an Asian guy who was quite wealthy. They were having a house built and during construction she walked through the second-floor bedroom, not realizing they had taken the floor out, and she fell to her death.

(ANSWER TO QUESTION ON PAGE 198)

The beautiful multiracial dancer and singer was Angela Bofill.

An irresistible young deejay named Herb Kent takes the airwaves by storm. (Herb Kent Private Collection)

One of my very first girlfriends, Barbara. (Herb Kent Private Collection)

Jack L. Cooper, who in 1929 became the first black radio deejay in Chicago. (Photo courtesy of the *Chicago Defender*)

"The Old Swingmaster" deejay Al Benson (right), in the studio with singer Lil Palmer and a cat you might remember named Cab Calloway. (Photo courtesy of the *Chicago Defender*)

Music businessman Leonard
Chess, owner of Chess Records
and the WVON radio station.
(Photo courtesy of Lucky Cordell)

The WVON Good Guys ruled radio from 1963 to 1977.
(Photo courtesy of Lucky Cordell)

About to take it to Rodney Jones (on the right) during an exhibition boxing match. (Photo courtesy of the *Chicago Defender*)

Guess what the Harlem Globetrotters did to me after this picture was taken? You can find the answer in chapter 5 of this book! (Photo courtesy of Lucky Cordell)

Here I am eating a barbecue rib with my Fu Manchu look.
(Photo courtesy of Lucky Cordell)

I was the Superfly of the microphone. Thanks to my friend "Hustling Oscar" for this picture. (Herb Kent Private Collection)

Singer and writer extraordinaire
Smokey Robinson clowning
around in my fur and a funny
hat. (Herb Kent Private Collection)

My favorite singer,
Luther Vandross.
(Photo courtesy,
© Martha Brock)

The Hot Buttered Soul
Man, Mr. Shaft himself,
Isaac Hayes. (Herb Kent
Private Collection)

Crooner Tyrone Davis and the Godfather of Soul, James Brown.
(Herb Kent Private Collection)

Chicago mayor and soul music enthusiast Richard Daley.
(Herb Kent Private Collection)

The late, great Chicago Bear,
Walter "Sweetness" Payton.
(Herb Kent Private Collection)

The Pied Piper
of R & B, R. Kelly.
(Herb Kent Private
Collection)

Earl Jones is a great boss to work with at Clear Channel Radio Chicago. (Photo courtesy of Clear Channel Radio Chicago, © David J. Snoble)

Maze lead vocalist Frankie Beverly. (Herb Kent Private Collection)

Marshall Thompson and the Chi-Lites are always sartorially resplendent!
(Herb Kent Private Collection)

California's "Governator," Arnold Schwarzenegger. (Photo courtesy, © Dot Ward)

My wonderful, lovely daughter, Robin. (Photo courtesy, © Richard Shay)

It's my honor to stand with two of the best deejays in radio history, Doug Banks (left) and the Flyjock, Tom Joyner. (Photo courtesy, © Richard Shay)

Inspiring young people through radio has always been my priority.
(Herb Kent Private Collection)

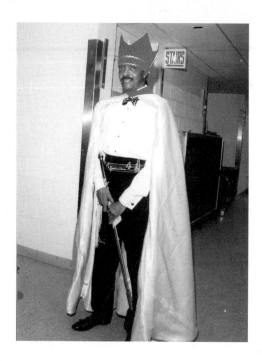

Yes, I *am* the King of the Dusties!
(Herb Kent Private Collection)

Radio executive Marv Dyson has been my boss, my competitor, and my friend. I wouldn't be here today without him. (Herb Kent Private Collection)

I'm also considered the Godfather of Steppin', and I've helped elevate this dance craze into an international art form. Here I am leading a steppers set, with the dancers doing their thing. Notice the moves and the fabulous outfits.
(Herb Kent Private Collection)

In the sunset of my years, I'm in the Radio Hall of Fame, a radio professor at Chicago State University, still on top of my radio ratings, and content just jamming with my band, the Herbie Babies. (Herb Kent Private Collection)

7

♦♦♦

HITTING
ROCK BOTTOM

Jailhouse Rock

Name three leading R & B singers who spent time in a juvenile home.

(ANSWER ON PAGE 210)

Enjoy your good times while they last. Because, brother, they don't last! As I was cruising along at WVON as king of the deejays, a funny thing happened—my life fell completely apart. This was in the 1970s, which was not a good decade for me at all. A number of things happened that shattered my world and damn near destroyed me on several occasions.

The first was a bogus run-in I had with the police right as the seventies first started off. Remember Eddie Murphy and Martin Lawrence's movie *Life*? It reminded me of this incident. After a party one night, I went motorcycle riding with a couple of friends. Back in the day, I craved excitement, so we got on those motorcycles and just rode. But on this trip, my two friends were involved in a horrible accident with a car.

I was devastated and was zooming down the Dan Ryan Expressway to the hospital when I was stopped by a policeman. He asked where I was going, and I told him I was rushing to be of assistance to my friends. This cop had the nerve to tell me that I wasn't a doctor, so what could I do? We got into an argument and I ended up at the police station. I was so shook up and angry that I refused to bond myself out.

I knew a lot of the policemen at the station, and they told me just to accept my court date, pay the fine, and go home. I said no, I'll show everybody, I'm going to jail tonight. I was angry and hurt, and I believed that I had a reason for speeding to the hospital.

I kept on screaming "Put me in jail!" so they took me in the back and actually put me in jail. Well, the jailer was a young guy who let me come out and sit and talk with him for hours. But finally he told me it was time to lock me up, so he put me in the cell, locked the door, and well, damn, I was incarcerated!

The only thing in the cell was a cold steel bench for you to sit or lie on and a toilet that stood out in the open. Later, as I was trying to sleep on this real hard steel, my cell opened and they handcuffed me to someone else. Then we were led to this police van and away we went in the predawn.

Those old vans had small windows up near the top so we couldn't see anything except lampposts or make out where we were. We just rumbled along, stopping at other police stations to pick up more prisoners. Eventually the van filled, and we were chained together with no distinction made between the type of criminals. I was a traffic case, but I might have been chained to a murderer. I learned you had to cooperate with the guy you were handcuffed to. If you needed to get your smokes, your hand would have to follow the motions of his hand.

There was no violence, and I must admit there was some strange form of comradeship between the prisoners. By this time, I had regained control of my emotions and realized what a stupid thing I had done. The van finally stopped and we were in the alley of police headquarters down on State Street. They took us upstairs to a room full of people who had also been rounded up the night before and took our handcuffs off.

A couple of hours later, a group of white policemen came to get us with tons of handcuffs draped over their arms, tons of them, just like slave chains. They handcuffed us again and took us downstairs and stuffed us in some holding cells so jam-packed that we had to face each other; there wasn't enough space to even sit down. We took turns sitting on a bucket in the corner.

After a while they brought us bologna sandwiches, just thin-sliced, tasteless meat on dry white bread, but at the time it felt good to eat something. We were waiting to go in front of the judge, and I thought my turn would never come, but it finally did. I was taken down a hallway, through a door, and suddenly bathed in light.

I was so ashamed. It was so dehumanizing. You haven't slept, you're in the same clothes from the day before, can't comb your hair or wash or brush your teeth. I don't think anyone recognized me because I kept my head turned away from the people sitting behind me in the courtroom. I went before the judge and was out of there without even a fine.

When I got home and walked through my front door, I never felt so dirty and grimy in my life. Going to jail was not fun—it was humiliating and stupefying. You lose your dignity as a human being. You feel separated from society. You have absolutely nothing to do except feel time pass, and it passes real slow in jail, real slow. And it's scary because you feel helplessly, hopelessly isolated, and you know they can do anything they want to you in there.

By the way, 80 percent of the prisoners were black, 19 percent Hispanic, and the remaining 1 percent was poor white. If you fit these categories, I suggest you stay out of trouble.

(ANSWER TO QUESTION ON PAGE 208)

Barry White, James Brown, and Jay Blackfoot were all in juvie homes.

The Two Dead Girls

How old were singers Minnie Riperton and Florence
Ballard when they passed away?

(ANSWER ON PAGE 213)

Two other incidents happened in the early seventies, not too far apart from each other, that devastated me and altered me in a way that I still feel today. This is a sad thing here, and I get very emotional telling it, but to the best of my knowledge, during my heyday at WVON, two girls were killed in relationship to some of the dance sets that I gave, and I have lived with that for a long, long time.

One of them was at the Time Square, my teenage nightclub, which was still a very successful operation. But street gangs were getting a real foothold in the city of Chicago around that time, and many of the gang members came to party at Time Square. But I would stand up and talk to them, saying things like "I know that you all like to fight, but this is your place. This is neutral ground; this is Switzerland. As long as you don't fight and don't cause any disturbance, you can come here and enjoy dancing, and I can bring you acts." And these kids liked that, gangbangers and all. They respected the place.

But one Sunday, I was inside counting my receipts and getting ready to leave the office when the police walked in and announced to me that a girl had been killed on the way home from the set

211

I had just finished. I think she just got caught in the middle of gang crossfire—they had ended up fighting just a few blocks away from the club.

A couple years later, a gentleman approached me who was building a skating rink in the Chicago suburb of Markham. He wanted me to come out there and spin records. We did a series of sets called Midnight Rambles—which was nothing new to the city of Chicago. The sets started at midnight, and people just piled in and skated until three or four in the morning. The kids loved it, and the thing that I had there was just huge. I'd announce the event on the radio, and we'd be jam-packed. I can't really convey just how big a disc jockey I was and how big my following was, but during the Midnight Rambles, sometimes we were so crowded on the skating rink that we had to lead some of the people off to dance in one of the side rooms.

On this occasion, it was a big night again, jam-packed. The evening was winding down, and I was packing my records up to leave when I felt concussions through the walls of the skating rink. It was BOOM! BOOM! You could hear it and feel it. The owner and I ran outside. A beautiful girl had been shot, and obviously she was dying.

We pieced the story together. A guy who had been shuffled off to the side room asked this girl to dance and she said no. He became infuriated, got his gun, and waited for her to come outside. He said, "You dissed me," then he shot and killed her. She was really pretty. He was a gang member, and I understand that he later was arrested and went to prison for a long time.

I can't tell you how much I regret what happened to these two girls. I felt so bad about it for so long. I thought that if I didn't do these things, these sets, that wouldn't have happened. So I closed down the Time Square. The deaths are something that I still live with today.

In the death of the first girl, I had help from a policeman in the district. He was the perfect man to talk to because, unfortunately, he saw similar things happen all the time. He said, "What you got to do, Herb, is send some flowers. It was not your fault, and you get over it, these things happen."

He was a wonderful man like that, but he wasn't around for the second death. No one was. I know this stuff affected me. Sometimes I question myself: maybe I tried to ruin my life after that because I felt so guilty about these two young girls.

(ANSWER TO QUESTION ON PAGE 211)

My good friend Minnie Riperton, who displayed her five-octave range on hits like "Lovin' You," died from breast cancer in 1979 at the age of thirty-one. Florence Ballard, an original member of the Supremes, was thirty-two when she died in 1976 from a blood clot in one of her coronary arteries.

Drinking and Drugging, Big-Time

Singer Candi Staton was married for a short time to another entertainer who was abusive to her. Who was that man?

(ANSWER ON PAGE 222)

have often said that the 1970s was *the* decade for black music—when it just exploded more so than at any other time in history. Had I realized the decade was so good while it was passing by, I would have appreciated things and tried to enjoy the 1970s more.

Only problem is that I was messed up throughout the entire decade. And most of the 1980s. And much of the 1960s. Messed up, as in fucked up. Drunk. High. Doctors diagnosed me as having a dual addiction to alcohol and drugs.

The murders of the two young girls at my record hops didn't begin this downward spiral of addiction for me, but they certainly threw a couple of logs on the fire to keep it stoked. I had all of the classic reasons why a person descends into this madness. I was a momma's boy, a scaredy-type guy with low self-esteem. Stress. Pressure. Access. Being a celebrity with a high-flying lifestyle.

When I was young, I didn't like alcohol at all. I had my first drink when I was eight or nine. It was during the holidays at my great-auntie's house. During Christmas dinners, they would have red wine and would give the kids some. I think that was just tradition with a lot of families back then—they'd give the dog some, the cat some, the kids some! I thought it was nasty.

We drank in high school to be stylish. When we got out of school, we'd go car riding and stop at the drugstore. For less than a dollar, you could get a whole fifth of wine and some paper cups, so we'd just ride up and down the lakefront, drinking wine out of paper cups. Might have got a slight buzz on and had a good time, which is just normal for kids to do.

It wasn't until I was at WBEE in the mid-fifties that I started to drink a little bit more seriously because I was starting to feel the stress of working constantly. I worked seven days a week with no rest. It wasn't a fear of success or anything like that; it was just the actual damn work. Having to be at the station all the time, dreaming up gimmicks, working with demanding bosses—they were all white and the place was kind of racist.

And they kept all kinds of pressure on. Radio is a pressure game; they put you in a pressure cooker. They'll tell you there are things you can say, things you can't say, and there's always this pressure to keep you where they feel you should be so they'll get the best ratings. Radio is definitely not just a bed of roses!

Most of the time, after my show, I'd go straight home because of the stress. I remember once I really wanted to date this girl, and I went by her house and said I just can't take you out. She asked why, and I said, I just can't, they're working me too hard. And I went home and went to bed.

I was still finding alcohol very hard to drink, but I was drinking it anyway. During the Budland nightclub days, I would always get a double scotch on the rocks, and after about three of those, I was in a good mood and could talk to anybody. I could talk to the ladies. At that time drinking made me feel relaxed and more confident. Maybe it seems funny that on the air I seem extroverted, but off the air, I've always been very quiet. Glib behind that microphone, but not the same off the mic.

I started drinking heavier in 1960, which was pretty late; I was thirty-one. People warned me against it, and I'd just say yeah, yeah, yeah. I wasn't paying attention, of course. This was at WHFC before it changed to WVON. I remember the lady who ran the station could see the signs and tried to warn me against it. She would give me breath mints and stuff like that. I kept doing it without realizing I was becoming an alcoholic.

I had learned to like the taste of alcohol by then, and I used to keep bottles in brown paper bags around—in my car, at the station, WVON especially, where I'd leave the brown paper bag in the wastebasket so it'd be there when I got on the air. I was doing a lot of shows just bombed out of my skull. But I got used to doing it and could do it pretty good . . . or so I thought.

This was the mid-sixties, and I was drinking and having fun—not only because I was king of the hill, but also to relieve the always-there pressure from radio and my terrible marriage.

I first started using drugs in the late sixties, early seventies. I would go into a back room at WVON where a bunch of the guys were and it would seem as though they would get quiet until after I left, and then I could hear them get more animated. Finally, one day I went in the room, and everybody looked funny, and I said, "What's wrong with you guys?"

One of them said, "I'm tired of this, we're not going to cover this up anymore," so he lifted up this sheet of paper, and there was white powder underneath. He said, "You should just sit down here and try some of this." I said OK, and I had my first snort of cocaine. That's how that terrible habit started. They said, "Now we don't have to hide it when you come into the room anymore." And from there, we were off to the races.

After my initial indoctrination, I just started following the crowd. I gradually started doing more with the guys in the room but didn't think too much about it. I was like, OK, this is what's happening here—you get your little money together, you go buy it, and sit around and do it. It was fun doing it with a bunch of the guys. Then you go do it with a lady, and it's really good. So it just increased.

Back in the day, cocaine was hard to find, so sometimes I'd go get it for all the guys, or one of them would get it—whoever had the connect. You'd call around in the morning, then sit around all day waiting, and it might not get to you until later that night.

So that was the start of it. At the height of me using, I could go to Wisconsin and inside of two minutes I could tell you if there were any drugs there and where I could get them. By the time I finished I could make a call and for fifty dollars I could get three grams of cocaine delivered by a female who would then give me a blowjob if I wanted it—you'd have to give a little something extra to the lady for that—but you could get it in fifteen minutes! It was guaranteed to be to you in less time than the pizza joint takes, always on time and delivered by different women. I hope you don't even know what a gram of cocaine is, but let's just say it's a lot. To get three grams of cocaine for fifty bucks was unheard of.

Plus, the dealer gave you like a ticket stub and at the end of the week if they called your number, you won an ounce of cocaine. I never won, but what they were trying to do was turn you into a dealer and expand their network. And these folks were never out, never out. They must have had some kind of fabulous connection. Unfortunately, I tapped into this mother lode, and it was nothing for me to go through the mother lode.

This is when my addiction really got bad. That much quantity for that little money, that was just too easy. My nose was bleeding constantly because I did so much of it. I'm surprised I still have nostrils left. I copped from these folks every day—three grams of coke a day—and sometimes I would buy twice a day if I had the money. That's six grams in a day. Think that's a lot? A guy gave me an ounce once, and I went in the house and stayed in there for a week and did it all.

If I wanted to sell it, I could have made money, but I wanted to snort it all. Some guys not as addicted as me would have been smart and just took a gram for themselves and sold the other two for a hundred bucks a gram, which would have let them get high for free and make a profit.

Actually, I don't think my habit was as big as it could have been—fifty bucks a day, sometimes a hundred? At one nightclub set I did, when I finished I had four dealers waiting for me. They came in one at a time, and I got fifty dollars' worth from him, twenty-five from him, sixty from him. I spent the whole pay I made from that gig and went home with my little packages and stayed up all night. That's how it is when you do cocaine, you stay up until it's all done—two days, three days, whatever.

One of the problems of being well-known is that people would just give me drugs; if I didn't have the money to buy them, they gave them to me. Sometimes I'd be in situations where they'd say, "Your money don't spend here!"

Another problem is that being in the business I'm in, everywhere I went there were drugs on the premises pretty much anyway, and they'd just be offered to you. It used to be that back in the day, at most of the parties, there'd be a little "get-high room" in the place somewhere—the basement or the bedroom—and everybody would be crowded around the bed or whatever getting high. But after a while, there was no get-high room—it was just right there in front of you when you walked in the door. You could get as much as you wanted while you were there.

One guy owned a little private club and gave a party for me with all the cocaine I wanted, and this nice-looking girl gravitated toward me. We were messing around at four o'clock in the morning, and in walks Ike Turner, who says, "I want Herb Kent's woman." I grabbed that girl and said, "Man, you're not getting this woman, oh no!"

The upshot was I took her in a room, and we had fun. I took my time, and the old pimp running the show said, "Man, what took you so long?" He couldn't lock up or anything like that and was waiting for me.

Drugs, alcohol, a combination of both, a nice woman—you're just in a whole other world. And that's why people get high. It's fun. Damn right, it's fun.

A lot of us guys thought that because cocaine works on the nervous system and heightens everything it made us smarter. We thought that's why white people used it. I remember a bunch of guys you wouldn't believe sitting around saying, "You know something, white people have had this shit for a long time and it made them smart. Now we're smart." It increased our energy, and we thought it was not habit-forming, that we wouldn't become addicted.

Wrong on all counts! In reality, cocaine was the worst devil there was in life. That was the start of a whole downhill fate for many of us. The only hard drug I did was cocaine. Reefer never really appealed to me—only toward the latter stages of my drug addiction, and mostly just because it was there. But I could live without it.

By the late 1960s drugs had exploded on the American scene, and cocaine was considered a rich man's drug. The typical disc jockeys, singers, and artists were into cocaine. I've done it with so many notable people—doctors, lawyers, cops, you name it. I would say that at one point almost everybody I knew in every walk of life did cocaine.

As an addict, you spend most of your time looking for cocaine, and you go to any lengths to get it. You will go to any neighborhood. You will go into the projects. And this was really scary—sometimes I'd go to a place I didn't know, knock on a door covered with iron bars, and a low voice would say, "What can I do for you?"

I'd say, "I'd like twenty-five dollars of cocaine." The voice would answer, "Put the money in here," and slowly a little tray slid out of the door. I'd put my money in it, it would slide back, and then

I'd hear footsteps, *tap, tap, tap.* The tray would slide out, and my little package would be there. That was really scary to me. Here I was, dealing with people I couldn't see. But I did that.

And I'd go into these huge apartment buildings, and that's scary. I didn't know who was up in there. Cops could be there, gang members, robbers, killers—I didn't know. I could have been murdered in there, and nobody would even have known. I couldn't even see who was on the stairs or what. There was a funny incident once, though not funny really, when I was buying in one of these kinds of locations. I placed my order, and the voice on the other side of the door said in surprise, "Are you Herb Kent?"

That's another point I'd like to get across, too. You think when you do drugs that nobody knows it. Shit, *everybody* knows it! Especially if you're in the limelight like I was. Some of the dealers would even brag, "Hell, I fixed *Herb Kent* a package the other night. That's *my* man!"

One night I was with some buddies at the Godfather Lounge, and we were taking some cute little girls home. One of them came up to me and asked, "Are you Herb Kent?" I smiled and said, "Yes, I am." She said, "Ooooh, yeah, I hear you do *big* drugs!" You don't want to be that kind of spokesman, that kind of celebrity endorser. Oh jeez!

And in addition to the dangerous situations and your reputation, another bad thing about being hooked on drugs is the way you look. You don't take care of yourself. Hygiene is just not what it should be.

Drug addiction is just a life-threatening thing, and sooner or later, if you stay in it, the drugs are going to kill you—or someone where you buy your drugs will kill you. You'll lose your job, you'll lose respect, you'll lose your money, and you might end up in prison.

I got stopped by the police twice. One time, they knew I had cocaine, and they were laying for me. I was at this big dance and a lot of off-duty cops were there. Some of the cops were selling drugs. I never bought any from them; I was afraid of that kind of situation. But evidently they saw me purchase drugs from someone else, or something, however they work these things.

I got in my car to go home through Jackson Park along the lake, and the police were waiting for me. They knew damn well I had drugs because they had just seen me purchase them at the dance. Two cops stopped me and started searching me. I had it in my socks and the cop got it. Matter of fact, I had two packets and I said, "Man, don't take them both." He didn't say anything but he looked in the trunk where I had some LPs and he helped himself to those, too.

The other cop was standing back, he didn't want any part of this shakedown. So I said, "Hey man, can I buy my cocaine back?" He said, "How much money you got?" I said, "Twenty dollars." He said, "Shit no."

I said, "C'mon man, why don't you just give it back to me?" He said, "I'm not giving it back to you, what I'm doing is giving you your freedom! You want to go to jail?" I said, "No, sir." He said, "Then get the fuck out of here!" He got into his squad car and drove down half a block by a tree and started snorting that cocaine. Right then and there. He hadn't stopped to just look at the scenery at three o'clock in the morning.

The second cop incident was potentially far more devastating. One winter day, I just happened to visit a guy who had a place of business and was known to be a drug dealer. Fortunately I was just visiting. I didn't have any drugs at the time—I think I was trying to arrange to interview him on the air or something like that.

But the cops knew that I was in the game—when you hang around and are seen with different people when you buy cocaine and you're high-profile, people watch you. Cops, dames, they all know. So I went in to talk to this guy and came out and got in my car. Before I could turn on the ignition, police cars came at me from everywhere.

A white cop came up to the window, put a gun to my head, and said, "Get out the car, nigger!" They searched the car, tore the wires out, pulled the heater out. They handcuffed me and put me in the back of the squad car. They took me to the police station to search me, but I was clean, so they walked me to the back to my car, took the cuffs off, and I got in my car and drove off, with no heat. Thank God, that one time I wasn't carrying. Any other of a million times, I probably would have had drugs and would have been sent away to the Big House in disgrace, my career ruined.

I'm not the first one those kinds of police incidents have happened to. One of the guys we used to run with in the DEA used to tell me, "Drugs is a funky business, man, it's a funky business. That's the best way to describe it—people telling on each other, losing friendships, messing up relationships, losing jobs and money and status, and the fact that you can go to jail, or get hurt, or get killed—there's nothing cool about it at all."

I hung with some big-time drug dealers, and I don't know how I didn't get killed.

(ANSWER TO QUESTION ON PAGE 214)

Candi Staton's abusive husband was Clarence Carter.

My Sixth Life

Who warned Otis Redding not to get on the fatal airplane that crashed, killing him and members of the Barkays?

(ANSWER ON PAGE 226)

Based on what I just told you, you're correct if you're guessing that the sixth life I used up was due to a drug overdose. Twice somebody slipped me different drugs than what I thought I was taking.

I didn't really like to do coke on the air, but it got so that if I was tired I would do it when I was broadcasting. Sometimes, after doing a lot of sets I'd be worn out, and if I had some coke I'd take it and it would spark me up for five minutes at a time. That rush didn't last so long, so I'd have to keep doing it.

But I got out of the habit of doing it on the air when a guy I knew, a fairly well-known blues singer from the projects, visited me at the station, said I got something nice here, and offered me some white powder while I was on the air. He was basically a nice guy, and it looked like cocaine, so I took some.

But what he had was half coke, half angel dust. I remember getting up to go to the bathroom, and I was gone! My head was this BIG, and my feet were this *small*. Some people enjoy stuff like that, and apparently he did, but I said to him, "Man, I'll kill you, what'd you give me?" And he said, "Herb, I didn't know! I just

223

thought you'd like it!" He thought he was doing me a favor. But I'll never forget that big, big head and little bitty feet.

I made it all the way through my show, and afterward the program director said, "Hey, that was a pretty mellow show you just did, Herb!" I was afraid I'd done something wrong, but I'd been in radio for such a long time by then that I was able to pull it off. It was all instinct, but it's still remarkable to me that I made it work.

The second time, I wasn't so fortunate. I did a set, a good set, at this motel that had a dance hall. A guy came up and asked if I wanted some cocaine. He had this real fancy little kit—the little leather pouch and the mirror, a snorter, a spoon. And he was dressed pretty smooth.

He poured some out, I hit it, and he said, "You want some more?" I said yeah. But it turns out that this was THC, not coke. And I'm not a THC fan, but I know you're only supposed to do just a little bit of that stuff. But he had put a bunch of it on the mirror, and thinking it was coke I snorted it like it was going out of style, taking big healthy hits. That's truly fucked up for somebody to do something like that to you; you can kill a person for doing that, for not being up front about the drugs they're giving you.

Well, my hands just started melting into the records, and I lost all track of everything. At the end of the set, I remember the guy who hired me had to push me up against the wall and stuff the money into my shirt pocket to pay me because I was unable to do anything.

Fortunately, I was with some friends, and I told them, "Let's go." We were on the way to the car, and the next thing I knew I was fighting, man, and I was holding my own! I had my keys in my hand the whole time—fighting like mad, strong as a bull, and I was winning.

Finally I shouted, "Somebody get the police!" And the folks I was fighting said, "We are the police!" Some kind of way they let me go because they recognized me as Herb Kent.

So we got into the car and headed to this party in the south suburbs, and to me, we were on the clouds. I was on this big, white, soft cloud, and I'd see a green sign with white printing on it go by every now and then.

We got to the party, and my friend said, "Come on!" I said, "Man, I ain't going nowhere, I'm cool." So they left me in the car. But it was well below zero and I was out there freezing to death. I don't know how much time passed, but I couldn't feel a thing.

A guy who saw me came out of his house, knocked on the window, and said, "Man you'll die out here. Your boys shouldn't have left you." I said, "Take me to the party." He said, "If I take you to the party, you'll probably freak out. You're in bad shape." I said, "Take me to the hospital, then." He said, "No, man, they'll find out who you are!"

At that point, I heard everything he said to me as garbled. He knew I was overdosing and wouldn't let me go. Let me tell you, this guy's name was Bernio, and he was a real man. He took me into his house and made a little bed for me on the couch. I just lay down and really tripped.

I heard a whole bunch of nickels falling down around me, then I was flying downtown. I flew all around the Wrigley Building, the Tribune Tower, over the Chicago River—I could see these things, I could feel them like this was astral projection, like I was there, and everything was in color. The next morning I was better but was out of it. I was still so high that when I shut my eyes I could see through my eyelids, then the image would break away into a thousand pieces. It was three days before I fully recovered, and I was just so ashamed of myself.

I still see Bernio around, and he's a great guy, a wonderful, wonderful guy. He wouldn't take any money or anything for saving my life. And that he did. By all rights, I could have—and if it wasn't for Bernio probably would have—frozen to death that night.

(ANSWER TO QUESTION ON PAGE 223)

James Brown saw the plane before the flight, said it looked rickety and raggedy, and begged Otis not to take it.

The Great Deejay Massacre at WVON

> When Tammi Terrell got too sick to sing on her
> recording sessions with Marvin Gaye, who filled in
> for her?
>
> *(ANSWER ON PAGE 230)*

In 1973, a little FM station came on the air in Oak Park, a suburb
of Chicago. It was called WBMX, which stood for the Black
Music Xperience. It was in stereo, had a slick sound, and played a
different type of music—longer album cuts, disco—with deejays
who only tended to the music. We had been around for years just
talking shit, when they came in slick. WBMX kicked WVON's
ass, just kicked our natural ass. We couldn't compete—FM was
the hot new thing in radio—and the Black Giant, this behemoth
of a station, was slain by this little David called WBMX.

I got beat in the ratings by a girl I taught—LaDonna Tittle.
I schooled LaDonna on how to be a deejay. Our friendship has
never wavered, though. She was a gorgeous, gorgeous woman, and
she wanted to learn how to be a deejay. I spent many an hour with
her and got her together. And when she got on WBMX, she kicked
my ass. I had mixed emotions, but I didn't take it personally.

WVON management made an attempt to brighten us up. They
brought some folks in to teach us the modern way, the contempo-

rary way, of approaching radio, and I learned it. The other deejays didn't want to learn and kind of looked down on me for going along with it.

But I said, "You know, man, it's here. They're not spending this kind of money to teach us for nothing. This is a new day." Fortunately I could look ahead, but they said, "Naw, man. That's not right."

So our ratings continued to slide. We were in the throes of an FM revolution. BMX was coming on with records we didn't play, and they just took over. In 1977, management called us all in to tell us the station was being sold. The new owners showed us our ratings. We had plummeted from like tens and twelves down to ones and twos; even if you don't understand ratings, you can tell that's obviously not good. They thought we were too old and said unless something changes, it's going to be over. That was the start of them getting rid of us.

◆◆◆

Shortly after that meeting, I was on a plane to New York. My mother was ill. After I had moved to Gary, Indiana, to work my first professional radio job, my mother Katherine went to live in New York City. She had family there, dated, and had boyfriends.

In 1973, I had gotten a call was from the lady my mother worked for. She told me at the time that she thought my mother was very sick. She told me that my mother kept favoring her side, and that she thought my mother had breast cancer.

My mother, being a devout Christian Scientist, would not see a doctor. Instead, she got into some Christian Science sanitarium. I went up there to get her, but they chased me away because she didn't want to leave. She did have breast cancer, and ultimately, she got so sick she had to leave anyway. That's when the battle began. I put her in the hospital, and she wouldn't let them take that breast off, which she should have done.

But the pain got so bad that when her doctor came in and told her, you know, I can take that breast and you're just going to feel so much better, she finally said OK, and they took it. For three or four years, she went back to being herself. But she had waited too long and it metastasized and then she went down again. That's why I was flying to New York.

While I was there, I would go by the hospital to see her and sit by the bed and cry. The nurses said, "You shouldn't let your mother see you do that, she needs you to be strong." I was just a mess, my clothes needed pressing and stuff like that.

After a while, she couldn't recognize anybody, but one day I went to see her, and she called out my name. The next day, she was dead.

This was in 1977, which wasn't my best year. Shortly before my mother died, my wife left for good—we had been estranged for quite a while—and shortly after my mother died, I broke up with my girlfriend at the time.

◆◆◆

Almost at the same time, the new owners of WVON decided that the Good Guys group of announcers were too old, so we were involuntarily retired—fired. They got new jocks, but that really wasn't the answer either. FM just made it a new day; AM radio was down in the dumps and it's never really come back up.

The way they got rid of us was very brutal. One of the first to go was Jay Jay Jackson, then a couple of other guys, and then me. I found out later that I was not supposed to be fired. Someone just had a personal vendetta against me and used the opportunity to wipe me out.

This happened a month after my mother died. I had gotten so depressed over her death that you could hear how down I was on the air. A lot of folks said I should have been given a leave of absence, and I probably could have got it together. But I was gone.

The owners hired Pinkerton guards with pistols and they set our belongings out the front door. Management was afraid; the deejays were so popular they thought their fans would come and start some mess.

We were all just crushed. They brought in new guys—that's when Tom Joyner came to WVON. He was good, and they brought some other guys in, but nobody with the exception of Tom made any noise like we did. But by then, AM radio was out of the ballpark anyway.

I can't describe what an empty feeling being fired and not being on the air was. I was so used to going to work that I just got up the next day and drove to the station. Then reality set in. I drove on by and went down the street to Red's Diner and got some bacon and eggs. Then I got back in my car and drove back home. It was devastating.

Those things you never forget. They're beyond the point of fair or unfair. They just happen, and if anything, I was determined that the situation would make me tougher in this radio game—if I ever found work again.

When we got fired, some of the white disc jockeys around the city said, "Well, don't feel bad, we get fired all the time. You guys had a long run of it." But then again, when a white jock got fired, he could go across town and get another job. But there weren't many black stations in town, and the white stations wouldn't hire black disc jockeys. I had to work at a real small station, or not at all, or leave town.

And irony of ironies, the 102.7 frequency that WBMX used to broadcast on, which caused me to get fired in the first place, is now home to WVAZ/V103, where I have been working for the past twenty years.

(ANSWER TO QUESTION ON PAGE 227)

Valerie Simpson of Ashford and Simpson filled in for a sick Tammi Terrell, and Marvin Gaye said he was unable to tell who was who on the playback.

One Lonely Night

Which of these duos made "You Don't Know Like I
Know" popular?

A. Rufus and Carla Thomas
B. James and Bobby Purify
C. Sam and Dave
D. Ashford and Simpson

(ANSWER ON PAGE 236)

L ife at this point was one big ball of tragedy, and it would only
get worse. Talk about falling apart. The wife leaving, the girlfriend leaving, my mother dying, being fired, all happened in
lockstep, one right after the other. All the while, I'm in a stupor of
booze and drugs. I don't see how I lived through this rough period
of my life, but I did.

Shortly after I got fired, my cowriter of this book, David Smallwood, hooked me up with a couple of weekly sets at a roller skating rink in the south suburbs and at a nightclub in downtown
Chicago called the Gazebo, which was on Wacker Drive.

We had met the year before, in 1976, when David wrote a cover
story for the *Chicago Sun-Times Midwest* magazine supplement
about Chicago's great black radio scene, in which I was featured
prominently. David was a bright spot in my life, because here
was a young, twenty-two-year-old guy just starting out in his own

career as a journalist who said, "Man, I really dig your work. Let's do stuff!"

He wasn't much of an agent and didn't get me a radio job, but he doesn't realize how much he was inspiring me to try to get back out there and do things, because at that point it just seemed almost impossible to me that I would ever, ever, ever do anything again. I was only out of work on the radio for five months or so, but that was long enough for all my systems to go down. I was terribly depressed.

I was still drinking and drugging, man, just really out of it. Sometimes I'd fall asleep in a booth while I was doing the after-work set at the Gazebo. But David and I had some fun and each met women who had some sort of impact on our lives. It was a short-lived gig, but I have fond memories every time I pass by where the Gazebo used to be.

One day in the late fall of 1977, I got a call from the Millionaire's Club out in a Chicago suburb called Niles. It was a pretty exclusive joint. This guy said he got my name from someplace, and they wanted to go disco with their sets. They wanted me to run it. So I took this job as a deejay for the Millionaire's Club and worked there every Friday and Saturday. That's how I ate and stayed alive. I was making eighty dollars a night, just enough to keep me eating and putting gas in my car.

I will never forget it. When the Millionaire's Club called, I was down to my last unemployment check. I had no money. I had *no* money. I met a guy who worked in the unemployment office and he was involved in some fraud there. He knew how to plug into the system and get checks. He asked me if I wanted to go that way, and I said hell, no. Seems like they could easily find you eventually and off you'd go, straight to jail!

As the weather got colder and my prospects dimmer, I woke up one day ready to end my life. I had had it. I had really had it. I had no friends coming around and everybody seemed to be so insensitive to me. Let me tell you: everybody loves a winner, that's true as hell. Everybody loves you when you're on top. But never let them see you sweat, because when you're down you ain't shit. There was almost nobody, man, it was just me. I can only remember very few people who reached out.

I had this beautiful pearl-handled .357 Magnum, complete with a holster, that I used to carry. This particular day when I woke up, I called one of those few remaining friends of mine to come get the gun. I told him, "If you don't, I just might use it on myself."

I can see why people commit suicide. I was out of it. I felt like electricity was going through my body. I was buzzing. I was being pushed and I just couldn't stand it anymore; it was just too much. So in a last attempt to save myself, I got in the car and I drove to Jackson Park Hospital on Stony Island. I went to the mental health floor and said I needed to see a psychiatrist.

The nurse said, "You're going to have to wait three weeks." I said, "In three weeks, baby, I will not be here." I was rapidly using up my seventh life. They came and got me right away. The doctor sat down and told me that it was too much I was trying to bear and that I was not protecting myself. He said, "You have to protect yourself, man! You will destroy yourself like this." It was just obvious to him. He said, "Too many things have happened to you at one time."

After he talked to me, he gave me a little bottle of pills, little yellow things, not as big as a grain of rice. I took one, and immediately, I felt great. I came down, I mean, I came down.

The next morning I took another one, and I took that bottle and hid it. I said, No one is ever going to get these little pills from me. But I only took two; I never needed them after that. I don't know what the hell they were, some kind of tranquilizers.

Unfortunately, I don't remember the doctor, either. But that guy saved my life, and he wouldn't even let me pay for that visit.

◆◆◆

The girlfriend I broke up with a few months earlier had told me I needed to go to AA. She was angry at the time and being sarcastic, but at this point I did take her advice and began attending Alcoholics Anonymous meetings. It wasn't because I got religion all of a sudden and wanted to change my ways—I just wanted to get the girl back. Truth is, we didn't "break up." Actually, she outright dumped my ass.

So, with that being my main motivation, I was not really in it when I went to AA and never really surrendered. I'd go to the meetings sober, get up and make speeches and stuff like that, but leave and go drinking again. One guy at the meetings saw I was just bullshitting and called me on it, saying, "You're not fooling me." I was in AA for less than a year and actually stopped drinking for a while a couple of times, but I couldn't stay stopped.

I usually drank topshelf scotch and gin, but switched to Rhine wine, which I thought would make me less drunk since it was softer than hard liquor, but there's no such animal. Actually I just got drunker more often because the Rhine wine was cheaper, plentiful, and it did the job. Eventually, it didn't matter at all what I drank, as long as I had something.

I knew all the places to go buy alcohol when I needed it, around five or six in the morning, when it's illegal to sell it. Of course they charged you extra for it. But I knew all these folks. I'd wake up in the morning sometimes and buy a gallon of white wine, go back, and get in bed, and by the time Bozo came on at noon, I was soused! I just drank that shit all day long.

I lost weight. I'm thin anyway, but I lost so much weight that I couldn't sit in a chair without sitting on my bones. It was so painful to sit that I'd have to lie down instead. I mean, I just really abused myself. And I still was in denial of the fact that I was an alcoholic and a drug addict, even though I was fucked up every day, almost all day.

Remember earlier I said I was the king of the deejays and always had a fly ride? At this point in my life, I would buy a car for two or three hundred dollars, drive it till it died, and then just leave it wherever it stopped. I'll never forget—I got this car and it made just an awful sound. I took it to a back-alley mechanic to find out what was wrong, and he said, "The crankshaft is broke." I asked, "What can I do?" and he said, "Junk it." So I did. And I went out and bought another one, just as cheap.

And all the fly women? Skeezers, hookers, crack whores. I was a male crack whore a couple of times, even though I didn't smoke any kind of cocaine out of the pipe. However, it happened many times that I'd go to clubs or sets, and women would give me drugs to have sex with them. Sometimes I did it more for the drugs than the sex.

I was in a beauty shop one day getting my hair done—the salon was one of my longtime radio advertisers and they would do my hair weaves and jheri curls for free, even though I was no longer on the air. I took a shine to a lady working there and she said she'd come over to the house. She came and sat on my couch and asked, "Do you *date?*"

I said, "Yeah, I take the ladies out." She said, "No, do you date?" I said, "Ohhhh." But I still wanted her, so I said, "How much?"

She said, "Twenty-five dollars." I said, "What can I do?" She said, "Anything you want to do!" And the party was on.

After a time, she started to like me, and she stopped charging. I was so lonely at home that on December 24, 1977, I asked her to come by and we spent that Christmas Eve together. She told me lots of stories and since everything was closed down, we just watched TV. She started doing my hair since she was a hairdresser, and she said, "Your hair is falling out." My hair was so thin that it just kept coming out because I was so worried about things.

I don't know what happened to her, but she was a necessary person in my life at that time. She was good to talk to.

After the winter holidays, in 1978, I was living alone in my house in a fancy southern suburb and could not pay my heating bill. Not only did I not have any money, I wasn't being rational about paying the bills. By the time you buy all your alcohol and cocaine, which is expensive, you don't have anything left to pay secondary things, like your mortgage and your gas.

So the guy came and turned off the gas. I remember he said, "Sorry, old man." I had a cat named Fluffy and an electric heater. That night the temperature went to ten or fifteen below zero, and I could hear the pipes freezing throughout the house. I could hear them explode. The kitchen faucet froze and flew off across the room.

The only reason I didn't die that night was because they didn't turn off the electricity, so I plugged in the heater and had it blow on my face. Then I got in bed and the cat slept on my stomach, and we made it through the night.

But the bursting pipes flooded out the whole bottom half of my house. The water was up to six feet and ruined most of my possessions. I certainly didn't have any money to clean up the mess, much less any money to pay any other bills, so I just walked away from the house.

I called my friend Emmanuel Arrington, who was one of the comedians in the Electric Crazy People. He lived nearby and agreed to let me stay in his basement until I got myself together. For that I was extremely grateful.

I lost the big fancy house to foreclosure within a month, and when I went to Emmanuel's basement, where I lived for almost a year, all I had to my name were a few suits and a shopping bag full of records.

I had truly hit rock bottom. I was at the lowest point of my life—almost fifty years old and didn't know which way to turn.

(ANSWER TO QUESTION ON PAGE 231)

C. Sam and Dave sang "You Don't Know Like I Know."

8

♦♦♦

REDEMPTION

Burning a Car, Saving a Life

Which of these groups recorded the top ten R & B and pop hit "Mama Said"?

A. The Chantels
B. The Marvelettes
C. The Shirelles
D. The Emotions

(ANSWER ON PAGE 241)

In this period of my life, everything that could go wrong just about did. It was a time that would have tested the faith of Job, but two incidents happened back to back that gave me signs of hope that maybe things could turn around.

One night, in early spring 1978, I had to drive into Chicago. I don't even remember what for. But I had barely made it into the city limits when my car began to overheat. I was just able to make it to a gas station. Clouds of steam were everywhere, and the car was too hot to put water in the radiator.

So I asked the attendant if it was OK for me to leave it there to cool off. He said it was, and I had noticed a small tavern across the street. So I was sitting at the bar drinking, thinking about my plight—definitely sitting on the pity pot—when I heard the sounds of sirens and fire engines. I could even see the red swirling lights reflecting off buildings.

As I drank more, I started to feel sorry for the person whose house apparently was on fire. "Poor bastard's got it about as bad as me," I thought. I drank for another hour or so, figuring by then the car would be cool enough for me to add water to the radiator.

As I crossed the street, I saw that it was my car that had been on fire, and it was now half burned up. The top half of the engine was gone, the carburetor had melted, the wires were all cut and burned—it was just a holocaust under my hood.

The fire engines had been headed to my car, and I had stayed in the bar drinking the whole time. The gas station attendant had noticed sparks coming out from under my hood and called the fire department. Had he not acted quickly, my car would have been totally burned rather than half burned, and likely there would have been an explosion. I bet then I would have come out of that tavern, wouldn't I?

Well, I just stood there and looked at that mess. I had maybe three or four dollars in my pocket. Without my car, whatever chance I still had in the ballgame of life was quickly fading.

I got that suicidal feeling again, thought about just cashing in all my chips, but the thought didn't linger this time, and I didn't even need the little yellow pills. Something inside me said I had to fight, told me I was not a coward, a quitter.

I left the car there—like I had any other choice—and got home somehow. I begged, pleaded, and borrowed money to get my car towed to a shop so that I could get back and forth to the little gig I had at the Millionaire's Club at the time. The next afternoon, I was at a repair shop around Ninety-Fifth and Halsted, where my jacked-up car had been towed. I had no money for repairs, but I was still resolved not to give up. As luck would have it, the owner of the shop was a friend of a good old friend from my better days. He was also an automotive genius.

He looked at the car and said it was an absolute mess, but that he might be able to get it to run again. I told him honestly, "Man, I don't know how I'm going to pay you." He knew I was *the* Herb Kent, even though I didn't look as suave as I do today; in fact, I was looking kind of tawdry. He looked at me and said, "Tell you what, can you come and spin records at a party for me and my wife?" I said yes, and we struck a deal. Somehow he fixed the car; the outside was a little scarred, but who cares how it looked, my life was back on track.

This was a real turning point for me. I had a lot of other problems, and I wasn't out of the woods by any means. But this guy and this incident helped me get from point A to point B.

The man's name is John Kidd. For more than thirty-five years he ran a car diagnostic center, and he taught auto shop at Chicago's Kennedy-King College for thirty years. For whatever reason, John and his wife never threw a party for me to spin at. But to repay him, one of these days I am going to do a big jam for some of the kids that he works with in the community.

John told me it took three days to repair that car, and while it was sitting on the lot one of his sons noticed an odor around the shop. He went and looked in the backseat of my car and found a big pot of red beans and rice, with some cornbread wrapped in aluminum foil. To this day I don't have a clue about how it got there. Maybe one of my listeners or fans gave me this pot of food to help me through this trying period. If it was you, please let me know.

A few weeks later, it was an unusually hot day. I was walking to the store and stopped at the corner of a very busy intersection at Seventy-First Street and Jeffrey. The stoplight was red, and this little girl came by me and walked right out into the path of all these cars just as the light was about to change. You can just imagine.

They were sitting there gunning their engines, and the exhaust smoke was filling the air. The girl tried to run to beat the light, but just as it changed, the cars raced off! I swooped down and picked her up just in the nick of time—her legs were still running in the air, I lifted her that quick. I held her, just held her close to me. It was such a horrible moment, but a good one, because I had her and could feel her little heart just beating so fast.

I don't know what she was doing out there by herself at that young age—I guess seven or eight years old. I sat down with her on a corner bench until the cars left and the light changed to green again. Then she got up and safely ran across the street.

An old man who was sitting on the bench too looked at me and said, "That was a good thing you did there, sonny." My heart lightened, and I was more encouraged about life than I had been in a long time.

> *(ANSWER TO QUESTION ON PAGE 238)*
>
> C. The Shirelles sang "Mama Said (There'll Be Days Like This)."

Climbing Back and Punking Out

> What two groups have maintained the same personnel for more than forty years?
>
> *(ANSWER ON PAGE 244)*

don't see how I hung in there through this disastrous period, but some kind of way I came through it, even though it took a few years to come back. It takes a long time. You can be thrust down, and you must realize that it takes a while to get back up. You have to have a lot of belief in yourself to not just let go, and fortunately I kept that belief.

It was always there, and I attribute that to my mother. She always said, "I know you're going to be great one day." So the belief was always there and I never completely gave up. But it was pretty scary and shaky there for a while. I would wonder if I had been great but lost it, wouldn't get it back. Other times I would sense that maybe I had hit just about as low as I could go, and maybe now I would be on some kind of upswing.

I was itching to get back into radio and thought that to get back on the air, why not go back to my roots and just broker my way back on? My good friend E. Rodney Jones from WVON hipped me to this FM station called WXFM. So I bought time on it, just a couple of hours, but it was the first time I had been back on the air in about five months. Brother, it felt terrific!

At first I did a regular black music show, but I remember being at a club, and they were playing "Whip It" by Devo. The black teens there were just jumping up and down and going nuts over it. I said, "Hmm, let me play that on the show." I did, and it turned out to be one of my hottest shows. So I started playing a lot of white New Wave and rock artists—Pat Benatar, the B-52's, Depeche Mode, the Vapors, the Tubes—and there was the black group, the BusBoys.

On the air, I called this Punk Out music, and, man, it was as hot as any show I've ever had anywhere. One of my most popular shows ever. It was a huge hit for WXFM, and one of the hottest things going in Chicago at the time. Most areas of radio that I get into I manage to do pretty well; I've just got a God-given talent to do radio.

But I was so good that the people over at WXFM started giving me holy hell. Some of the other white announcers were saying, "We don't want no punks around here." The environment for me there got to be just terrible. I left WXFM after less than two years because—of all reasons—my Punk Out show was absolutely killing rival FM station WGCI in the ratings, and WGCI was a black-oriented station. Yet they were losing their valuable listeners to me over at the white station.

So WGCI hired me themselves, just to kill the competition. I went to WGCI in 1980, but I really had to start back at the bottom. They hired me because I was doing so well at WXFM, but they didn't plan to push me ahead to help them. They were pushing and promoting everybody else except me and weren't giving me my props. First, they put me on the AM side. I did the night shift, seven to eleven, then they put me on middays.

It was just awful because I had to play records and couldn't say anything. I'm a creative person, it's just natural with me, but they choked that off at WGCI. That's like not being allowed to eat, you know? It was very painful for me. They told me, "Just play music, don't talk too much."

So the first couple of years were pretty bad. Finally, they lightened up and put me on the FM side and let me do a Sunday dusties show. They paid me a bit more money, and I had a bit more freedom. It wasn't all bad and I was able to do a lot with it.

I can't really belittle the station, though, over the way I perceived that I was being treated. Some of it was maybe me. In fact, I was about to find out that quite a bit of it was me.

(ANSWER TO QUESTION ON PAGE 242)

The Four Tops and the Dells have had the same singers for more than forty years.

The Intervention

Damn, They Caught Me!

> Dennis Edwards of the Temptations had a solo hit
> with vocalist Siedah Garrett. What was the name of
> that record?
>
> *(ANSWER ON PAGE 250)*

Despite the fact that I had had a hit show on WXFM with the Punk Out thing and was starting to get back in my groove doing Sunday dusties on WGCI, even after I was making a little money again I was still boozing and snorting. It was about 1987. I was living with a lady, drinking really hard, and doing a lot of drugs. I would say to myself, "I know this cannot go on forever; whatever this is, it's going to end one way or the other."

I had started to see things—I was having the DTs. I remember seeing a bug crawling on a red carpet. I remember seeing faces at the window. I remember seeing a cross in 3-D just all lit up. I was in bad shape. And I had started to see stuff like that *as far back as 1975!* But I wouldn't stop.

That kept on and kept on until my daughter, Robin, told Marv Dyson, the station manager at WGCI, who was my boss. I did not know that she had told him. Marv called one Sunday night and told me he had to meet with me the next morning. So I got down to the station at eight o'clock, and all the WGCI executives were sitting around. After a bit, Marv stood up and said, "Herb, you've been doing drugs, and you're drinking."

He said, "I will fire you right now if you do not go into treatment. If you go into treatment, we've got everything arranged. You'll come out, and everything will be like it was, like it didn't even happen." Folks started crying and shit. They had talked to the crisis intervention person from human resources previously, and this guy was there in the room. There were also department heads and my daughter, so they had planned this out pretty well. I'm not sure who made what other comments after Marv; I was so stunned, don't know whether everybody put in their own two cents on the matter or what.

You'd think that you would hate to go through an intervention like that, but you know what, at least they were there. That was my second thought after this all happened. My very first thought was, "They caught me, goddamn it!" That was it; I felt like I was caught with my hand in the cookie jar, trapped.

And silently, inside my head, I'm belligerent, thinking: "I mean, I knew I did it, yeah, I do drugs, yeah." But in order for me to stay in radio—and as you know by now, I'm obsessed with staying in radio—I had to rehab, and that's the only reason I agreed to go in at the time. I didn't want to be fired—and they had caught me dead to rights.

Marv said, "You can go to drug treatment in Chicago, Detroit, L.A., we don't care. And if your insurance won't pay for it, I'll pay for it." So I said, "OK, I'll stay here and do it in Chicago."

"Can you go this afternoon?" Marv asked. I said, "No, I have some things to take care of, so if that's the case, you all just have to fire me. I'll go Sunday." They said OK. So I'm being clever, right, and I go buy all the cocaine and alcohol I can find. This was a Monday, and I'm thinking I'll just stay fucked up until next Sunday.

But you know something? I bought all the stuff but I couldn't get high. The healing process had already started. It was the most amazing thing. I didn't want the booze; I halfheartedly did the cocaine. I didn't feel anything because I knew the jig was up.

Well, Sunday came and my daughter Robin and her boyfriend came to get me at the appointed time. I told them, "Why are you all coming today? You know hospitals don't take people in on Sundays!" They said, "Oh, yeah, that's right," and headed back to their car. Then they thought about it and said, "He's lying to us," and came and got my ass! At ten o'clock that Sunday night we checked me in at the old Osteopathic Hospital in Hyde Park.

I went in and peed in the bottle. The hospital staff took my vitals, and my blood pressure was down, my body temperature was down. I was in very, very bad shape. I was given a room, and some big, big guy from Detroit was camping in there. I said, "Oh shit, I don't want to be in here. I need my damn privacy." But that wasn't happening. A nurse came in and shot me right in the butt with a big needle and that was so painful.

Everybody in this ward was in there for that shit, same as me, and you had to stay in for thirty-one, thirty-two days. They gave you meds that kept you down all day. You could get up and eat and take a shower, and they had classes all day long on drugs.

For the first two days, I'd just sit up and nod in the class. Gradually, the stuff metabolized out of my system, which was supposed to happen. I never will forget that on the third day I woke up and for the first time I could smell the grass outside the window. I thought to myself, "OK, I'm good, I'm ready to get out of here now." But if I walked out, I'd get fired. There are no locks on the door, but it's a jail. If I walked out of there, they'd call my boss, my insurance would be canceled, and I'd be fired.

So I had to stay and go to all them damn classes. But it was a transcendent experience. After a while I was elected senior peer, and for the last week or so they made me the head guy in charge of everybody. They always bestow that on somebody just before they get out. And they gave me this big long quiz before they let me out, and I worried I had failed it.

Considering what the people are in there for, this isn't exactly a churchlike environment to be in for a month. Once I almost got into a fight with this guy. He was just a little asshole; I don't know what was wrong with him. He said something about your arms too short to box with God. I said, "But they're long enough to beat your ass!"

There were about thirty or forty people in there at the time with me, and it was a little frightening. They were having sex *and* they were doing drugs—see, the people who came to visit them brought them drugs. They hospital people spot-checked us with random urine tests and if you were using they would eventually find you. When they *knew* there were drugs there, they'd have a lockdown, man. And they'd go through the whole place and turn everything upside down until they found them goddamn drugs.

And the folks having sex—I'll never forget that this nurse came in and said, "It is against the law to say who has or who doesn't have AIDS in here, but you can believe one thing: some of these women you need to be careful of." It wasn't a bluff. I knew one woman and she was one that *I* initially wanted to fuck, but they discreetly got the message to me: *Don't fuck her, she has AIDS.* She was doing my hair and stuff like that before I found out.

So I didn't have sex with anybody there. I didn't do any drugs while I was there. I was in there to be cured, man. I'm not a dumb person. I wanted to get back in radio. Plus, the cure had taken hold already, you know. I just had to bide my time in there.

Well, you're never cured, but I had lost my desire for drugs, just in those three days when I first entered rehab, while they were getting them out of my system. I never wanted to be in that position again, being basically locked up with all them drug addicts—and I was one of them. So I tried to make the most of my time.

Ironically, I wasn't embarrassed to be Herb Kent the Drug Addict in there. Actually, sometimes it was kind of fun—or at least not bad. We ate really good, played games, watched TV. I learned how to use a washer and dryer. My daughter came every Sunday to see me, and I'd be given an hour that we would use to walk down to the drugstore on Fifty-Third Street in Hyde Park or someplace like that. We had to be back at a certain time, though; I told you it was like being in jail.

But I wasn't embarrassed at all. I made friends in there. And I learned that out of every forty people who enter, you're lucky if three of them manage to get out. It's usually an overwhelmingly losing battle, because a lot of addicts are there to satisfy their mothers, fathers, husbands, wives, or judges. I also found out that after you get out of there, you shouldn't go back to your girlfriend or boyfriend, whatever the case may be. And you need to stay away from people, places, and things you used to frequent because you'll fall right back into the same habits that brought you down originally. I know a big-time lady drug dealer who was in love with me for a while. She is very nice, but I don't go by or keep up with her anymore.

I lost a lot of friends and some were angry at me. But when the time came, I said, "You know, we just can't do anything anymore." And from the way I said it, they went away. It was a little hard for some people. They'd come back, and I'd have to say, "Somebody's feelings are going to get hurt here!" to emphasize how serious I was.

So I lost friends. And I have to point out that everybody who does drugs is not a bad guy or girl, of course. You have folks that you hang with, and they're responsible people to a point, I suppose. They're not dragons and ogres and terrors that live underneath the bridge. They're people just like you and me. But if they do drugs, they're going to pull you down, so you have to get away from them.

In rehab, I believed everything they taught me. I practiced everything they taught me. After I got out, I went to follow-up aftercare meetings for a straight 365 days right there in the hospital. Then I went every Sunday until they changed my schedule at the station, and I couldn't go anymore. I would sporadically go to meetings, and I would still practice the principles.

I haven't had a drink since then. I haven't done drugs since then. If I did, I could get right back into that thing again. So I just don't do anything. I've learned to live without alcohol and drugs, and it's been more than twenty years now that I've been dry and working on my sobriety. No more hangovers, no more sick stomachs or vomiting. I feel great.

And one of the proudest moments of my life was being able to tell my good friend the DEA agent, who knew I was a drug addict but stayed my friend in spite of it, that I no longer use.

I'm forever grateful to Marv Dyson and my daughter Robin for what they did for me.

(ANSWER TO QUESTION ON PAGE 245)

Dennis and Siedih scored with the hit "Don't Look Any Further."

My Private Dance
with the Big C

What number one R & B single clocked in at the
shortest time?

(ANSWER ON PAGE 258)

I stayed at WGCI for about ten years, and it was a trying period for me. I lived in this guy's basement for the first year or so when I worked there, trying to pull my life back together. I was doing all right with the station after I completed rehab, but in 1989, Barry Mayo called and asked me to come onboard at V103, and I jumped. That's when I really got back in the radio ballgame.

Barry put me in a good position, gave me some general guidelines, then said, "Now, be Herb Kent." That's all I needed, man. It's been good for me and the radio station ever since. But my personal drama was hardly over because shortly after I arrived at V103, I was about to face my biggest crisis, and it was one that had been building for a while.

When they release you from rehab, they give you a physical. In my case, the doctor had seen something and advised me to go see my private doctor. This was maybe 1988 or 1989. I didn't go at first. A year or so after rehab, I started lifting weights and taking weight supplements to build myself up. But it became difficult to drink and eat certain things. I'd get a real bad pain when I did.

It didn't hurt to swallow, it wasn't in my throat; it just hurt going down, halfway between my throat and stomach.

It would just burn like crazy, an unnatural burn, like hot sauce or something. Then other things began to burn. I had no idea what it was. I thought maybe an ulcer, but it just became a constant pain, and I knew I had to see a doctor. I went to several doctors before I ended up with this one guy. He examined me, sent me to get chest X-rays, and from what they saw, they decided to put that tube down my throat and take a look, do a biopsy.

So they knocked me out, put the tube in, then woke me up and showed me the pictures. The X-rays showed something just awful-looking. He said he wasn't sure what it was; it might be cancer. Sometimes these doctors kinda know, they just want to be sure, and later he told me he figured that's what it was from all the symptoms I told him I had.

I asked him if he could just burn it out, and he said it's more complicated than that. He told me to relax and come back to see him in a few days. When I went back, he was just about in tears as he told me I had cancer in two places in my esophagus. And what I had was about 100 percent fatal.

The esophagus is a long tube that leads from your throat to your stomach. It has muscles in it, and when you eat, it forces the food down automatically. So when food would hit these tumors in my esophagus, that was the holy hell I felt. How did mine turn cancerous? Everybody argued about that. I smoked a lot, but I stopped smoking cigarettes in 1965. One doctor said perhaps it was because I drank a lot, and the alcohol might have destroyed the lining of the esophagus. I did have an ulcer once. A doctor treated it and it went away. However, I remember him saying, "I can't see it anymore, but that doesn't mean that it's not there." So that might have stayed and turned bad.

I told the doctor that my mother died of cancer. He didn't feel it was hereditary but said that families who live together and all die of cancer had to have done or experienced something together to get the disease. A common thread—some kind of food they ate, the air they breathed, just something in common in their mutual environment that affected everybody that they didn't know about.

Also, I was run over by that car when I was six years old. The car ran across my chest, so I thought it might have bruised my esophagus way back then. But we never did determine an actual cause.

Now, the trick of the thing is when you have cancer, there are going to be several treatment options. You have to pick the right one; it might mean life or death. You don't know.

The doctor originally said they could do an operation to take part of my intestine and use it in place of the esophagus, but that didn't sound too appealing to me. For one thing, there would have been no muscles to force the food down, so what are you going to do, put a plunger down there?

Then he consulted another doctor, and they decided on a treatment of chemotherapy and radiation, which they put me on immediately. They went right at it. Once they confirmed that I had the cancer, they had to line up some doctors, line up the treatment, and line up the hospital. I would say that within two weeks of being diagnosed, I was in treatment.

But I certainly didn't like the treatment. You take chemo for a few days, then you have to rest because it's so hard on your body. Then you take radiation, and you rest, and you alternate between the two. When they first gave me the chemo, I stayed in the hospital for a couple of days. They also gave me an antinausea medicine because the chemo makes you so sick.

No one knew that I had cancer, and I told the doctors I didn't want anyone to know. I guess it depends on what you're like— some people want the whole world to know. I didn't want anyone to know, especially people at my job. At this point, not even my daughter knew. The doctors cooperated with my wishes. They gave me something to wear under my clothes that automatically pumped chemo into my system. To do that, I had to go through another operation. I had a catheter put in my chest, and I still have the scars. They put a tube deep in my chest, and I wore this thing on my side. It was about the size of a small book and slipped onto my belt. It had a battery and it had chemo in it, and a schedule of when it needed to pump the stuff into me.

Every other day, a nurse came to the house and took pads to dress the catheter to make sure that I didn't get an infection or anything like that. This went on for a long time, and the nurse and I became friendly. She was a very pretty lady and she wouldn't even wear her uniform because everybody was trying to cooperate with me so that news wouldn't get out to the public that Herb Kent had cancer. (Only one lady knew, but I swore her to secrecy and she never told.)

The radio station didn't know. When I started messing stuff up working on the radio control board, they thought I was just getting old. Because I was so weak, it was very difficult to run the board and go through everything that I had to do. Thank goodness we had a great relationship, and I had great ratings, so the station gave me an engineer to take over that part. I've had these engineers ever since and found that I can do a lot of creative things to make my show more interesting because I don't have to worry about recording this or watching that.

I only told the boss, Barry Mayo, ten years later, and he was just so amazed. He said they had noticed some difference, but never thought it was because of anything like cancer. I went to work every day, never missed a day. I did my gigs at clubs. I did everything and nobody ever had a clue. Except I bent over once at the station and I had on a big heavy sweater that rose up. One of the program directors saw the tubes and said, "My God, what is that?" I just quickly said, "I got diabetes, man, I didn't want anybody to know." He bought it. I guess it made sense.

But back to the treatment—after this pump would cut off with the chemo, I would go for radiation, and that's a trip because they put you in all kinds of crazy positions that you have to hold for a long time while they shoot this radiation in you. They do a lot of damage to the healthy surrounding parts, too. They have to shoot into the tumors, and to get to mine they had to shoot through my heart. I remember at night my heart would go crazy sometimes because of the radiation. It would just start booming; the rhythm of the beat would change and I knew that's what that was. The doctors didn't have any choice, but that made me real nervous. The oncologist said she didn't think I would lose much hair, and fortunately, only a little fell out.

I saw so many X-rays of my esophagus and so many many doctors, each a specialist of one sort or another. My nurse was very sympathetic, and when I was hospitalized, she brought her little girl to visit me.

While I was in the hospital I had to sign a living will, which the hospital has you do if you might not make it. One doctor came in, in fact, and told me just that. I asked, "How am I doing?" This doctor, and she was my oncologist, said, "You ain't doing. It won't be long and you can take that to the bank." I'll never forget how she phrased it. I asked some other doctors if I had two years, and they shook their heads no. The best they figured me for was a year because most people die pretty quickly from esophageal cancer.

Dr. Terry Mason, who is now Chicago's Public Health Director and an internationally known urologist, came to visit me in the hospital. Terry used to help me carry my records to my various sets when he was a high school student. I was so out of it at the time that I didn't know Terry had even come to visit until he told me recently. He said that when he saw me, I looked like a "very, very, very sick man."

You know how I felt? Like I was getting ready to leave this big party, if you really want to know. Once I found out that I probably would not make it, my big thought was, "Boy, life has been a great party, and I sure hate to leave it."

That was the thought that went through my mind—that I just hated to leave this motherfucker. I'm spinning records, I'm a disc jockey, there are a lot of nice-looking ladies, I've had some nice cars—and I thought, "My God, now I've got to leave this party."

But you know what? I never, never really believed deep down that this was going to happen, and that might be what saved me. My spirit didn't feel it; there was nothing inside me saying, "You're going to die here." It wasn't that I was putting up this steely determination, like "Dammit, I'm not going to die!" It was more that I just didn't feel like I was dying. My life wasn't passing before my eyes or anything like that.

If I had accepted that I was going to die, I might have. All the doctors said I would. The nurses looked at it a different way, though. They all talked to me and said so many people came in there who just gave up and died. They always told me, "Please don't give up!" They felt that you had to have faith, and you had to fight it mentally, and that's what pulled people through.

I was lying in the hospital bed one day when this white lady priest came in. She said, "I understand you're quite sick."

"Well, that depends," I said. "Are you ready to talk to Jesus?" she asked. "Well, not quite," I answered. She asked, "Why?"

"Because I'm just not ready to die," I replied. So she said, "Well, are you denying Jesus?" I said, "Naw, lady, I'm not denying Jesus; I'm just not ready to talk to him! And I think you need to get the hell out of here!" And she stormed out. I don't know what she was trying to do, but I wasn't ready. I never saw her again and to this day I think she was crazy. She wasn't concerned about me or my feelings; she was just concerned about Jesus. I love Jesus—but just tell him I said hi! Give him a message for me! I'll meet him one day, but not today.

I also never felt sorry for myself. I drove myself to the hospital, since nobody knew I was sick, took my treatments, and came back.

The doctors were really a lot of fun to talk to. When they put the catheter in, they made me get in a wheelchair, which I didn't want to do, but I had to. They wheeled me in and gave me a local anesthetic. I felt a sharp pain and said, "Hey you just stuck me." A doctor laughed and said, "Yeah, we do stick 'em around here every now and then!"

All this went on for a while, and I was still in pain. The only way I could eat during this time was to go to McDonald's and get those little gushburgers they have because they're so soft. I was living off McDonald's and would drink milk, coffee, or tea. I couldn't take anything harder because it would be too painful. I couldn't eat peanuts, steaks, and stuff, but I could choke down these little hamburgers with the soft buns. White Castles, too.

Then one Saturday, I was doing a gig at a skating rink on Chicago's North Side. I was feeling pretty good, still feeling a little pain, but suddenly I got hungry. Without even thinking about it, I went and got a hot dog—and I ate the whole thing! And it didn't hurt. I told the doctor when I saw him the next week, and he was happier than I was. Shortly after that, I woke up one morning and I was pain-free. I went to the doctor and he said, "I now pronounce you completely in remission." That one made me cry. It's like pronouncing you either dead or alive.

According to the nine out of ten doctors who attended me, I didn't have any chance at all. Of all these doctors, just one said, "I'm going to cure you." Everybody else was saying, "Not long," shaking their heads, but this one doctor said, "I'm going to cure you," and he was dedicated to it.

The whole process took maybe three months. The chemo softens up the tumors and the radiation finishes the job. It all makes you so weak, though. I took so much radiation I couldn't swallow; my throat swelled up and I had to take additional medication.

Afterward, I saw the oncologist—the one who said I could take it to the bank that I was about to die. She said, "You're blessed. God has blessed you," and she took her stethoscope down.

My esophagus took a beating, and I still get heartburn easily. And because the radiation killed so many red blood cells, I'm slightly anemic and get little sleepy spells. But by and large since then, and it's now more than fifteen years later, nothing's happened. I feel good.

I kept the secret for years, until I got bronchitis somehow, and the doctor sent me to Mercy Hospital, which is where I spent my time with cancer. While I was there to check on the bronchitis, I leaned over to my daughter, Robin, who had come with me, and said, "I've got something to tell you . . ." At my seventy-fifth birthday party that the station threw for me, I stood up and told everybody there that I was a cancer survivor.

When I think about what happened, as I recount this story, I want to cry. I knew I had been in a battle, but in that particular battle, I had never given in mentally. I had said, *Jesus, I don't want to leave.* I've been fairly religious ever since I was about three years old. I'm a Christian Scientist, but one that goes to the doctor. My faith has brought me through a lot of things, a lot of things other than sickness. I mean the challenging things in life that happen to you. God has been very good to me.

And you know what? Recovering from drugs, alcohol, and cancer made me more sensitive to other people's feelings. Before all this happened to me, I wasn't sensitive enough as to what other people go through and what their feelings are as they're fighting their battles, whatever those may be. After I lived through my eighth life, which surely could have killed me, I became a different, changed person for what I went through. A little older, wiser, calmer, a little more determined. It changed me in that way. It made me work a little harder. I'm a man who doesn't stay on his knees; I'm one who gets back up.

One goal I had was that I wanted to own another house after I had lost mine on the way to hitting the bottom. The battles I went through made me more set on getting that house, getting more antique radios. The challenges just drove me to do those things.

When I had the cancer, I remember thinking, *Gee, I won't get that house now.* I was in my sixties and couldn't even get a mortgage. But after rehab and beating cancer, I got my credit and everything straightened out, and I walked into South Shore Bank. Half an hour later, I walked out with a mortgage.

I had the feeling that Herb Kent was back.

(ANSWER TO QUESTION ON PAGE 251)

"Stay," by Maurice Williams and the Zodiac, a number one hit in 1960, was only one hundred seconds long.

9
♦♦♦

BACK TO
THE FUTURE

Twenty Years with My V103 Radio Home

> How many R & B hits reached number one on the
> Billboard charts from 1942 through 1995?
>
> *(ANSWER ON PAGE 263)*

My move to WVAZ/V103 following rehab was a good one; it changed my life. This is a laid-back adult contemporary station that plays the best variety of R & B and dusties, so it fits my personality wonderfully. We're like peanut butter and jelly, as far as I'm concerned.

I've been here for twenty years now, longer than the fourteen years I was at WVON, and I feel appreciated, loved, and wanted, which can do wonders for anybody in any field of endeavor. I felt appreciated at the ten other stations I've worked for during my career, but not to the degree that I do at V103. Since I've been here, I've been a weekend man, doing a show on Saturday and a classic black music show on Sunday each week.

Since my cancer went into remission, I've grown into a top-rated, prominent deejay all over again at V103. I've gotten to be, once again, really big. So at this point in my career, it has been a savior for me. V103 has given me the opportunity to express myself the way I do best and enabled me to really do my thing. I play records from the 1960s through the mid-1980s. I talk about them, and I can play the records that I have found out personally that people like to hear. I've had a lot of freedom from the station in that regard. You may not know this, but I'm one of the few disc jockeys who actually has choices in the music he is allowed to play.

The station has let me be creative, and in return they have what you call a branded deejay. I'm perhaps the best-known black disc jockey in Chicago and one of the best known in the entire city, black or white. And that reputation has grown nationwide as so many people I've entertained through the years have migrated out of Chicago and now live all around the country.

Even though I only work Saturdays and Sundays, and do occasional fill-ins as needed, I feel what I do carries so much impact in the city and I think that shows in my ratings, which are consistently just phenomenal.

One of the most popular things I've ever done in radio, which I do here at V103, is something called the Battle of the Best. For an hour, we pick two similar artists—say Michael Jackson versus Prince—and alternate playing their hit records. People call in and vote for their favorite.

In never ceases to amaze me the different types of listeners who get involved. Educators, police, doctors, lawyers, laborers, teens, seniors, everybody. The battle truly turns into a no-holds-barred, slam-bang, argumentative, knock-down, kick-'em-while-they're-down contest, and I play the devil's advocate, taking one side over the other and agitating the listeners with my opinions.

The results are interesting. Nobody beats Aretha, for instance, and the Isley Brothers have only been beaten once, by Frankie Beverly and Maze. But the thing about the battles is that it doesn't matter who wins; it's an hour of really good music that you're hooked into. It's something we've been doing for years now—I've always put creative things out there on radio to let them find their own level, and when I hit on something good, I go there more frequently.

In my twenty years here, V103 has offered friendships and closeness that I cherish. I met a really good person who is my right hand and that's Raquel Lopez, my multitalented, excellent engineer. Program director Ron Atkins suggested I do a tease into my music, and that really turned the tide for me. I'll ask why David Ruffin left the Temptations, then in the next hour I'll play a Temptations' record and explain why. The listeners love this, so I study and use my memory and have been given the unofficial designation as music historian. I first came to V103 under station honcho Barry Mayo, one of the most brilliant men I've ever worked for. After he left, my bosses were Max Myrick, then Don Moore, and I think I'm older than Max and Don combined. But they are nice guys.

When WVAZ and WGCI merged under Clear Channel Radio ownership, my boss became, again, Marv Dyson. That was too ironic, because I left Marv at WGCI to come to WVAZ. He never really appreciated my leaving, and after I came over I was really kicking his station's butt in the ratings. Marv didn't like that either!

But after he sent me to rehab and said if I completed it everything would be cool, Marv kept his promise. He has been a very good friend, and I still go to him for advice. Marv was my boss for six or seven years after the merger before he retired. But he couldn't stay still long and now runs the radio and TV department and the radio station for Kennedy-King College in Chicago.

Now my guy is Earl Jones, a gifted man who went into radio after his football days were over. He was an outstanding defensive back for the Atlanta Falcons in the 1980s.

Earl is the first black president of Clear Channel Radio in Chicago and runs this station and the other stations in Clear Channel's Chicago cluster very effectively. He's done a lot for us already, and he'll do a lot more in the coming years. He's the kind of manager that everybody likes, and when he comes down the hall it's like, "Hey Earl!" And he returns that love. All people, all bosses, are not like that. Earl's a good guy.

For my seventy-fifth birthday, the station gave me a trip to China—Beijing, Hong Kong—and Thailand, and that was fascinating because I got a chance to see what Communist China was about, and it wasn't bad.

And at V103, I have a chance to be at the same station with Tom Joyner again. We were in a recent Bud Billiken Day Parade together. The station had a car in the parade just for Tom and me, and we had some great conversation and got a lot of attention during the course of the parade. Tom is very businesslike, very outgoing. Very talented. I've known Tom since the late 1970s at WVON, and he's been an inspiration to me. I've also been an inspiration to him, I found out. One time I had a talk with him and Doug Banks together. They were amazed by what I told them about old-time radio and the stuff that I went through.

Doug Banks, who also works at V103, is one of the most dynamic disc jockeys I've ever seen. I remember working overnight once, and Doug came in to do his morning show. It was like he was cranked with electricity—I've never seen anything like it. You ever see anybody come to work bouncing and with sparks flying? He and Tom are just unusually gifted people, tailor-made for the radio game. I don't think you'll find the likes of them again for a very long time.

I'll always be indebted to this station and its people for helping me get back to the top.

(ANSWER TO QUESTION ON PAGE 260)

In the fifty-three years from 1942 to 1995, 1,002 R & B singles hit number one on the Billboard list.

Star of TV and Movies

Who was the first African American composer to ever win an Academy Award? Hint: He won it in 1971.

(ANSWER ON PAGE 269)

Well, not really a star, but as a result of my newfound success, I have done some TV and movie work. For four years in the late nineties, I hosted two shows called *Steppin' at Club Seven* and *The New Dance Club*, and producers Anna Morris and June Mohn taught me how to be a TV performer. These shows both brought the art of steppin' to the forefront and were huge hits.

But I almost didn't get on TV. Even though I've been thrust in the role of a kind of grandfather of the steppers movement, and when stepper events come around I'm usually involved, I still had to audition for the shows. To tell the truth, I didn't even know about the programs until it was almost too late. A promotions lady name Merry Green told me that they were about to close auditions for a new TV dance show and that I should get myself down there, so I went.

I don't audition well, so I didn't expect too much. June Mohn was the man—yeah, he's a guy—to audition me, and he put me through my paces in front of the camera. I was nervous, and June asked me why was I squinting so much with my right eye. I wasn't even aware I was doing it. I don't how, but I got the job.

The art of steppin' is indigenous to Chicago. It evolved from earlier dances called the Walk and the Bop. The show's format included steppin' by dancers, dance instructions, spotlight dancers, videos, and we gave Latin dance instructions as well. We had guests—singers, tap dancers, comedians, magicians—and in addition to my "deep dusty," an interview segment.

We filmed in a huge TV studio cleverly set up to resemble a nightclub. Raqi Lopez was my assistant and floor director when we shot these things. When we arrived, the studio people were alive and full of energy and electricity was in the air. I would make it to my dressing room and drop off my garment bag, then head for the makeup room. Sometimes I would get a facial the week before a taping because you know I had to look good.

In the background you would hear people shouting, "Hurry up, Herb, we need you!" Then I would run up two flights of stairs to my dressing room, where Bruce, the owner of a nice clothing store called Mario Uomo, was waiting to dress me in some really fly fashions. We would try on a few outfits, and Bruce would ask me how they felt because it is important to feel natural and comfortable, not out of place or ill-fitted. He did such an excellent job of dressing me that part of the show's success was based on what I was wearing—it became that vital to the show.

Fully decked out and made up, I'd run downstairs to start taping. By this time, more and more of the folks who were going to dance in the first taping were streaming in. Knowing they were going to be on TV, they were dressed to kill, too, and it was truly exciting.

People would speak and I'd shake hands while making my way to the teleprompter. I would see a rough draft of the show beforehand and might even write part of it, but I had to read it through minutes before we started taping so that I would be smooth.

Bob, the head floor director, would hand me my microphone, the script would begin rolling on the teleprompter, and I would read it without appearing to read it. Some of the dialogue I ad-libbed; it wasn't all prewritten. In the meantime, the music started so the dancers could warm up. The producers' intent was to roll continuously with the tape on one day until we had two or three shows canned. So the dancers danced almost continuously and were really put to the test.

I think everybody in Chicago wanted to dance on our show. Sometimes people would literally beg me to please, please get them on the show. The truth of the matter is that Mary Lucas, one of the producers, would go to every steppin' club and event there was and handpick the dancers. And we would get a lot of them from the annual V103 steppin' contests.

Also, in the steppin' game, there are people who have made names for themselves as steppin' gurus or masters, so we chose them too. One of the big problems we had in taping was that steppers always like to put on a cool steppin' face and the producers were always trying to get them to look more "viewer-friendly."

Steppin' is such a laid-back dance, but the producers needed them to show more energy and look more lively, which put the dancers in a catch-22, because you can't just be going wild with your steppin'. Also, the dancers never knew how long they would have to dance once they got started, and it could be exhausting.

One time a woman dressed entirely in leather flat ran out of steam after about forty-five straight minutes of steppin' and sweating—I know she lost some pounds—and she had to sit out the rest of the show. A few others suffered the same fate.

I would go over to the deejay and check out what music he had, with Raqi at my side the whole time relaying information like where I should stand and when they needed me.

June Mohn would shout, "Stand by, everybody," and it was time to start the show. Cue music, cue camera, *Hi, this is Herb Kent*, and whoops! hold it—something went wrong somewhere. That would mean we had to take a moment to get started again. TV is not like radio—if you make a mistake, so many things have to be reset and rewound.

Here we'd go again. Lights, camera, music, announce. If the second time it came off perfectly, we'd be on our way. After my intro, with the dancers going at it, I'd wait to be told where to go next. Bob might send me quickly to the far end of the studio, and I wouldn't have much time to get there. So I'd negotiate my way past dancers, lights, coils of cords, sometimes ducking really low or flattening myself against the side of the wall to stay out of camera range. One time a programming assistant grabbed me by the arm and said, "We need you over by the deejay," while another one said, "No, we need you by the monitors." I thought I was going to be split in two before the second guy won the tug-of-war and I was over by the monitors.

Hosting these TV gigs was hard work, but I loved it. I gradually caught on to some of the technique of working in front of a camera, which really involved a lot of teamwork behind the camera. After really prodigious work on everybody's part in producing a couple of shows in one day, we'd take a rest and food break. We'd have chicken, ribs, greens, coleslaw, salad, as many soft drinks as we wanted, and it was all good. After resting and eating, everybody got real sluggish and tired, which made it hard to get back to work. We would change dancers for every show, so at least they were fresh. And we always managed to tape that last show of the day and do it well. No one ever complained. It was a labor of love.

◆◆◆

Now, people are excited when they get to talk on the radio, thrilled when they get a chance to be on TV. But let somebody tell you that you're going to be in a movie, and the excitement is beyond belief. That tops everything.

Here is my "distinguished" history in the cinema. In the 1960s, a record promoter said there was going to be a movie with a lot of disc jockeys starring it, including yours truly. I was ecstatic, but it turned out the movie producer previously had only made pornographic movies and before he got around to producing this disc jockey movie he was arrested and sent to jail. And so ended my movie career—for a while.

Years later, I got a call from an agent to portray myself in a sho-nuff real movie called *Love Jones*, starring Larenz Tate and Nia Long. I was to portray the deejay in a dance scene about steppin'. The scene was shot in a downtown hotel ballroom, and preliminaries for the shoot included dancers who came down and auditioned to music that I helped pick. At the designated time, I showed up on the set—had my own dressing room and everything. I changed clothes and scooted over to the makeup trailer to be made up like a big-time movie star. There were three of us in that trailer getting done up—Larenz Tate, Nia Long, and myself.

Then we were ready, and they shot scene after scene of people steppin' and dancing. Then came time for my Oscar-winning performance. My line was, "A party is just a party, but steppin' is a way of life!" Let me tell you, all of this consumed more than twelve hours, just shooting this little simple scene, but it was worth it because I was finally in the movies!

Now it's time for the premiere—showtime, right? So the movie opens and I go to the premiere, anxiously awaiting my appearance on the silver screen. And then it happened—the whole dance scene lasted all of forty seconds. And not only did they cut my line out, but they blurred my face. Later, all my friends said, "I thought you were in that movie. What happened?"

Then I was tabbed for another movie about steppin', actually called *Steppin'*, and I was to play a deejay again—DJ Kool, kind of a lovable, dirty old man—and this time it was a very meaty part with a lot of lines, so many that if they cut my lines, there wouldn't be a movie. The associate producer was the gifted and popular actor Antonio Fargas, who the world remembers best as the character Huggy Bear on the old *Starsky and Hutch* TV show. Antonio was a Shakespearean actor who went to public schools in different cities reading Shakespeare to inner-city students. But he told me the only two things anybody ever asked him about were, number one, being Huggy Bear and, number two, where the shoes were with the fish swimming in the heels that he wore in the movie *I'm Gonna Git You, Sucka!* This movie, *Steppin'*, unfortunately never got made because of financing problems.

And I was an extra in *Beauty Shop*. They got a beautiful shot of me sitting and getting my shoes shined, but supposedly I was in Cedric the Entertainer's dream, and they blurred me so you couldn't see my face. But some little kid in the screening I saw hollered out, "Ain't that Herb Kent?"

After that, I said, well, my movie days are done. Then Robert Townsend came in and put me in his movie *Of Boys and Men*, and I have one big line that they didn't cut out. In that movie, I say, "My name is Herb Kent. I'm a deejay in Chicago and I play dusty records." Finally, I'm a Hollywood star!

(ANSWER TO QUESTION ON PAGE 264)

Isaac Hayes was the first black cat to score a Best Music Oscar, for the theme song to *Shaft*.

From the Hall of Fame to the Mayor of Bronzeville

> What Chicago group did Marvin Gaye sing in for a while?
>
> *(ANSWER ON PAGE 275)*

One morning in November 1995, I got a call from Bruce DuMont, president of the Museum of Broadcast Communications. It was a complete surprise. He woke me up and said, "Good morning, Mr. Kent. You've just been elected into the National Radio Hall of Fame." That was stupefying. I couldn't speak.

The Radio Hall of Fame is no fluke, no fly-by-night thing. This is a really big deal. The hall exists to honor the giants of radio throughout its history, and so many nationally known people are in it: Abbott and Costello, Gene Autry, Jack Benny, Edgar Bergen, Jack Buck, Harry Caray, Dick Clark, Bing Crosby, Tommy Dorsey, Arthur Godfrey, Benny Goodman, Paul Harvey, Bob Hope, Murray the K, Garrison Keillor, Larry King, Groucho Marx, Edward R. Murrow, Red Skelton, Kate Smith, Orson Welles, Wolfman Jack, Walter Winchell. That's some rarified company there!

When I accepted my award, I sat next to June Lockhart, who used to be the mother on the *Lassie* TV show. Eve Arden—from the 1950s TV show *Our Miss Brooks* and, before that, a longtime radio icon—was also in my induction class. So were the St. Louis Cardinals baseball announcer Jack Buck and satirist Stan Freberg.

I entered the hall of fame with the first class of black radio inductees, including Jesse Blayton, the first black owner of a radio station in the United States; my friend Yvonne Daniels; and Andrew Carter, a Kansas City broadcaster. They were all deceased and inducted posthumously. Hal Jackson and I were the only living black honorees.

The ceremony was broadcast live from coast to coast and hosted by Tom Snyder, Susan Stamberg from National Public Radio, and Tom Joyner. We had a ceremony and a big scrumptious dinner. As we got our individual presentations, they read a little bit about who you were and what you did, then called you up to give you this wonderful Lucite trophy with a pair of earphones on it, engraved with your name and the date of your inauguration. It was awesome, a little like going to your own funeral and getting the keys to the pearly gates! I got a chance to meet Paul Harvey, the only guy who's been on radio longer than me.

Rush Limbaugh was there and didn't speak to me much. I told him, "You do a good radio show, but there's a lot of stuff that I don't like," and he got pissed. He had a bodyguard with him. I said, "I just don't agree with everything you say." He turned away and didn't say anything, but I could tell he didn't like it.

I gave a nice speech that people complimented. But I tell you what—I was in a daze from the moment Bruce told me I was being inducted to the moment I walked out of there with that trophy. A total daze—me, a kid from the projects being honored with some of the people I listened to, like Les Tremayne, who was also inducted in my class posthumously. He had this radio show called *Grand Central Station* that I listened to as a kid. At the time I thought I really didn't deserve it as much as some other people who hadn't gotten in, like Al Benson, who definitely should be in. He was a mean guy, but he was an icon, too.

I'm glad that I have the award, and it's probably the high point of my career. But if you ask me if it validated everything I went through in radio, I'd have to say not really. I struggled in radio, with racism and all the rest I endured. A lot of black people in radio today don't have those experiences; they don't know anything about it. But still, the honor was more than satisfactory; and it wasn't the end of my career—my career really just took off again after I got that thing.

A lot of people don't know it, but I'm in another hall of fame, the Gwendolyn Brooks Hall of Fame at Chicago State University. It's a literary hall of fame named after the great poetess and former poet laureate of Illinois. I'm in that one for creating and writing all these pieces about the Wahoo Man, the Gym Shoe Creeper, and those other creative bits I did back in the 1960s at WVON. They consider that writing, which I guess it is, like writing any kind of character for a movie or TV show. But I was surprised at that induction, too.

If you wonder whether being inducted into the National Radio Hall of Fame made me think of my college professor who told me I wouldn't make it in radio because I was a Negro, the answer is no. I just grew right on by that one. At the point where you receive an award or an honor like that, you know you've worked really hard for it and don't really think about people who told you that you'd never make it. I never believed them when they said that kind of stuff anyway.

◆◆◆

The next year a long stretch of a Chicago street was named after me, an honor initiated by Chicago alderman Arenda Troutman. And this was truly an honor, as I was joining the ranks of the likes of Emmett Till, who has a long, long section named in his honor along Seventy-First Street. That street was chosen because it was the location of the A. A. Rayner Funeral Home, which held Emmett's open casket funeral.

Alderman Troutman asked where I wanted my street located, and I picked the area in front of my old high school, Hyde Park, hoping it might be an inspiration to the students who go there now. If just one kid is inspired by looking up at the street sign that says Herb Kent Drive, then that's really good.

◆◆◆

In 1999, I became a mayor—the mayor of Bronzeville—and I still hold that lofty office. For decades in the early part of the twentieth century, Bronzeville was the center of black Chicago. It's the neighborhood I grew up in as a child and where I live now, as a matter of fact. In its heyday, from the 1920s through the early 1960s, Bronzeville was just overflowing with life and activity: merchants, music clubs, theaters, cultural institutions. A lot of entertainers came out of Bronzeville, from Nat King Cole to Redd Foxx. That's all long gone, but the area is being revitalized now.

The position of the mayor of Bronzeville was originally started by the *Chicago Defender* newspaper in the 1930s, and the first mayor was the gentleman who owned the legendary Gerri's Palm Tavern on Forty-Seventh Street. He was followed by many prominent people including disc jockey Al Benson. It was really big back in the day, with the mayors' pictures printed in the *Defender* and *Jet* magazine. One of the winners once received as many as fifteen thousand votes.

Somehow the thing kind of fizzled for many years, until it was revived in 1999 by the Bronzeville Merchants Association. There are all kinds of things encompassed in the Bronzeville area—schools, high-rises, brownstones, graystones, businesses, the very upscale Gap area, and many buildings with landmark status. Plans are underway for Bronzeville to be designated a National Heritage area by the federal government, and the community is rapidly becoming a national, even international, tourist destination.

I got a call one day from Sandra Hutchins at the Bronzeville Merchants Association, who said that I had been chosen to run for mayor against some other well-known community people. Betty Harris, the assistant controller at V103, became my official campaign manager, and the entire station rallied behind me.

The winner was announced at a big gala with the candidates dressed in nostalgic clothing provided by Mangelo, who says he did the wardrobe for *Hoodlum* and other films. Mangelo outfitted me in a long smoking jacket with a 1930s flare. On the night of the affair, I was whisked away in a beautiful shiny limo. The ceremony began, and as if I was dreaming, I heard my name announced as the mayor of Bronzeville. I was stunned.

My family over at V103 gave me an honorary inaugural ball at the House of Blues before an Incognito concert. I took my oath of office in front of hundreds of people, including Chicago news anchors Cheryl Burton and Bill Campbell, a very special friend of mine. Everyone got into the spirit of the event.

At one point a white girl asked me, "What is the mayor of Bronzeville?" I said, "It's a symbolic honor in a historic area of the city for black people." She said, "Gee, oh golly, that's great!" After the inauguration, a guy came up to me and said, "Herb this is all about love."

Then Incognito came on and jammed like a big dog. At the Bud Billiken Parade, I rode on the V103 float to the end, then after I finished with V103, I went all the way back to the beginning of that very long parade to the mayor of Bronzeville float. I hopped on and rode that parade again!

◆◆◆

I did take some measure of satisfaction against my old teacher, however, when I was asked to be a distinguished professor at Chicago State University in 2002. Since then, I've taught radio and TV courses where my students learn vocabulary, articulation, breathing, and many other pointers necessary to become a professional broadcast announcer. In addition, Chicago State a few years back staged a play of my life called *Old School Memories: The Herb Kent Story.*

So I guess you can say in a way that I've come full circle, and that the old adage is true, that what goes around, comes around.

(ANSWER TO QUESTION ON PAGE 270)

A very young Marvin Gaye sang in the Moonglows.

10

◆◆◆

LOOKING BACK
ON A LONG ROAD

Sweet Soul Music
You Must Have
on a Desert Island

What two artists have had the most consecutive
number one hits?

(ANSWER ON PAGE 283)

Let's leave on a final note about the thing I love most next to radio, and that's music. I have loved music since I was three years old and have lived it 24/7 ever since.

I believe that if there is any true magic in the world, it is music. There is no real time machine, but until they invent one, the magic of music puts us anywhere in time we want to be. In the 1940s, we heard music by Nat King Cole, the Ink Spots, Louis Jordan. In the 1950s we moved to Fats Domino, the Platters, Chuck Berry, and Brook Benton before doo-wops took over. In the 1960s it was the Motown Sound. In the 1970s, black music just exploded—in 1945, there were eight black records that hit number one; in 1975 there were forty-five black records that made number one R & B.

Rap began to take hold in the 1980s, and house music was big. Hip-hop and sampling dominated the 1990s and the first decade of the twenty-first century, and nouveau soul is starting to bring back traditional R & B sounds.

Certain songs just generate charges of electricity in my body. Music triggers your emotions and can instantly change your mood, from tears to laughter or the other way around. It takes you into another world and gives you an escape. It makes you want to make love, gives you a sense of beauty, and probes the depths of your emotions. Some music fits your soul like a piece to a puzzle and paints such a picture that even a blind man can see it. If that's not magic, I don't know what is.

Music offers you one-hit wonders, like "Function at the Junction" by Shorty Long, "The Book of Love" by the Monotones, "Float On" by the Floaters, "Play That Funky Music" by Wild Cherry, and "Rapper's Delight" by Sugarhill Gang.

Music offers the "oh, wow" records: the first time you hear them you go, "Oh, wow!" and then you play them until you can't stand them anymore—like "Sexual Healing" by Marvin Gaye, "Walk On By" and "Shaft" by Isaac Hayes, "You Send Me" by Sam Cooke, "Georgia on My Mind" by Ray Charles, "Ribbon in the Sky" by Stevie Wonder, Gene Chandler's "Duke of Earl," "For the Love of Money" by the O'Jays, "Flash Light" and "Atomic Dog" by George Clinton.

Music makes you contort your body in all kinds of freaky ways to dances like the jitterbug, the Bristol Stomp, the Roach, the Watusi, the Continental, the Madison, the twist, the Hustle, the Bus Stop, the Jerk, the Spank, the Electric Slide, the Casper Slide, the monkey, the Bump, the Macarena, the Running Man, the Uncle Willy—they said I was the Uncle Willy champion!

There's poplocking, breakdancing, and, of course, the twine. When Alvin Cash, who invented the dance and the record, died, everybody at his funeral got up and did the twine—and we all knew we would even before we got there.

Music reflects the signs of the times, as in Marvin Gaye's *What's Goin' On* album, which gives a good feel of what the world was like when the album was recorded. In short, music really is a soundtrack to your life, which brings me to one of my favorite stories.

A white doctor friend of mine was doing a liver transplant and wanted to tune in to my show. But first he asked the two younger doctors working with him if they liked Herb Kent. They approved, so the doctor turned on my show, and they jammed through the whole operation, which was a success.

On that note, and in an ode to music, let me offer you the two following lists. The first is what I consider to be the best of the best of black soul music artists. The second is the twenty-five black artists you must have music by if you're ever stranded on a desert island. Not the twenty-five albums, but the artists, and I have chosen albums that I think best represent their work. Let me know if you agree or disagree.

All-Time Best of the Best Soul Music Artists

The Royalty
James Brown
Aretha Franklin

Writers
Smokey Robinson
Stevie Wonder
Prince

Best Groups
The Temptations
The Supremes

Arrangers
Quincy Jones
Barry White

Singing Groups
The O'Jays
The Isley Brothers
The Four Tops
The Spinners

The Impressions
The Stylistics

Music Groups
Parliament/Funkadelic
Earth, Wind & Fire

Soul Singers
Luther Vandross
Marvin Gaye
Stevie Wonder
Ray Charles
Prince
Al Green
Michael Jackson

Divas
Gladys Knight
Dionne Warwick
Diana Ross

Historic
Sam Cooke
The Spaniels
The Shirelles

Honorable Mention
The Flamingos
Chuck Jackson
The Whispers
Chaka Khan
Minnie Riperton
Kool & the Gang
Johnnie Taylor
Jackie Wilson
Bobby Womack
War

Isaac Hayes
Bill Withers
Wilson Pickett
The Ohio Players
Teddy Pendergrass
R. Kelly

Classic Black Musicians' Albums You Must Have on a Desert Island

James Brown, *Sex Machine* (Polydor, 1970)

Aretha Franklin, *I Never Loved a Man the Way I Love You* (Atlantic, 1967)

The Temptations, *The Temptin' Temptations* (Motown, 1965) and *Psychedelic Shack* (Motown, 1970)

The Supremes, *Where Did Our Love Go?* (Motown, 1964)

Smokey Robinson, *A Quiet Storm* (Motown, 1975)

Marvin Gaye, *What's Going On* (Motown, 1971)

Stevie Wonder, *Innervisions* (Motown, 1973)

Prince, *Purple Rain* (Warner Brothers, 1984)

Isaac Hayes, *Hot Buttered Soul* (Stax, 1969)

R. Kelly, *R. in R&B Collection Vol. 1* (Jive, 2003)

Al Green, *I'm Still in Love with You* (Capitol, 1972)

Four Tops, *Still Waters Run Deep* (Motown, 1970)

The Stylistics, Round Two (Amherst, 1972)

Michael Jackson, *Thriller* (Sony, 1982)

Barry White, *All-Time Greatest Hits* (Island/Mercury, 1994)

Parliament/Funkadelic and George Clinton, *Mothership Connection* (Casablanca, 1976)

Gladys Knight, *Imagination* (Buddah, 1973)

Ray Charles, *What'd I Say* (Atlantic, 1959)

The Dells, *Love Is Blue* (Cadet, 1969)

Dionne Warwick, *Make Way for Dionne Warwick* (Collector's Choice, 1964)

Luther Vandross, *The Best of Luther Vandross: The Best of Love* (Sony, 1989)
The Isley Brothers, *The Heat Is On* (T-Neck, 1975)
Curtis Mayfield/Impressions, *Superfly* (Rhino/Wea, 1972)
The O'Jays, *Ship Ahoy* (Sony, 1973)
Earth, Wind & Fire, *Gratitude* (Sony, 1975)

(ANSWER TO QUESTION ON PAGE 278)

Louis Jordan had six number one records from 1944 to 1946, and Janet Jackson had six from 1987 to 1990.

Joy Inside My Tears

Appreciations and Regrets

> What group from Baltimore, Maryland, had the
> distinction of being called the first R & B vocal group?
>
> *(ANSWER ON PAGE 288)*

Well, that's my story. I'm eight years younger than radio, and before radio, there was silence. Radio was the first instant medium shared by millions and brought us closer together as people and a nation through news, music, stories, and talk.

I'm fortunate to have lived through several decades of radio—hell, at my age, I'm fortunate to be alive. But the changes in radio have been tremendous, challenging, and fun. Today's jocks must express themselves in a much shorter time and be smoother and more articulate than in the past.

Today, the race is to play more music with less talk. I've had to curtail a lot of my talking; I can't be a 1960s deejay in 2010. It isn't like it used to be where we sat there and talked until our mouths got tired. If you do that today, somebody on the other station is playing music, and they'll get your audience.

I'm grateful that God gave me the vision and revelation of radio at an early age. I'm grateful that I've met so many people from all over, and from my relationships with these people, I've been able to draw inspiration. I'm grateful that I've been able to witness people realizing their ambitions.

I'm grateful for the advent of radio and its growth from little wooden boxes hooked up to storage batteries to the Bluetooth radios you wear in your ear today. I've seen all of that, and I've played music in every format—78s, 45s, LPs, cassettes, dats, hard drives, I've worked with them all in radio.

I've seen life before television, and I remember seeing the first color television. I worked at NBC as an office boy, and the president was Jules Herbuveaux, a very nice man. I was delivering mail to his office, and he asked me, "You want to see something?" I said, "Sure would." He told me to sit down and he turned the TV on, and that big NBC peacock jumped up on the screen. The color was just fascinating. I was grateful to see that.

One of the things I'm proudest of is that I've seen the roles of black men and women expand in radio and TV. When TV first came around, there weren't any black people on it—so few that *Jet* listed them on the last page of the magazine any time a black person was to be on TV. When you saw that listing, you knew it was a historic occasion.

When radio first came on, there weren't any black people on it, either, but in the late 1920s, or probably early 1930s, you began to hear a black disc jockey here and there. Today, I can't tell you how many black people there are in radio, not only behind the mic but in the sales department, programming, everywhere. My boss Earl Jones, who runs Clear Channel, is black, which to me seemed almost impossible where I first came from.

I'm grateful for the way the music industry has grown up with radio—the big recording companies like Atlantic, Motown, many others—and the growth of the black executives there, too. The roles of black men and women in communications have just expanded, so a kid can come out of college, come out of high school, aim for a career in communication, and make it. It's not just a fantasy. When I started, it was just a fantasy, and for me to get in it and succeed—really just to get in it—was like hitting the lottery or the jackpot.

I don't have a whole lot of regrets; I haven't done a lot of wrong to people. My mother taught me pretty well, and I haven't been a bastard. Tried not to anyway. I mean, I'm not perfect, but there was never anything that significant.

My first paid job was for thirty-five dollars a week in 1949 in Gary, Indiana, and I've been working every year since then. I was thinking the other day about how happy I was when I was at WBEE making eighty-five dollars a week. I lived in Lake Meadows, I had a car, I had a great-looking girlfriend, and I was happy.

But sometimes you can't really live that happiness because you're always waiting for this great day when you're gonna really get ahead and be really great, and stuff like that. I was just always driven to succeed, so much so that I don't think I enjoyed life as much as I should have. I was always looking to get ahead, get a foothold in this business, trying to be great in it, whatever.

And I've never reached a point where I ever said, I have succeeded, I am great at this. I don't even say that today. There is no point in this game where you can sit and rest on your laurels; the industry keeps changing, and you have to adapt to stay alive in it.

I do regret that because I was driven so much to get in radio, because I just wanted to play records, I failed to heed some advice that was given to me. I remember Hugh Downs advised me to get into news because he could see even back in the early 1950s that the best way for black people to get started was in the news. But I wanted to play records, so I followed that line instead. Had I followed the news path, I would have made millions of dollars. I would be retired now, probably dictating this book on some huge yacht off the coast of Florida somewhere.

I regret that I got caught up in drugs and alcoholism; I regret that sincerely, but I have lived through that phase of my life and have successfully moved on.

I regret that even though blacks are more heavily involved in radio, TV, and movies, we haven't forged ahead as much as we could have in these fields. We're still second-class citizens as far as many things are concerned. Racism is still out there. It is not nearly as bad as it used to be, and I regret that that bugaboo still exists. But it is still there, believe me.

There is one last *gigantic* regret I've had for a long time, and I don't think anything can be done about this one. It's an incident that occurred in the 1960s when I had just risen so big. I was on Chicago's West Side, walking to my car, and two little black kids came up—eight years old or so—and asked for my autograph.

Well, I was late, and I said, "You know, I'm sorry, but I'm running late." At that point a couple of policemen came up and said, "OK, come on, Herb, give the kids some autographs." I said, "I told you I was late." Then it got to be like a test of wills, where I felt they were trying to force me to do something. I was late, so I said to myself, "screw this." I got into the car and drove away. I did not sign that autograph for those kids, and I have regretted it to this day.

But it taught me something. Ever since, whenever I'm out, I don't care who comes up to me or what I'm doing—if you want an autograph, I'll give it to you. Even if I'm running and have to scribble it, then I'll just scribble it. But I've regretted that incident for years and years and years, and if by some wild chance either of you kids is reading this—I'm sorry. I am so sorry.

We all have things we'd like to undo. But rather than undo, in my case, there are things I should have done. I think there are certain females I should have married. Seems like if you have more than one woman and you have to pick between them, you always pick the wrong one. I let a lot of good women go.

I've been a little mischievous, but I can honestly say that I have not been a bad guy. I abused myself more than anyone else. I'm completely sober now; healthwise, I'm fine. And now that I'm on my ninth and last life, the trick is for me to focus, look at where I'm going, at what I'm doing, without anything stopping me or fogging my brain.

My cowriter, David, told me a story about legendary *Chicago Sun-Times* columnist and talk show host Irv Kupcinet. David and Kup were in the *Sun-Times* bathroom taking a leak at adjacent urinals when David asked him, "How long are you going to keep doing your column?" And Kup replied, "Until I die."

And with the help of his protégé Stella Foster, Kup did write his column until his end. I second Kup's emotion. I'm going to keep broadcasting until I die. I can't think of anything else I'd rather do. Maybe I'll keel over during the middle of my show, but since you can never have dead air on the radio, my last instinct will probably be to push the button to go to commercial. Dead jock, OK; dead air, a no-no!

But until that happens, I'll continue jackin' this music like a big dog and remaining your humble radio servant. Thank you for reading, thank you for listening.

(ANSWER TO QUESTION ON PAGE 284)

Sonny Til and the Orioles was considered the first R & B singing group. If you don't remember them, you're not alone!

Index

A

A. A. Rayner Funeral Home, 272
AA (Alcoholics Anonymous), joining,
    233–234
Adderley, Julian "Cannonball," 3
addiction. *See* alcohol abuse; cocaine; drug
    abuse
AIDS, threat of, 248
airline ticket offices, robberies of, 192–193
air-raid wardens, during World War II, 25
alcohol abuse
    beginning of problems with, 215–216
    crisis intervention in, 246
    regrets about, 287
    stopping, 250
Ali, Muhammad, xvi, 142
Allen, Steve, 8
Allied Radio shop, 14, 196
Allison, Verne (the Dells), 173, 175
AM radio, demise of, 230
Amos 'n' Andy, debut of, 2, 10
Amphitheater, appearance of Michael Jackson
    at, 98–100
angel dust, snorting with cocaine, 223–224
Angelou, Maya, 2
announcer position, auditioning for, 35
announcers, voices of, 47
Arden, Eve, 270–271
Armstrong, Louis, 2
arrest in 1970s, 208–210
Arrington, Emmanuel, 133–134, 236
Art Institute, receiving scholarship to, 10
artist, being, 68
Atkins, Charlie, 175
Atkins, Cholly, 149, 154
Atkins, Ron, 262
Atlantic Records, doo-wop singers on, 60

Aunt Dora, 9
Aunt Mary, 4
Austin, Patti, 106
autographs, signing, 287

B

"Baby Come to Me," 110
Bacharach, Burt, 3
Bacon's Casino, 102
Baker, LaVern, 150
Ballard, Florence, 88, 173, 211, 213
Banks, Doug, 263
Banks, Ron, 141, 156
barbecue house, sponsor at, 152–153
Barkays, the, 223, 226
Barksdale, Chuck, 156, 172–173, 176
basketball, playing, 141–142
Bass, Fontella, 87–88
Battle of the Best, 261
Be Brave game, playing with cousins, 9–10
Beauty Shop, 269
Beige Room nightclub, 149–150
Beijing, trip to, 263
"beloved icon," xiv
Bennett, Lerone, Jr., 3
Benson, Al, 43–44, 53–54, 271, 273
Bernio, rescue by, 225
Berry, Chuck, 51, 57
Best, Willie, 36
Beverly, Frankie, 60, 141, 261
Beyoncé, 171
Big Bike Rides, duration of, 113
Big Three disc jockey lineup, 53
bike rides, promotion of, 111–113
Biondi, Dick, xiii
"bird groups," doo-woppers as, 59
Birdsong, Cindy, 89, 92

black deejays. *See also* deejay style; Good
    Guys of WVON
  in 1947, 43
  book about, 48
  Cooper, Jack L., 43
  fundraising for black power movement,
    114–118
  Jack L. Cooper, 11
"Black Giant," WVON as, 80
Black Music Xperience, 227
black musicians, classics, 282–283
black people. *See also* Bronzeville; racism
  neighborhoods of, 9
  schools of, 8
  on TV and radio, 285
  in World War II, 27
black power movement, collecting money for,
    114–118
black R & B station, WVON as, 80
black radio
  commercials in, 48–50
  stations, 53
  versus white radio, 70–71, 230
black talk show, *Hotline*, 83
"black" versus "white" voice, 44–46
black women, debasing of, 74
Blackfoot, Jay, 210
blackouts, during World War II, 25–26
Blackstone Rangers street gang,
    192–193
Blake, Cicero, 59
Blatty, William Peter, 3
Blayton, Jesse, 271
Blige, Mary J., 171
blind date, going on, 199–200
Block, Martin, 15
boardinghouse
  childhood experiences in, 4–6
  moving from, 18–19
Bobbettes, the, 60
bodyguard, hiring at dance, 194
Bofill, Angela, 205
Bop, the, 265
Boss Lady (Loretta Kraft), 43, 103
Bourne, Carlton, 26
bowling alley, in Pershing Hotel, 149–150
Boy Scouts, crystal radio sets made by, 14
Brand, Oscar, xiv
"Brandy," 101, 105
Braxton, Toni, 172

Brenda and Nitro, 127–128
broadcast radio
  current state of, 284
  decisive moment about career in, 21
  early availability of, 14
  growth of, 13
  life dedication to, 288
Broadcasting magazine, placing ad in, 37
broadcasting stations
  first example of, 12
  growth of, 13
brokered system, explanation of, 53–54
bronchitis, treatment of, 257
Bronzeville, mayor of, 273–274. *See also* black
    people
Brooks, Arthur and Richard, 177, 180
Brooks, Gwendolyn, 272
Brown, James, 280, 282
  birth of, 3
  crossover hits of, 23
  incarceration in Aiken, South Carolina,
    163–169
  interview of, 139, 142–143
  lyrics of, 72
  popularity of, 108
  premonition about Otis Redding, 226
  release from prison, 167
  spontaneous songs of, 162
  trivia about, 210
  visiting in jail, 162–169
Brown, Ruth, 197
Browner, Rudolph, 133–135
Buck, Jack, 271
Buckner, Milt, 175
Bud Billiken Parade, 6–7, 263, 274
Budland nightclub, 150, 215–216
Bundini Brown, Drew, 2
Burke, Kirkland, 91, 112
Burton, Cheryl, 274
business. *See* music business
Butler, Billy, 113
Butler, Jerry, 60, 156, 177–179

C
Cadillac Seth, 195–196
Cadillacs
  mixup of, 147–148
  promotion for, 94
Camden, South Carolina, 13
Campbell, Bill, 85, 274

cancer
  being in remission from, 257, 260
  diagnosis of, 252
  surviving, 257
  treatment of, 253–254
Capitol Records, doo-wop singers on, 60
Capone, Al, 2
car, getting run over by, 5, 253
Carbondale, Kappa Karnival in, 106–108
career
  beginning of, xiii
  regrets about, 286–287
cars
  junking, 234–235
  overheating, 238
Carter, Andrew, 271
Carter, Clarence, 222
Carter, Johnny, 174–175
Carter, Vivian, 52–53, 172
Cash, Alvin, 279
Cash, Fred, 179–181
Casper the Slide Man, 156
cat (Fluffy), 236
CB (citizens band) terminology, use of,
  124–125
Cedric the Entertainer, 269
Central City Productions, head of, 83
Chamberlain, Wilt, 198
Chan, Charlie, 36
Chandler, Gene, 61, 103, 112, 156
Chantelles, the, 60
Chaplin, Frank, 112
Chapman, Sam, 111–113
Charles (friend), 196, 200
Charles, Ray, 281–282
Charles A. Hayes Family Investment Center,
  101, 105
Checker, Chubby, 126, 141
chemotherapy and radiation
  effectiveness of, 257
  receiving, 253–255
Chess, Leonard, 81–84, 87–88, 172, 176
Chess Records, doo-wop singers on, 60
Chicago, arrival of Jackson family in, 98–99
Chicago State University
  play staged by, 274–275
  teaching at, 274
childhood
  from ages four to ten, 6–7
  early memories of, 4–5

education, 8–9
  independence during, 6–7
  personality during, 6, 9
Chili Mac's, 127–128
Chi-Lites, the, 156
China, trip to, 263
Christian Science Church, 15, 258
Christmas mice, 6
citizens band (CB) terminology, use of,
  124–125
Clair, Marian, 21
Clark, Delecta (Dee), 59–61, 179
Clark, Dick, xiii
Clear Channel Radio, 262, 285
Clinton, George, 140
clubs, working at, 63–65
Cobb, Joe, 82
Coburn, James, 3
cocaine
  addiction to, 217–218
  beginning of problems with, 216–217
  doing on air, 223
  getting and snorting, 219–220
  perceptions of, 219
Cockettes, the, 127, 132
Cole, Nat King, 273
college
  attending, 34
  discouragement in, xv
  racism in, 34
Collier, Mitty, 140
comedians, influence on radio, 47–48
commercials, in early black radio, 48–50
Commodores, the, 60
Conrad, Frank, 13
Cook, Ed "Nassau Daddy," 83–84, 116
Cooke, Sam, 42, 281
Cool Gent, coining of, 55
Cool School music, xiv
Coolidge, Calvin, 2
Cooper, Jack L., 11, 43–44
cops
  hanging out with, 193–195
  involvement with drugs, 220–221
  run-in with, 208–210
Cordell, Lucky, 83, 116
Cornelius, Don, 83
Correll, Charles, 10
Cosey, Pete, 58
cousins, relationship with, 9–10

Crane, Bill "Butterball," 82, 114, 116
crisis intervention, 246
Crocker, Frankie, 140
Crown Propeller, 150
crystal radio sets, making, 13–14. See also
    radios
cursing on radio, 70–72
Curtom production company, 180

D
Daley, Richard, 140
dance floor, keeping full, 68
dances, types of, 279. See also steppin'
Daniels, Yvonne, 82, 271
Davis, Tyrone, 139, 156, 171
Daylie, Daddy-O, 43
D-Day, movie about, 26
DEA (Drug Enforcement Agency), friend at,
    194–195
Dean, Jimmy, 3
deejay style, explanation of, 66. See also black
    deejays; Good Guys of WVON
Deep South
    attitudes toward, 163–164
    experiences with James Brown in,
    167
Dells, the, 156, 172–175, 241, 244, 282
depression. See 1970s; suicide
derogatory remarks, avoiding on radio,
    70–73
Devo, 243
diamond record, requirement for, 118
Diddley, Bo, 3
"disc jockey," coining of, 15
disco, era of, 61
"Disco Lady," 113
Dixon, Willie, 4
DJ Kool, 268
doctors, relationships with, 256
Doggett, Bill, 58, 150
Domino, Fats, 2
Dominoes, the, 60–61
Donald (friend), 196
"Don't Look Any Further," 250
doo-wop
    books about, 61
    corruption of lead singers, 60
    end of, 60
    era of, 61
    golden era of, 58

record companies for, 60
    style of, 59–60
Dora (Aunt), 9
Dorsey, Georgia Tom, 2
Downs, Hugh, 34, 286
Dr. Bop, death of, 89–90
Dramatics, the, 156, 171
dreams
    about radio, 20
    beginning of, 17–19
Drifters, the, 60
drinking. See alcohol abuse
drug abuse
    crisis intervention in, 246
    stopping, 250
Drug Enforcement Agency (DEA), friend at,
    194–195
drug treatment, receiving, 246–250
drugs
    in 1960s, 219
    avoiding arrest related to, 221–222
    beginning of problems with, 216–217
    business of, 222
    continued problems with, 235
    corruption associated with, 220–221
    regrets about, 287
DTs, having, 245
Dukays, the, 61
"Duke of Earl," 61, 156
DuMont, Bruce, 270
"dusty records," 55–56
Dyson, Marv, 246, 250, 262

E
Earth, Wind & Fire, 281, 283
"Earth Angel," 59
Easter-egg hunt, promotion for, 94
Ed Sullivan Show, 59
education
    involvement in, 85–86
    personal, 8–9
Edwards, Dennis, 141, 245, 250
8MK radio station, beginning of, 13
Electric Crazy People, 133–136, 236. See also
    Theater of the Mind on Radio
The 11:60 Club, 55
Ellington, Duke, 2, 56–58
El-Rays, the, 173
Emotions, the, 156
engineers, at WVON, 84

esophagus, cancer of, 252
Evans, Darwin, 196
Evans, Ernest (Chubby Checker), 126
Evans, Sam, 53–54

F
faith, importance of, 242, 258
fame
    interactions with fans, 186
    loss of privacy and anonymity, 184–185
family
    heritage of, 3
    "killer cousins," 9
fans, interactions with, 186–187, 200–201.
    See also female fans
fantasies about radio, beginning of, 17–18
Fargas, Antonio, 268
FCC regulation, exemptions from, 70
Federal Building, visit to, 195
female fans. See also fans
female fans, interactions with, 200–202. See
    also women
Ferguson, Maynard, 2
"fesneckies," 125
Fiestas ("So Fine"), 62–63
50 Yard Line nightclub, spinning at, 63–64
Fitzhugh, McKee, 83
The Five Heartbeats, 177
Five Stairsteps, 103
Flamingos, the, 281
flight cases, carrying, 63
Fluffy the cat, 236
FM revolution, beginning of, 227–228
food, scarcity in childhood, 5–6
football, fantasies about, 19–20
foreclosure of house, 235–236
Forman, James, 3
Foster, Stella, 288
Foster, Tyrone, 111–113
Four Tops, the, 241, 244, 280, 282
four-letter words, refraining from use of,
    72
Foxx, Redd, 273
Franklin, Aretha, xvi, 85–86, 280, 282
number-one R & B hits, 16
at record hops, 156
winner of Battle of the Best, 261
Freberg, Stan, 271
freedom of speech, controversy about, 74
Funches, Johnny, 173–174, 176

G
Gamble, Kenny, 176
gangs
    in 1970s, 211
    Blackstone Rangers, 192
    rapport with, 193
Gangster Disciples, 193
gangsters
    glorification in music, 74–75
    offer from, 191–192
Garfield Hotel, 200
Garner, James, 3
Garrett, JoAnne, 103
Garrett, Siedah, 245, 250
Garroway, Dave, 34, 55–56
Gary, Indiana, accepting job in, 35–36, 51
Gaye, Marvin, 227, 230, 270, 275, 279, 281–282
Gazebo nightclub, the, 231–232
Gems, the, 144
General Hospital, 106, 110
Gerri's Palm Tavern, 273
girl, saving from traffic accident, 240–241
girl cousins, relationship with, 9–10
Girls Gone Wild commercials, 74
Godfather Lounge
    hanging out at, 220
    working at, 188
Godfather of Soul. See Brown, James
golf outing, at NBC, 35–36
Good Guys of WVON, 84–85, 88, 90, 99. See
    also black deejays; deejay style; WVON
    fundraising by, 116
    getting fired from, 229–230
    sexual encounters of, 201
Gooden, Sam, 177, 180
"Goodnight, Sweetheart, Goodnight," 58–59
Gordy, Berry, 21, 159, 170, 181, 184, 190
Gosden, Freeman, 10
gospel program, following, 66
gousters, apparel of, 121–123
Grand Central Station, 271
Great Depression, 5
Great Migration, 3
Green, Al, 281–282
Green, Garland, 156
Green, Merry, 264
Green Bunny, Wahoo Man at,
    130
groupies, dealing with, 187–188
grunchions, 125–126

Guy, Jasmine, 138
Gwendolyn Brooks Hall of Fame, 272
Gym Shoe Creeper, 126, 272

H
hairdresser, relationship with, 235
Hale, Cecil, 83, 99
Hamilton, Lynn, 52
Hamilton, Roy, 150
Hammer, MC, 166
"hammers" versus "nails," 125
Hammond, Indiana, 56–57
Hancock, Herbie, 8
Harlem Globetrotters, xvi, 141–142
Harold Melvin and the Blue Notes, 176
Harper's Ferry, West Virginia, 3
Harris, Betty, 274
Harris, Major, 139
Harvey, Illinois
    Dells Day in, 177
    Dells' office in, 175
    working for WBEE in, 54
Harvey, Paul, xiv, 271
Harvey, Steve, 45
Harvey, William (longtime friend), 15–16,
    194–196
Hathaway, Donny, 113, 180
Hathaway, Lalah, 113
Hayes, Charles, 102
Hayes, Isaac, 269, 282
Hearns, Tommy "Hitman," 141
Heavyweights, the, 103
helicopter, flying, 142
Henderson, Woody, 133–134
Hendrix, Jimi, 69, 77
Henry, Patrick, 129
Herb Kent Drive, 273
The Herb Kent Story (play), 275
Herbuveaux, Jules, 35, 285
Herman (friend), 196, 200
Herrold, Charles, 12
high school (Hyde Park), 8
    joining radio club at, 21
    protection from racism at, 30
    racism at, 22
Hippodrome, party at, 107–108
Hitler, 24
Hitler Youth, experience with, 32
Holland, Eddie, 90–91

"Honky Tonk," 58
Hoover, Herbert, 2
hotel rooms, renting in youth, 200
Hotline, 83
house, losing, 235–236
House of Blues, 274
housing projects, move to, 18–19
"How Could I Let You Get Away?" 100
Howling Wolf, 55
Hudson, Al, 140
Hudson, Leroy, 180
Huggy Bear, 268–269
Hutchins, Sandra, 274
Hyde Park High School, 8
    joining radio club at, 21
    protection from racism at, 30
    racism at, 22

I
"I Miss You," 176
Ida B. Wells projects, move to, 18–19
"I'll Be Around," 98
I'm Gonna Git You, Sucka!, 269
imagination, development of, 17–18
Impressions, the, 61, 103, 177–179, 281,
    283
Imus, Don, 70–71, 73–74
Incognito, 274
Indiana (Gary), accepting job in, 35–36, 51
Indiana County Fair, covering in 1959, 56
Indiana Dunes, losing virginity at, 199
Ingram, James, 106
insurance company, job at, 31–33
intervention in drug abuse, 246
Isley Brothers, the, 261, 280, 283
Ivy Leaguers, apparel of, 122

J
jackin' music, 64
Jackson, Chuck, 281
Jackson, Don, 83
Jackson, Hal, xiii–xiv, 271
Jackson, Janet, 283
Jackson, Jay Jay, 229
Jackson, Jesse, 86, 115
Jackson, Mahalia, 54–55
Jackson, Michael, 98–99, 140, 281–282
Jackson, Millie, 140
Jackson, Walter, 156

Jackson 5, xvi, 103
Jackson family, arrival in Chicago, 98–99
Jackson Park Hospital, 233
jail, brief time in, 208–210
Japanese attack on Pearl Harbor, 25
Jerry the Tailor, 123
Joe (police cadet), hanging out with,
   194–196
Johnson, Isabel Joseph, 83
Johnson, Jay, 83, 99
Johnson-Black, Zenobia, 101–102
Jones, E. Rodney, 82–84, 90, 92, 116, 201,
   242–243
Jones, Earl, 262, 285
Jones, Quincy, 175, 280
Jones, Ruth Lee, 62, 68
Jones, Thad, 175
Jordan, Louis, 283
Joyner, Tom, 230, 263, 271
Junior, Marvin, 173–177

K
Kappa Karnival, 106–109
Kasem, Casey, xiii
KCBS, broadcasts from, 12
KDKA, creation of, 12–13
Kelly, R., 282
Kendricks, Eddie, 157, 159
Kennedy, Jayne, 159
Kennedy, Leon Isaac, 159
Kent, Herbert Rogers, birthday of, 3
Kent, Katherine (mother), 3–4, 228–229,
   242
Kev-heads, 31
Keyes, Johnny, 61
Keyman Club, 113
Khan, Chaka, 281
KHJ, broadcast of Rose Bowl on, 13
Kidd, John, 240
King, Ben E., 60
King, Martin Luther, Jr., 145–146
King of the Dusties, 55
Knight, Gladys, 139, 281–282
Kool & the Gang, 60, 141, 281
Kool Gents, the, 59, 172, 179
Korean War, getting drafted in, 27–28
Kraft, Loretta (Boss Lady), 103
Kukla, Fran, and Ollie, 34
Kupcinet, Irv, 288

L
LaBelle, Patti, 156
labor organizations, location of, 102
Lance, Major, 156
Langford, Larry, 133
language
   black versus white, 45
   in rap music and videos, 75
"Lanky Lou," 19
Lassie, 270
Lawrence (friend), 196, 200
Leak, Spencer, 130
LeBlanc, Carolyn, 133
Lee, Bill "Doc," 83, 116
Levert, Eddie, 141, 143–144, 156
Lewis, Jerry Lee, 123
Limbaugh, Rush, 271
Lindbergh, Charles, 15
listeners
   delivering music to, xiv
   at V103, 261
little girl, saving from traffic, 240–241
Little Richard
   booking at Time Square, 103
   interview of, 140
liver transplant, playing music during, 280
Lockhart, June, 270
Lonely Drifter (the O'Jays), 143
Long, Nia, 268
The Longest Day, 26
Lopez, Raquel, 262, 265–266
"Lost Inside of You," 140
Love Jones, 268
"Love Won't Let Me Wait," 139
Lucas, Mary, 266
Lymon, Frankie, 150

M
Madison, Wisconsin, 13
Magnificent Montague, 83, 116
Make Believe Ballroom, 15
"Mama Said," 238, 241
Mangelo, 274
Marie, Teena, 140
Markham, skating rink in, 212
marriage, failure of, 188, 216
Martell cases, carrying, 63
Martha Reeves and the Vandellas, 103
Mary (Aunt), 4

Mason, Terry (doctor), 255
Matthews, Kevin, 31
Maurice (motorcyclist), 147
Maxwell, Holly, 156
Mayfield, Curtis, 156, 283
    accident of, 180
    insight into music business, 171
    interviewing, 141
    and the Impressions, 61, 177–179,
    touring with Jerry Butler, 180
Mayo, Barry, 251, 254, 262
Maze, Frankie Beverly and, 261. See also
    Beverly, Frankie
McCarthy, Franklin "Sugar Daddy," 83
McCormick, Seth, 195–196
McCoy, Sid, 43, 124
McDonald's, eating at, 256
McGill, Mickey, 173, 175
Melvin, Harold and the Blue Notes, 176
Merchant Marines, attempt at joining, 26–27
Mercy Hospital, 257
microphones, making, 14–15
Midnight Rambles, 212
military
    blacks in, 27
    segregation in World War II, 26–27
Miller, Dorie (black war hero), 27
Millionaire's Club, 231–232, 239
Miner, Raynard, 87–88, 144–146
Miracles, the, 103, 158
Mohn, June, 264, 266
Moonglows, the, 156, 275
Moore, Don, 262
Moore, Melba, 140
Mootry, Charles, 95–96
Moreland, Mantan, 36
Morris, Anna, 264
mortgage, receiving, 258
mother, (Katherine Kent), 3–4, 228–229, 242
motorcycle rally, in South Dakota, 31
Motown Records, 21, 87, 157
movies, appearances in, 268–269
Mueller, Kurt, 35
Murchinson, Ira, 105
murders, occurrence in 1970s, 211–213
Murrow, Edward R., 26
Museum of Broadcast Communications, 270
music
    impact of, 279
    love of, 278

    playing during liver transplant, 280
    steppin', 65
music business
    age factor in, 171
    bankrupt artists in, 172–173
    evolution with radio, 285–286
    nature of, 171, 181
    music groups, problems in, 176
"My Girl," 159
Myrick, Max, 262

N
"nails" versus "hammers," 125
"nappy-headed hos" remark, 70, 73–74
"narrowcasting," 12
National Radio Hall of Fame, induction
    into, 270–272
NBC in Chicago
    getting job at, 33
    golf outing at, 35–36
    leaving for WGES, 54
    returning to job at, 53
The New Dance Club, 264
news, advice to get into, 286
nicknames, list of, xiii–xiv
nightclubs, working at, 63–65
9/11 versus Pearl Harbor, 26
nine lives
    burning car incident, 238–239
    car incident in West Virginia, 38
    getting hit by car, 5
    last of, 288
    overcoming suicidal tendency,
        233
    pig ear sandwich and car insurance,
        92
    surviving "Be Brave" with cousins, 10
    surviving cancer, 258
    surviving drug overdose, 223–225
Nitro, 127–128, 192
Northwestern University, attending, 34
n-word
    abolishing use of, 76
    original meaning of, 76–77
    refraining from use of, 72, 75

O
Of Boys and Men, 269
Ohio Players, the, 140, 282
O'Jays, the, xvi, 105, 143–144, 280, 283

Old School Memories: The Herb Kent Story
(play), 275
oncologist, remarks of, 255, 257
Open the Door, Richard!, 53
Operation Breadbasket
beginning of, 86
collecting money for, 115
Orioles, the, 288
Osteopathic Hospital, checking into,
247
Our Miss Brooks, 270–271
overdosing on drugs, 225

P
Packing House, 102
paper circus, gift of, 17
Parker, Maceo, 166
Parliament/Funkadelic, 281–282
Pearl Harbor
versus 9/11, 26
Japanese attack on, 25
Pegue, Richard, 83
Pendergrass, Teddy, 175–176, 282
Penguins ("Earth Angel"), 59
Peppermint Lounge, 190
Pershing Hotel Ballroom, 149–151
Petty, Bob, 112
Phillips, Esther, 150
Pickett, Wilson, 282
"Play That Funky Music White Boy," 97
police
hanging out with, 193–195
involvement with drugs, 220–221
run-in with, 208–210
poverty in childhood, 5–6
Presley, Elvis, 30
priest, visit by, 256
Prince, 280–282
profanity, addressing on radio,
70–72
projects, move to, 18–19
promotions
bike rides, 112–113
at Kappa Karnival, 108
power of, 93–94, 108
Roller Derby, 95–96
at V103, 97
window stickers, 97
Pruter, Robert, 61
Pryor, Richard, 73, 75

Punk Out music, 243
PUSH program, beginning of, 86

Q
Queen Bee Merri Dee, 43

R
R & B station, WVON as, 80
"race show," 45
racism. *See also* black people; white people
in college, xv, 34
at country club, 35
in hiring at radio stations, 230
at Hyde Park High School, 21
impact on career, 272
at insurance company, 31–33
power struggle related to, 30–31
related to drug use, 221–222
on South Side of Chicago, 145
in World War II, 26–27
after World War II, 27
radiation and chemotherapy
effectiveness of, 257
receiving, 253–255
radio
black people on, 285
contemporary influences on, 47–48
pressures of working in, 215
radio breaks, coming out of, 67
radio broadcasting
current state of, 284
decisive moment about career in, 21
early availability of, 14
growth of, 13
life dedication to, 288
radio business, evolution with music,
285–286
radio club, joining, 21–22
radio courses, teaching, 274–275
Radio Hall of Fame, induction into, xiii,
270–272
radio listeners
delivering music to, xiv
at V103, 261
radio news program, first example of, 13
radio promotions
bike rides, 112–113
at Kappa Karnival, 108
power of, 93–94, 108
Roller Derby, 95–96

at V103, 97
    window stickers, 97
radio shows
    personal goal of, 68
    preparing for, 66–67
radio stations, growth of, 13
radio transmissions, early use of,
    12
radio tubes, getting repaired, 29
radios. See also crystal radio sets
    early paid advertising on, 13
    gift from mother, 6
    making, 11–12
    one-tube, 14–15
    repairing, 29
"Raindrops," 59, 179
"Raindrops Keep Falling on My Head," 92
rap music, language used in, 75
rappers, influence on radio,
    47–48
ratings, rise in, xiv
Rayner Funeral Home, 272
Rawls, Lou, 50
record companies. See music business
record hops
    doing, 62, 85–86
    use of two turntables at, 103
records
    art of playing, 68
    breaking, 87
Red (barbecue house sponsor), 152–154
Red, Tampa, 2
Red Hot & Lowdown, 11
Red Top Lounge, working at, 187
Redding, Otis, 223, 226
Red's Diner, 230
Reeves, Martha, 103, 140, 156
regrets
    about career, 286–287
    about drugs and alcohol, 287
    about not signing autograph, 287
    about women, 287
rehab
    receiving, 246–250
    release from, 251
Reid, Tim, 140
remission from cancer, being in,
    257
"Rescue Me," 88, 144–145
Reyes, Orlando, 133

Rib Supreme, 134
Richards, Michael, 75
Richie, Lionel, 60
Riperton, Minnie, 8, 140, 144–145, 211, 213,
    281
The Rise and Fall of Vee-Jay Records, 180
Robin (daughter), 193–194, 246–247, 249–250,
    257
Robinson, Don, 105
Robinson, Smokey, xvi, 104, 157–161, 280, 282
Robinson Peete, Holly, 138
rock bottom, hitting, 236
Roller Derby, promotion for, 95–96
Roosevelt, Franklin D. (president), 24
Roosters, the, 177–178
Rose Bowl, first broadcast of, 13
Ross, Diana, 88, 141, 281
ROTC
    field trip in, 20–21
    joining, 19
Rowe, James, 83
Ruffin, David, 262
"Runaway Child, Running Wild," 87
Rush Street, club on, 158

S
S&S Hotel, 200
Sam and Dave, 103, 236
Sam 'n' Henry, debut of, 10
San Jose Calling, 12
Sassoon, Vidal, 3
schools, interviewing kids in, 85
"Selfish One," 144–145
747, racing in Roller Derby, 95–96
sex, having at WVON, 201
sexist remarks, avoiding on radio, 70–73
Sexton, Ben, 133
Sexton grammar school, graduation from, 8
sexual encounters. See also white girls; women
    with bisexual woman, 204–205
    with cocaine addict, 202–203
    in rehab, 248
    at WBEE, 202–204
    at WGES, 202
    at WHFC, 203
    at WVON, 201, 203
Sha Na Na, 59
Shaft, 269
"Shaqwanda," 153–154
Shirells, the, 60, 241, 281

"shock-jock" radio, development of, 69
"Shotgun," (Junior Walker), 136
Silver, Horace, 3
Simmons, Jerry, 103, 112, 194
Simpson, Valerie, 230
"skrunch," the, 103
Skyloft Players, membership in, 51–52, 120
slang, use of, 45–46
Smallwood, David, 231–232, 288
Smith, Jimmy, 156
Snatch-It-Back Corporation, skit about, 134
Snyder, Tom, 271
"So Fine" (Fiestas), 62–63
Soldier Field, rally for Dr. King at, 145
solo lead singers, careers of, 176
Something of the Air, 20–21
soul music artists, list of, 280–282
soul singers, favorites, 281
Soul Train, 83, 124
soundproof booth, building at Time Square, 103
South, Wesley, 83
South Carolina (Camden), 13
South Dakota, motorcycle rally in, 31
South Side of Chicago, racism on, 145
Spaniels, the, 61, 281
Spann, Pervis, xiii, 97–98, 116, 118
speaking voice
    "black" versus "white" sound of, 44–45
    gift of, 44
Spencer Hotel, 200
Spinners, the, 98, 100, 280
Springer, Jerry, 139
St. Valentine's Day Massacre, 2
Stallworth, Robert, 129–132
Stamberg, Susan, 271
Stamz, Richard, 53
Staple Singers, 112
Starsky and Hutch, 268
Staton, Candi, 214, 222
"Stay" (Maurice Williams), 251, 258
stealing, discouragement of, 4
steppin'. *See also* dances
    art of, 265
    contests, 266
    gurus and masters, 266
Steppin' at Club Seven, 264
Steppin' movie project, 268–269
steppin' music, playing, 65
Stern, Howard, 69

Storer College (West Virginia), 3
Stovall, Emmett, 143
street feel, origin of, 65–66
street gangs
    in 1970s, 211
    Blackstone Rangers, 192
    rapport with, 193
    style, explanation of, 66
Stylistics, the, 281–282
success
    perspective on, 286
    secrets of, xiv
Sugarfoot (Ohio Players), 140
suicide, contemplation of, 232–233, 239
Sunday Classics show, xiv
Supremes, the, 80, 88, 141, 280, 282
swearing on radio, 70–72
Sylvester, 132

T
talk shows, influence on radio, 47–48
Tampa Red, 2
Tate, Larenz, 268
Taylor, J. T. (Kool & the Gang), 60, 141
Taylor, Johnnie, 67, 113, 140, 156, 281
The Tea Box, 103
Teenagers, the, 150
Temple, Shirley, 3
Temptations, the, 87, 103, 148, 154, 262, 280, 282
Terrell, Ernie, 103
Terrell, Tammi, 227, 230
Tesla, Nikola, 12
Thailand, trip to, 263
THC, snorting by accident, 224
theater group, membership in, 51–52
Theater of the Mind on Radio, 120. *See also* Electric Crazy People
Thomas, B. J., 92
Thomas, Eddie, 112–113, 177–179, 181
Thomas Associates, 180
Thompson, Marshall, 98, 156
Til, Sonny (the Orioles), 288
Till, Emmett, 27, 164, 272
Tillstrom, Burr, 34
Time Square nightclub
    history of, 102
    murder of teenage girl at, 211–212
    popularity of, 103
    renovation of, 102–103

Tinley Park, 48
Tittle, LaDonna, 227
Tivoli theater, 150
Today Show, first host of, 34
"Tonight I Give In," 198
Torme, Mel, 8
Townsend, Robert, 177, 269
"Tracks of My Tears," 159
Tremayne, Les, 271
Trianon, the, 150
Troutman, Arenda, 272–273
Turner, Ike, 218
Turrentine, Stanley, 155–156
Tuskegee Airmen, 27
TV, roles of black people on, 285
TV courses, teaching, 274–275
TV gigs, hosting, 264–267
twine dance, 279

U
Uhles, Glen, 33
unions
    being approached by, 81
    United Packinghouse Workers of America,
        102
United Negro College Fund, 42
United Packinghouse Workers of America,
    102
Uomo, Mario, 265
Upchurch, Phil, 59, 180
urologist, visit by, 255

V
V103. See also WVAZ/V103
    friendships at, 262
    honor as mayor of Bronzeville, 274
    length of time at, xvi
    listeners to, 261
    promotions at, 97
    show on, 260–261
    working at, 230, 251
vacuum tubes, use in broadcast radio, 14
Vandellas, Martha Reeves and the, 103
Vandross, Luther, 281, 283
Vanelli, Gino, 140
Vanity, 138
Vaughan, Sarah, 55
Vee-Jay Records, 53, 60, 172, 178–179

Vibrations, the, 87
videos, language used in, 75
Vietnam, sending tapes to, 28–29
virginity, losing, 199
voice
    of announcers, 47
    "black" versus "white" sound of, 44–45
    communicating with, 46–47
    gift of, 44
"Voice of the Negro," WVON as, 82

W
Wahoo Man, 103, 128–130, 272
Walgreens, taking broken radio tubes to, 29
Walk, the, 265
Walker, Junior ("Shotgun"), 103,
    136
War, 281
war planes, fascination with, 26
Warwick, Dionne, 139, 281–282
Washington, Bernadine, 83, 201
Washington, Dinah, 68, 174–175
Washington, Harold, 81
Watson, Johnny "Guitar," 77, 138
"The Watusi," 87
wave trap, using with crystal radio, 13
WBEE
    announcing job at, 54–55
    female fans while at, 202–203
    getting fired from, 56
    returning to, 57
    strike at, 81
WBEZ Radio Workshops series, 22, 44
WBMX
    beginning of, 227
    frequency of, 230
WEAF, first paid ads on, 13
welfare-to-work assistance, availability of,
    101
Wesley, Fred, 166
West, Adam ("Batman"), 3
West Virginia, audition in, 37–38
West Virginia (Harper's Ferry), 3
WGCI
    length of time at, 251
    manager Marv Dyson at, 246
    merger with WVAZ, 262
    working at, 243–244

WGES
   Al Benson's show on, 43
   black programming at, 53
   female fans while at, 201
   versus WHFC-AM, 81
   working at, 152
WGN radio
   debut of Amos 'n' Andy on, 10
   field trip to, 20–21
WGRY
   getting job at, 42, 51
   leaving, 53
   reputation at, 54
   voice-over for dancing school, 46
   working at, 45
WHA, beginning of, 13
What's Goin' On, 279
WHFC-AM
   drinking problems at, 216
   purchase by Leonard Chess, 81–82
   working at, 81, 203
"Whip It," 243
Whispers, the, 281
White, Barry, 180, 210, 280, 282
White Castles, eating at, 256
white girls, sleeping with, 201–203. *See also*
   sexual encounters
white people. *See also* black people; racism
   neighborhoods of, 9
   schools of, 8
white versus black radio, 70–71, 230
"white" versus "black" voice, 44–46
Wild Cherry, 97
Williams, Herbert (father), 3
Williams, Maurice ("Stay"), 251,
   258
Williams, Rick, 135–136
Williams Cadillac, 48
Williamson, Rudolph, 110
Wilson, Jackie, 60–61, 173, 184, 190, 281
Wilson, Mary, 88, 141
Wilson, Nancy, 139
Winchell, Walter, 15
WIND in Chicago, audition at, 38–39
Winfrey, Oprah, 139
Wings, 2
Wisconsin, University of, 13
Withers, Bill, 156–157, 282

WJOB
   getting job at, 56–57, 81
   leaving, 57
WKRP in Cincinnati, 140
WLS, interaction with, 86
WLUP, evolution of, 82
Womack, Bobby, 139, 156, 281
women. *See also* female fans; sexual
   encounters
   altercations with, 188–190
   debasing of, 74
   regrets about, 287
Wonder, Stevie, 145–146, 280–282
Wood, Roy, 83
World War II
   beginning of, 24
   racism during, 26–27
WSBC, first black disc jockey at, 43
WSDM, beginning of, 82
WVAZ/V103. *See also* V103
   frequency of, 230
   merger with WGCI, 262
   move to, 260
WVON. *See also* Electric Crazy People; Good
      Guys of WVON
   from 1963-1977, 88
   beginning of, 82
   as "the Black Giant," 80
   breaking records on, 87
   changes at, 229–230
   competition to be played on, 87
   drinking problems at, 216
   engineers at, 84
   getting fired from, 229–230
   having sex at, 201
   high ratings of, 86
   impact on success of Michael Jackson, 98
   involvement in community, 86
   mood and ambience at, 85
   open house at, 94–95
   sale of, 228
   versus WBMX, 227–228
   window-sticker promotion, 97
WVON Good Guys. *See* Good Guys of
      WVON
WVON tapes, sending to Vietnam, 28–29
WWJ, beginning of, 13
WXFM, working at, 242–243

X
XM shock jocks, suspension of,
    70

Y
"You Don't Know Like I Know,"
    231, 236

"Your Precious Love," 177
Youth Forum club, 15

Z
Zodiac, the, 258